PRAISE FOR *VERITA$: HARVARD'S F*

"Shin Eun-jung's careful study raises many important questions not just about Harvard but about elite educational institutions and their nature and roles more generally. A valuable and thought-provoking contribution."
—Noam Chomsky, Institute Professor of Linguistics (emeritus), MIT

"Eun-jung was a remarkable person. It was wonderful to have even a small role collaborating with her on *Verita$*, which I call 'Verita$ the Dollar.' I was impressed by every aspect, starting with the concept and the research she had done. She took on the huge subject of Harvard's corporatization. Later I watched with admiration as she drew this difficult material together into a cohesive whole and deployed immense persistence in showing it around the world and writing about the subject."
—Margaret Morgenroth Gullette, resident scholar, Women's Studies Research Center, Brandeis University; Harvard PhD, 1975; Radcliffe College, B.A., 1962

"What I loved about Eun-jung was her courage—the courage to follow her heart's desire and to leave her country and everything familiar to her, to come to our distant country where she amazed us all with her remarkable critical intelligence and energy. Overnight, it seemed, she learned English at Harvard and then became an award-winning filmmaker with her incisive analysis of that very institution."
—Inez Hedges, professor of French, German, and cinema studies, Northeastern University

COMMENTARY ON HARVARD IN THE BOOK'S INTERVIEWS

"Harvard is an organ of the American ruling class whose mission is to do the intellectual labor that class needs."
—Richard Levins, professor at Harvard School of Public Health

"Harvard has prestige. That is probably the single thing that brings back to mind the campaign of Harvard clerical workers when they tried to organize against poor working conditions. Their slogan was 'you can't eat prestige.'"
—Victor Wallis, professor at Berklee College of Music

VERITA$
HARVARD'S HIDDEN HISTORY

Shin Eun-jung

VERITA $: Harvard's Hidden History
Shin Eun-jung
© 2015 Eros Effect Foundation
All rights reserved. No part of this book may be transmitted by any means without
permission in writing from the publisher.

ISBN: 978-1-62963-040-3
Library of Congress Control Number: 2014908070

Cover by John Yates/Stealworks
Interior design by briandesign

10 9 8 7 6 5 4 3 2 1

PM Press
PO Box 23912
Oakland, CA 94623
www.pmpress.org

Printed in the USA by the Employee Owners of Thomson-Shore in Dexter, Michigan.
www.thomsonshore.com

CONTENTS

INTRODUCTION TO
THE U.S. EDITION OF *VERITA$*

John Trumpbour

Shortly before her sudden death at age forty, the Korean documentary film-maker and television writer Shin Eun-jung (1972–2012) produced a movie and a book about the global role of Harvard. The film *Verita$: Everybody Loves Harvard* won her the award of Best Director of a Documentary Film at the 2011 New York International Film Festival.

Eun-jung developed her political and artistic sensibility as a student activist in Gwangju, Korea. In her high school years studying Korean litera-ture and poetry, she delivered passionate speeches in support of teachers fighting for educational reform and striking for the right to join a union, the Jeongyojo (the Korean Teachers and Education Workers Union). In 1989, 1,139 teachers were sacked for supporting the union, but in 2002 a special committee under the Prime Minister's Office reinstated them and praised them as exemplars of educational reform and the rising democratic move-ment in South Korea.[1] Boston College professor emeritus of psychology Ramsay Liem explained Eun-jung's political passion this way: "A child of the Gwangju uprising in 1980 against martial law and U.S. abetted mili-tary dictatorship, she never abandoned her commitment to justice for all Koreans and, actually, I don't think she had a choice because it was a part of her very being." He elaborated, "It wasn't a youthful phase in her life or a response to an immediate crisis that would call most of us to action, but her way of life."[2]

After years of service as director of the Gwangju Human Rights Film Festival, she later created a thirtieth anniversary documentary on the Gwangju Uprising of May 18, 1980, a signal event in which government troops massacred student protesters against the authoritarian regime of Major General Chun Doo-hwan. The Martial Law Command officially listed 144 civilians, 22 soldiers, and 4 police as dead on June 2, 1980, though Asia Watch, a division of Human Rights Watch, later offered estimates that as many as 2,000 citizens perished in the brutal repression. Gi-Wook Shin, the founding director of the Korean Studies program at Stanford University, has examined the wide variations in the grisly death toll, observing, "The best estimates available today suggest about five hundred civilians dead and over three thousand injured. Many injured people still suffer from wounds, both physical and psychological."[3] University of Chicago historian Bruce Cumings explains the political upshot of the Gwangju Uprising for a rising generation of Korean dissidents: "Kwangju convinced a new generation of young people that the democratic movement had developed not with the support of Washington, as an older generation of more conservative Koreans thought, but in the face of daily American support for any dictator who could quell the democratic aspirations of the Korean people."[4]

Throughout her research, Eun-jung noticed that many leading apologists for anti-democratic repression in Asia were distinguished graduates and officials of Harvard University. Documents obtained under the Freedom of Information Act confirmed U.S. military and government awareness of the capacity of the Korean Special Forces for merciless crackdown on dissenters, but U.S. officials in several cables gave what the Martial Law Command could regard as a green light for the ensuing iron-fisted suppression. Indeed the Special Forces lacerated students with bayonet thrusts and scorched them with flamethrowers, while mowing down protesters with M1 and carbon rifles blazing with bullet fire.[5] In the months after the massacre, among the prominent Americans who met and seemed to give aid and comfort to Korean military strongman Chun Doo-hwan included former Harvard Board of Overseers chair David Rockefeller and then-current Harvard Board of Overseers member T. Jefferson Coolidge Jr. A major force in developing the postwar fertilizer industry in South Korea, Coolidge had in the mid-1970s negotiated with Seoul and the Korean Traders Association (KTA) to obtain a million-dollar grant for establishing Korean studies at Harvard.[6] The U.S. academic specialist in East Asian Studies most outspoken for bolstering the regime was University of California Berkeley professor of political science Robert Scalapino, who received his MA and PhD training at Harvard.

In the years after her graduation from Chonnam National University in Gwangju, Shin Eun-jung also took sharp notice of the mounting obsession in South Korean society with elite U.S. universities, most dramatically with Harvard. In much of the world, ambitious students pursue undergraduate studies in local universities and then later seek admission to graduate programs in the United States. But many affluent families in Korea start far earlier. In considerable numbers, Koreans send children in their early teens to the United States for high school. Eun-jung heard from many families that the ultimate prize would be an undergraduate seat at Harvard. She appreciated the arduous discipline and work ethic of many young Koreans but also worried that she was witnessing, to paraphrase beat poet Allen Ginsberg, the best minds of her generation destroyed by this uncritical quest to make their Harvard dream come true.

Korean elites are hardly alone in the belief that Harvard represents the pinnacle of educational accomplishment. Alex Beam of the *Boston Globe* captures this sensibility when he regularly calls the Crimson institution WGU ("World's Greatest University").[7] In the popular media, Harvard stands out for amassing the world's largest university endowment of $36.4 billion (2014), a figure exceeding the annual GDP of more than half the nations of the world in the global rankings of "Gross domestic product" from the World Bank. Yale is a distant second with $23.9 billion of endowment, though as of late magnificent investment returns have reduced the gap with Harvard.[8]

Several dramatic indicators reveal overwhelming global deference to Harvard. A very conventional search on the Anglophone-skewed Google using the phrase in quotations "Harvard educated" yields 394,000 hits (October 12, 2014). Other highly esteemed educational institutions may boast of Pulitzer Prize winners, Nobel laureates, prestigious faculties, and outstanding students, but the "Harvard educated" modifier is bestowed six to forty times more on the worldwide web than any of the names of elite U.S. rivals: "Yale educated" (61,400 hits); "Cornell educated" (48,700 hits); "Columbia educated" (38,800 hits); "Stanford educated" (33,200 hits); "Pennsylvania educated" (27,200 hits); "MIT educated" (24,900 hits); "Princeton educated" (23,300 hits); "Dartmouth educated" (18,500 hits); "Brown educated" (12,100 hits); and "Duke educated" (9,490 hits). There are indeed significant "false positives" in this Google exercise, but these actually increase the hits more markedly for places such as Brown, Columbia, and Pennsylvania. (Some aggrieved followers of the University of Pennsylvania may prefer the modifier "Penn educated," but that adds a mere 3,990 hits.) The only university in the world that gives Harvard competition in the Google search sweepstakes is Oxford: "Oxford educated" (163,000 hits). "Cambridge educated" yields 75,900 hits.

The disparities are often worse when consulting news media, with the notable exception of the Universities of Oxford and Cambridge that receive ample reference in U.K. and British Commonwealth press outlets. Factiva, self-described as a database of over eight thousand business and news publications in twenty-two languages, yields these results when probing how journalists and wire services describe the education of people in the news:

Factiva/Dow Jones (number of hits when searching all dates in the database; October 12, 2014)

"Harvard educated"	22,253
"Oxford educated"	13,923
"Cambridge educated"	6,221
"Yale educated"	3,940
"Stanford educated"	1,249
"MIT educated"	608
"Cornell educated"	226
"Columbia educated"	199
"Dartmouth educated"	153
"Brown educated"	68
"Pennsylvania educated"	54
(11 more if "Penn educated"; "Wharton educated" adds 10)	
"Duke educated"	46

Toward the end of his long presidency of Harvard, Derek C. Bok liked to talk about the internationalization of Harvard, resulting in a global presence with the sun never setting on the Crimson university. A *Harvard Crimson* journalist named Madeline W. Lissner in 2007 expressed this idea with a blunter edge: "The sun never sets on the Harvard empire."[9] While Harvard had less of an institutional presence than several rivals in terms of overseas centers and campuses for much of its history, its alumni have created a far denser networking and club presence in both the United States and in many parts of the globe. Harvard provides clubs or a dedicated alumni contact person in ninety-nine nations around the world, while Yale, the most clubbish of its university rivals, can claim forty-seven nations with a club or a dedicated alumni contact as of 2014. In India alone, Harvard has clubs in Mumbai, New Delhi, and Chennai, and a dedicated alumni contact in Bangalore. This does not include the very large Harvard Business School Club of India based in Mumbai with approximately a thousand members. In contrast, Yale only lists one contact person for the Yale Club of India, and there appear to be few ongoing activities, with LinkedIn listing 171 members nationwide. Given that Yale is named after East India Company agent Elihu Yale, it might surprise some that the Harvard networking presence in South Asia is much more substantial than its New Haven rival. Admittedly, the most elite social networkers of the Ivy League have access to clubs far more potent and exclusive than their university-sponsored organizations.[10]

Harvard can still outflank its elite rivals partly because many of its graduate schools are far larger than those of, say, Yale and Stanford. Harvard Law School has a student body nearly triple the size of the enrollment of the law schools at Yale and Stanford. Princeton does not offer business, medicine, and law degrees. There is not a school of government or of public health at Stanford, and Yale mainly trains public administrators at a broad-based management school covering both business and nonprofit endeavors. Yale's management school provides training of a high caliber, but it is regarded as no match in the corporate world for what is commonly called the West Point of U.S. capitalism, the Harvard Business School.

Thus, though many other social critics have delivered an indictment of several elite universities at once, Eun-jung thought that Harvard's impact required special focus.[11]

She came to appreciate some of the withering contemporary critique of U.S. universities delivered by Hacker and Dreifus, with the New York duo remarking, "We all fill our homes with inexpensive products that are fabricated overseas at Third World wages. At this point, we can't outsource History 101 to be taught in Bangalore. . . . What we do instead is hire our own citizens and give them Third World pay."[12]

But in contrast to these more recent denunciations of academic careerism and soulless education, Eun-jung became animated when discovering the ways in which seemingly benign intellectual institutions help inflict suffering and violence on the wretched of the earth by all too often delivering what a previous generation of Harvard radicals called "reason in the service of Empire." In his famous 1971 debate and dialogue with Noam Chomsky in the Netherlands, Michel Foucault reflected on the modern university:

> One knows . . . that the university, and in a general way, all teaching systems, which appear simply to disseminate knowledge, are made to maintain a certain social class in power; and to exclude the instruments of power of another social class. . . . The real political task in a society such as ours is to criticize the workings of institutions that appear to be both neutral and independent, to criticize and attack them in such a manner that the political violence that has always exercised itself obscurely through them will be unmasked, so that one can fight against them.[13]

Kingman Brewster, the president of Yale in the turbulent 1960s and 1970s and a role model for Harvard's Derek Bok, claimed that "Yale as an institution cannot let itself be 'mobilized' for any cause, no matter how noble, or for the achievement of a social objective extraneous to its purpose, no matter how worthy."[14] Contrast this declaration of the university's neutrality with the earnest Cold War stylings of Harvard president Nathan Marsh Pusey (1953–1971): "Today the sort of activity which goes on in the classrooms and laboratories of Cambridge is contributing vastly to the immense national efforts we are making and shall have to make to live up to our nation's acquired responsibilities in the world and to compete effectively in the life-and-death struggle in which it seems that we are to be engaged for a long time with our alien rival, the USSR." Pusey sought to remind the U.S. public that in the Age of the Cold War "Harvard is no stranger to such struggles, albeit this is the most serious one we have ever faced. Our university has done its part—and more—in every conflict in our nation's history."[15] Harvard dean McGeorge Bundy explained to an ROTC panel back in 1955, "A university which does not try to develop to a maximal degree the interest, the cooperation and understanding between its staff members and those of the National Defense forces is not doing its full job."[16]

In the twenty-first century, Shin Eun-jung found a new Harvard leadership quick to declare the institution's neutrality while cozying up to not only the big bankers and corporate interests but also with the national security elite. President Drew Gilpin Faust eagerly brought ROTC back to Harvard during 2011 and 2012, and in 2013 she beamed with pride when receiving the U.S. Navy Distinguished Public Service Award for her "total commitment to the NROTC" (Naval Reserve Officers Training Corps).[17] Honorable people may disagree about the university granting the military special access to higher education facilities, but such a privilege is hardly illustrative of Brewster's vaunted principle that an educational "institution cannot let itself be 'mobilized' for any cause, no matter how noble."

It has often been ignored that during the recent decades when ROTC students at Harvard went to other local campuses to receive training, Harvard soon offered plenty of welcoming programs for aspiring elites in the military and intelligence establishment, most notably the National Security Fellows Program and the Senior Executives in National and International Security program. In 2004, at the annual joint breakfast in the Harvard Faculty Club for ROTC and National Security Fellows, Harvard students openly brandished the ceremonial saber of Captain Constant Cordier, appointed in 1916 as the first Professor of Military Science at Harvard.[18] Arriving in 2007, the Faust era may not be like the days before U.S. entry into World War I when the *Harvard Crimson* (September 23, 1916) could report that "a new department known as the Military Department has been added to the University, and Captain Constant Cordier, U. S. A., has been designated by the Secretary of War, by direction of the President, as professor of military science and tactics and a regular member of the faculty, as well as commandant of the reserve officers' training corps at Harvard." But Faust has won hearts and minds by a muscular liberalism combining delight in the military with flourishes of liberal feminist inclusiveness towards gays and lesbians formerly excluded from the armed forces.[19]

Meanwhile, in planning the 375th anniversary events of Harvard during the 2011–2012 academic year, Faust made a personal pilgrimage to invite Henry Kissinger back to Harvard. She then delivered a star-studded academic welcome for the nation's eighth national security advisor amid a cheering Harvard throng packed into Sanders Theater. Kissinger is living evidence of the late historian Gabriel Kolko's suggestion that there is much more to fear in the civilian elite who dominate the higher circles of power than those who serve in the military. A few picketers and questioners tried to confront the audience with some of the bloodbaths conducted with the policy recommendations and cold complicity of Kissinger: well more than a million Vietnamese dead, the vast genocide in East Timor, the thousands killed in Chile including Harvard alumnus Charles Horman, and the three hundred thousand people vanquished by Pakistan's military in efforts to snuff out the movement for Bangladesh independence. Of the latter, few critics of U.S. foreign policy have held Kissinger accountable for his activities leading to the slaughterhouse in South Asia, though Gary J. Bass in *The Blood Telegram: Nixon, Kissinger, and a Forgotten Genocide* reveals the tapes and documents of the Kissinger machinations in ample detail. One might have thought Faust would have been moved by documents showing how the Kissinger-backed repression shattered university life. In Bass's subsequent description:

> The provost of the Hindu dormitory, a respected scholar of English, was dragged out of his residence and shot in the neck. [Consul General Archer K.] Blood listed six other faculty members "reliably reported killed by troops," with several more possibly dead. One American who had visited the campus said that students had been "mowed down" in their rooms or as they fled, with a residence hall in flames and youths being machine-gunned. "At least two mass graves on campus," Blood cabled. "Stench terrible."
>
> There were 148 corpses in one of these mass graves, according to the workmen forced to dig them. An official in the Dacca consulate estimated that five hundred students had been killed in the first two days of the crackdown, almost none of them fighting back.[20]

Lieutenant General J.F.R. Jacob, the Calcutta-born chief of staff of India's Eastern Army, confronted U.S. Ambassador Kenneth B. Keating about large-scale atrocities being carried out by the Pakistanis: "I told him that I was at a loss to understand why the Government of the world's most powerful democracy should support a brutal, repressive military regime which had completely disregarded the results of the elections in East

Pakistan."[21] Bass observes that "Kissinger began telling noticeable false-hoods about the administration's record just two weeks into the crisis, and has not stopped distorting since. Nixon and Kissinger, in their vigorous efforts after Watergate to rehabilitate their own respectability as foreign policy wizards, have left us a farrago of distortions, half-truths, and outright lies about their policy toward the Bengali atrocities."[22]

Fortunately for Kissinger, his authorized biography is now being written by Harvard historian Niall Ferguson, who was in the crowd for the celebration of Kissinger at the 375th anniversary event at Sanders Theater and was exultant over his performance. Lest there be any doubt where Ferguson stands in his historical craft, he observes that the preeminent social historian Eric Hobsbawm "sided with the workers and peasants, while I side with the bourgeoisie."[23]

Even after an audience questioner identified FBI documents from the 1950s released under a Freedom of Information Act request revealing that then Harvard professor Kissinger had volunteered to snoop and report on the putatively subversive activities of fellow Harvard faculty, President Faust in the general audience continued her joyous clapping for her favorite national security advisor. Some may well say that she was simply honoring Harvard traditions of cordiality towards invited guests. Professor Henry Louis Gates, often portrayed on Fox News as some kind of militant-left Black nationalist or, in Rush Limbaugh's words, an "angry racist,"[24] welcomed George W. Bush's national security advisor, Condoleezza Rice, to Harvard in 2010 by not just requesting but rather ordering a cheering ovation. In part one of Rice's lecture series on "American Foreign Policy and the Black Experience" cosponsored by the W.E.B. Du Bois Institute, Gates judged that the polite clapping initially given by the Harvard audience was for him too tepid. "You can all do better," he barked. "Give it up for Condoleezza Rice!"[25] Upon Gates's command, the compliant Harvard crowd then delivered rapturous applause for the elated 20th U.S. national security advisor and the first African American woman to serve as U.S. secretary of state. The belief that Harvard is a hostile place for the national security elite remains part of the folklore of American conservatism. In her work, Eun-jung continuously sought to expose Korean readers to the reality of Harvard's long dedication to interventionism, the abiding faith that unleashing U.S. warriors on foes far and wide will make the world a better place.

Koreans claim to have been invaded some four hundred times in five thousand years of history, and they sometimes like to add they have never invaded any nation.[26] The Korean left, nevertheless, blames the postwar South Korean government for breaking with the non-interventionist tradition by assisting the U.S. invasion of Vietnam. In the Age of Obama, warrior interventions are now giving way to drones as the strike-force of choice. A

Council on Foreign Relations study indicates that the Obama Administration has brought a sevenfold increase in the number of drone strikes over the hawkish Bush era.[27] Harvardians commonly treat the Nobel Peace Prize–winning Obama as more restrained and dove-like in foreign policy, even though Harvard Law School's favorite son has bombed many more nations than Bush. The Obama tally includes Afghanistan, Iraq, Pakistan, Somalia, Yemen, Libya, Syria, and, very briefly, the Philippines. While Bush liked to round up the usual suspects and ship them to Guantánamo, the Obama team prefers just to bomb and kill them. Drone operators have slang words for those on their screens who have been killed: the grainy image of doom is called a "bug splat."[28] The destabilization of the greater Middle East that began as a Bush project carries on under Obama's carapace of liberal humanitarian interventionism, with steady assistance from the laptop bombardiers of the Harvard Kennedy School.

Obama appointed as his fourth U.S. secretary of defense Ashton Carter, a Yalie and former chair of the International and Global Studies faculty at the Harvard Kennedy School. The physicist Carter counseled the Clinton Administration to start bombing North Korea back in 1994, and he followed up as an encore with new demands in June 2006 for surgical strikes on the missile platforms of the DPRK.[29]

Jonathan Alter reported that a quarter of Obama's appointments in the first term were fellow Harvard alumni or faculty.[30] For Chris Floyd, columnist for *CounterPunch* magazine, commenting on liberal-progressive complicity in the open-ended dirty wars and targeted assassination programs: "They cannot genuinely and effectively oppose the monstrous system of military Empire because, in the end, what is most important to them is not stopping the system—but making sure that one of 'theirs' is running it."[31]

During the hundredth anniversary of the Harvard Business School starting in the 2008–2009 academic year, the theme of its main program became encapsulated in a banner dangling over an HBS building: "Who Will Lead?" Stefan Stern of the *Financial Times* reported that the answer for the assembled Harvard alumni and professoriate was in no doubt, "HBS graduates will."[32] In particular, Niall Ferguson explained why this should be so: "A leader needs to understand the process of creative destruction. HBS, more than any other institution, has sought to illuminate, elucidate, and, above all, communicate this principle."[33] This bravado for Harvard-led creative destruction was striking if only because the timing of the centenary had coincided with the most devastating financial carnage since the Great Depression. For Stern, "You would have to have a heart of stone not to be amused by this piquant accident of timing. Here, at the spiritual home of the Masters of the Universe, distinguished graduates could only look on as that same universe threatened to implode."[34]

Eun-jung saw her book and documentary film project as a more radical variant of the tradition exposing "the revolt of the elites and the betrayal of democracy," to use Christopher Lasch's evocative phrasing. She found that too many critics of U.S. society like to dwell tediously on obvious shortcomings such as violent school shootings, fast-food gluttony, consumerist excess, and the crumbling decay of once-prosperous cities such as Detroit. Instead she asked people to reconsider how the most admired institutions of U.S. society such as Ivy League universities and "the best and the brightest" had contributed to the society's failure to meet its democratic promise. She thought that education had an essential role in inspiring democratic uplift, but instead the premier institutions had succumbed to the allure of Empire. Most Harvardians struck her as sleepwalking through history, unaware that their university had intimate connections with some of the most retrograde assaults on democracy and human decency: the Salem Witch Trials, the execution of Sacco and Vanzetti, the promotion of eugenics, the maintenance of ties with Nazi ideologues, and cooperation with McCarthyite smackdowns of left dissent.

Harvard has long been assailed in a vast array of right-wing books about its contribution to the leftist subversion of America. Harvardians tend to laugh off these criticisms and almost regard them as a compliment for ratifying their progressive and enlightened credentials. In contrast to the U.S. right, Shin Eun-jung saw Harvard as a servant of powerful corporate interests and the national security state. Her message and others like hers are typically far less welcome. When he identified corporate conformity as the dominant ethos at contemporary Harvard, John Summers, the embattled editor of the satirical magazine *The Baffler*, soon met howls of outrage filling the online *Times Higher Education Supplement*.[35] Harvardians pleaded that a generous sprinkling of graduates are kind people from modest backgrounds who help nonprofit foundations, the poor, and wider humanity. Eun-jung knew several Harvard activists and faculty whom she regarded as good people, including those increasingly sympathetic with democratic forces at Harvard's Korea Institute. Her book affirms the rise in diversity among the student body. But her indictment of Harvard as an institution serving corporate power and the welfare-warfare state is not vitiated by the presence of Harvard alumni working assiduously for homeless shelters and soup kitchens. For all the examples of individual Harvardians exhibiting dissident thoughts and kindness to strangers, the Harvard Corporation and the institution's leadership are there to make sure that Harvard will not waver in its modern mission: delivering reason in the service of Empire. Read on.

THE STATUE OF THREE LIES

"Welcome to Harvard University! We are about to embark on a fantastic adventure, learning about Harvard's rich history and tradition while touring Harvard Yard and other historical landmarks of this exceptional institution. Are you ready? Let's go!"

After clamorous cheering and applause, a group of parents, tourists, and Harvard hopefuls follow their guide from Massachusetts Avenue to Harvard Yard, center of Harvard University's main campus. This scene repeats itself several times each and every day: a pack of visitors being led by a Harvard student guide around the campus to discover the glorious history and culture of the world's most famous educational institution. So popular were the official tours of the campus that in 2006 two Harvard graduates established an unofficial tour group, which in 2010 alone shepherded forty thousand visitors around the campus—clear evidence of Harvard's draw, prestige, and popularity. Whether official or unofficial, the tours all have one thing in common: admiration and glorification of Harvard's history.

Shortly after the tour begins, visitors will hear the story of Harvard's very first class. With only twelve students and one professor, it was held in a hut-like classroom, since the monumental buildings that now make up the campus were yet to be constructed. In awe, visitors will learn about Harvard's colorful history while passing by Memorial Hall, erected in honor of the Harvard graduates who fought for the Union in the Civil War, and Memorial Church, built in honor of the Harvard men who died during World War I. Impressed by the dazzling beauty of these buildings, they'll then

A Harvard tour group.

pass by Widener Library and listen intently to its dramatic story: built with a gift from Eleanor Elkins Widener as a memorial to her son, Harry Elkins Widener, class of 1907, who died aboard the *Titanic*.

Beginning in Harvard Square, then exploring Harvard Yard, the group hurries toward the grand finale: the statue of John Harvard, the most celebrated and important symbol of the university. Cast in 1884 by American sculptor Daniel Chester French, the John Harvard Statue is a very popular photo-op among tourists seeking lasting proof of their visit to the world's most celebrated university. In fact, it is said to be the third most photographed statue in the United States. According to superstition, one who touches the left foot of the statue will likely be granted admission to the college, resulting in an extremely polished and shiny left foot—evidence of the massive desire to attend Harvard. However, don't forget to wash your hands after touching the holy foot, since it is known that mischievous students often urinate on it!

Memorial Hall (left) and Widener Library (right).

"The Statue of Three Lies." Because of the superstitious belief that anyone who touches the left foot of the statue will likely be granted admission to the college, the left foot is extremely polished and shiny.

As visitors take turns rubbing the foot of the statue, posing in front of cameras, the guide reveals some surprising facts. The John Harvard Statue is also known as the "Statue of Three Lies." What are those three lies? At the bottom of the statue, there are three key elements engraved: John Harvard, Founder, and 1638. However, John Harvard was merely a benefactor, not a founder of the university, and Harvard was established in 1636 not 1638 (the year John Harvard's estate was donated to the university). Last but not least, the model of the statue was not, in fact, John Harvard. The guide's humorous explanation brings a rupture of laughter among the tour group, and on this light note, the tour ends.

Yet, one must wonder, what does it really mean that Harvard's central symbol is full of lies? Why would Harvard place deceit at the heart of its campus? Moreover, the statue has proudly and ironically been engraved with Harvard's motto, "*Veritas*," meaning *truth*. Does the fact that the symbol of Harvard is full of lies shed some light on the true nature of this university?

We could easily dismiss this symbolic paradox as humorous and of little importance. Still, there are plenty of more surprising facts hidden behind the glorious façade of this institution. In the following pages, I will examine many more critical dimensions of its history that Harvard has kept well hidden from textbooks and the major media.

For example, during a Harvard tour, you won't hear how Harvard was involved in the Salem Witch Trials of the late seventeenth century. Though they often brag about how Harvard was the kingdom of heaven for abolitionists, they won't dare whisper that many Harvard presidents had their own slaves. Nor will they share how throughout history, Harvard students were at the forefront of breaking labor strikes. They'll say nothing about how Harvard professors promoted American eugenics in the early twentieth century, nor its huge impact on the creation of Nazi Germany. Can you believe that one Harvard graduate who became personally very close with Adolf Hitler was invited to Harvard's commencement and welcomed as a royal envoy? Believe it or not, it's unfortunately true.

In the following chapters, you will discover how Harvard professors have heavily influenced U.S. foreign policy. From converting the OSS into the CIA, to their solid relationships with the FBI, Harvard men produced the Cold War ideology that propelled the U.S. government to promote mistrust and war. We'll review the hidden history of the removal of leftist professors during the McCarthy Era, despite Harvard's pride in being a sanctuary of academic freedom.

Harvard's true character was clearly expressed when they invited the Shah of Iran in 1968 for commencement and awarded an honorary degree to a dictator who ruled his people with ruthless violence. Many Harvard scholars were also involved in the Vietnam War, justifying and advocating for the war and massive killing of civilians. As a result, Harvard became a hotbed of the anti-war movement during the 1960s. In 1969 hundreds of Harvard students occupied University Hall, where the administration was located. Nathan Pusey, the president of Harvard at that time, quickly called in police, whose bloody violence resulted in the first strike in Harvard's history.

The Vietnam War shook Harvard to its core, and consequently Harvard transformed its administrative strategy from defense management to corporate management. In 1989, the Berlin Wall crumbled, and two years later, the Cold War ended as the Soviet Union dissolved. During this time, Harvard's influence stretched over the globe. Harvard men played a key role in transforming the Russian economy into a neoliberal market economy, which resulted in great economic disparity and drove a majority of Russians into poverty. Using the university's influences and contacts, Harvard men engaged in prohibited investments that later resulted in their being sued by the U.S. government. In 2005, a settlement was made which compelled Harvard defendants to pay up to $31 million. Of course, you won't hear such history in the media or during the Harvard tour.

Part of this book will examine Harvard's power structure. Until 2010, the university was run by the "President and Fellows" or the "Harvard Corporation," a self-perpetuating oligarchy composed of seven people including the president. Most members were drawn from the corporate world rather than from academia, meaning Harvard often cooperated with key corporations, maintaining a close relationship to them even at the cost of academic freedom. For instance, following Enron's collapse in 2002, which dealt a huge blow to the U.S. economy, it came to light that many Harvard professors who were heavily sponsored by Enron had promoted deregulation in the energy sector, thereby playing their role in Enron's corporate agenda—not the public interest. Even more interestingly, Harvard had sold their Enron stock right before its crash, a move that brought huge suspicion of insider trading their way. As suspicion grew about the integrity and nondemocratic character of the Harvard Corporation, Harvard announced in 2010 the surprising news that after 360 years, it would expand its members from seven to thirteen.

I will also review how Harvard, a symbol of American left-liberalism, has treated its campus workers. A glimpse of this reality was revealed in 2001, when Harvard students occupied Massachusetts Hall for twenty-one days to demand a living wage for Harvard service workers. Their courageous fight was well supported by the broader community as it exposed how the richest university in the world has exploited its workers.

Finally, I will examine how Harvard has managed its billions of dollars of endowment. Since 1974, when the Harvard Management Company (HMC) was founded, Harvard has aggressively invested its portfolio in the search for greater profits. As a result, its endowment featured double-digit returns for many years starting at $1.4 billion in 1974 until it reached $36.9 billion in 2008. Soon after, the global financial crisis struck, and Harvard lost nearly 30 percent of its endowment. How did Harvard respond to this crisis? They got rid of nearly a thousand workers through layoffs and forced retirement. Surely you'd hear no such story on the Harvard campus tour.

This is just a sample of Harvard's hidden history that will be illuminated in the following pages. What you hold in your hands is the real Harvard tour that will guide you to discover the true character of the world's favorite university.

The true Harvard tour now begins.

CHAPTER 1

PROFILING HARVARD

"[Harvard] is an organ of the American ruling class whose mission is to do the intellectual labor that class needs."
—Richard Levins, professor at Harvard School of Public Health

"It's hard to say exactly how it happens. But after four years here you feel as though the world has been created to be led by Harvard men."
—A Harvard senior, as told to author Vivian Gornick[1]

"When I think of Harvard, unfortunately, what I think of is a $26 billion endowment. It's a small country."
—Michael Ansara, Harvard College Class of 1968

American historian Bernard DeVoto (1897–1955) once defined Harvard University as "a republic within the Republic."[2] This keen observation remains true to this day, as Harvard, with influence reaching all over the globe, is really more like a small country than a university. Throughout the twentieth and twenty-first centuries, Harvard has remained a leading brand in higher education—the ultimate "dream school" for parents and students alike—and not just in the United States.

In South Korea, for example, young students who strive to attend Harvard often enroll in special, exclusive preparatory schools that focus on churning out Harvard-eligible candidates. Some parents teach their babies the word "Harvard" right after "mama" and papa." In 2008, a *New York Times* article, "Elite Korean Schools, Forging Ivy League Skills," analyzed Koreans' zeal for prestigious American universities, especially Harvard. As Alexander Vershbow, then U.S. ambassador to South Korea, stated, "Preparing to get into the best American universities has become something of a national obsession in Korea."[3] Vershbow also implied that these highly motivated prep-school students often receive perfect SAT scores, but they may be insufficiently educated as responsible citizens. Further, it's not uncommon for accepted Korean students to write autobiographies

Side Glances

© 1966 by NEA, Inc. T.M. Reg. U.S. Pat. Off.

"Eight and a half pounds and that's not all! He has Harvard written all over him!"
A cartoon satirizing excessive enthusiasm for Harvard.

about their journey into Harvard, or for their parents to write step-by-step guidebooks on the process.

Yet, with all this enthusiasm for the university, how well do we actually know Harvard? When you think about Harvard University, if the words "genius" or "bookworm" come to mind, the book in your hands might be helpful in fleshing out a more accurate depiction of the institution. Obviously, Harvard is a prestigious university—but it is much more than just an ivory tower. It is also a training ground for American political, economic, and military elites, as well as a cornerstone of the military-industrial-educational complex that has long initiated U.S. wars and political interventions all over the world.

Nevertheless, Harvard somehow upholds a distinctly "progressive" reputation among U.S. universities. Harvard leaders often boast that they have been a spearhead in defending academic freedom. Conservatives have said that Harvard is radical, calling the university "The Kremlin on the Charles River." Although some conscientious intellectuals have openly criticized Harvard's close relationship with the U.S. government and for serving the empire's agenda, such voices are few and far between. The debate of whether Harvard is "progressive" or "conservative" effectively blocks us from grasping the university's true nature. In this chapter, we'll profile the university's social, historical, and political character in order to approach a more accurate understanding of what Harvard's really about.

Harvard, the Vatican of All Universities

In 2009, *Forbes* magazine reported on "Billionaire Universities." Not surprisingly, Harvard topped that list, and further, the article even began with the quote: "Want your kid to become one of the richest people in the world? Send them to Harvard."[4] According to their list, Harvard produced more than 5 percent of the world's billionaires that year—fifty-four in all, a number that increased to sixty-two the following year. The number of Harvard graduate billionaires is more than double that of Stanford University, which came in second on the *Forbes* list, far beyond the other top five universities.

The top five universities that produced the most billionaires in 2009

Harvard University	54
Stanford University	25
University of Pennsylvania	18
Columbia University	16
Yale University	16

The *Forbes* report is just one of many examples illustrating Harvard's incredible brand power. Harvard also ranked number one in *U.S. News & World Report*'s Best Colleges of 2011 rankings, among many other surveys. It's hard to imagine any other university surpassing Harvard's social status, reputation, and global influence.

Harvard is composed of eleven academic units: the Faculty of Arts and Science (which includes Harvard College, the Graduate School of Arts and Science, and the Harvard Division of Continuing Education), Harvard Medical School, Harvard School of Dental Medicine, Harvard Divinity School, Harvard Law School, Harvard Business School, the Graduate School of Design, Harvard Graduate School of Education, the School of Public Health, the Kennedy School of Government, and Radcliffe Institute for Advanced Study. Harvard Yard, the center of the university's main campus in Cambridge, Massachusetts, contains academic buildings, libraries, the

Harvard Yard.

Memorial Church, and freshmen dormitories. Each dormitory has its own dining hall, library, and many other facilities. The Business School and Harvard Stadium are across the Charles River in the Allston neighborhood of Boston, where Harvard is planning to create a new campus. The medical, dental, and public health schools are located in Boston's Longwood Medical Area, where some of the best hospitals and medical research institutes in the country can be found.

To view Harvard as a singular esteemed college would be to see only a fraction of the institution's vast scale and wealth. Take, for instance, the ninety or so libraries within the university's dominion or the hundreds of institutes and specialized graduate schools that pump out leading elites in their fields, in particular, Harvard Law School (HLS), the Business School (HBS), the Medical School (HMS), and the Kennedy School of Government (HKS), each of which has world-renowned reputations of their own.

Harvard is also the wealthiest university in the world. In 2008, its endowment peaked at a whopping $36.9 billion. Though Harvard lost about 30 percent of its monetary value during the ensuing financial crisis, its endowment remains astronomical. In 2011, it was valued at $32 billion— much greater than any American university, and even exceeding the GDP of Estonia. After the Roman Catholic Church and the Bill and Melinda Gates Foundation (founded by a Harvard dropout), Harvard has the third-largest endowment in the world among nonprofit organizations—and this doesn't include the plethora of magnificent buildings on campus or thousands of acres of prime land, not to mention the priceless art owned by

The eight U.S. presidents from Harvard: John Adams (2nd), John Quincy Adams (6th), Rutherford Hayes (19th), Theodore Roosevelt (26th), Franklin Roosevelt (32nd), John F. Kennedy (35th), George W. Bush (43rd), and Barack Obama (44th).

Harvard museums. Howard University, also known as "Black Harvard," has the largest endowment among black college and universities, about $420 million. Valencia College in Orlando, Florida, the best-endowed community college, has around $67 million, a mere 0.26 percent of Harvard's wealth.[5]

Harvard's distinguished network is another source of great pride for the university. Eight U.S. presidents have hailed from Harvard, more than from any other university, beginning with John Adams (1791–1801), and followed by John Quincy Adams (1825–29), Rutherford B. Hayes (1877–81), Theodore Roosevelt (1901–09), Franklin Roosevelt (1933–45), John F. Kennedy (1961–63), George W. Bush (2001–09), and Barack Obama (2009–17). Harvard churns out powerful and influential members of the political elite. In 1968, the Alumni Bulletin conducted a survey among 50,913 Harvard graduates, and it turned out that "10 percent have run for political office at the local level, and 7 out of 10 of those had been elected."[6]

Harvard's powerful network extends well beyond national borders. According to a report published by *Global Study Magazine*, "from 1945 through mid-2010, seventy-four heads of state and government from forty-two countries have attended, or earned degrees, or held a variety of special scholarships and fellowships at Harvard or Oxford."[7] While many of Oxford's graduates hail from the Commonwealth of Nations, Harvard students-turned-heads-of-state are considerably more diverse, and a significant number represent Latin America: Alejandro Toledo (former president of Peru), Juan Manuel Santos (president of Columbia), Felipe Calderón (former president of Mexico), and Sebastián Piñera (president of Chile)—to name only a few who've emerged from Harvard. It doesn't stop there. Ellen Johnson Sirleaf (president of Liberia), Ban Ki-moon (secretary-general of the UN), Lee Hsien Loong (prime minister of Singapore), and various other international leaders have risen to the top with Harvard degrees in hand— many from Harvard's Kennedy School. Harvard produced more than 11 percent of the U.S. political elite in the second half of the twentieth century, while its only competitor, Yale, educated less than 7 percent. Harvard Law School alone produced thirty-seven national leaders, while all of Yale's colleges combined produced thirty-eight.[8]

What about in business? In 2011, *U.S. News & World Report* surveyed where the CEOs of the largest five hundred companies had attended college, and Harvard University once again topped the charts with more than 11 percent. This is far beyond Columbia University, ranked number two with a mere 4 percent. Making it to graduation isn't even necessary to make a fortune. Take, for example, Bill Gates, one of the world's richest men, or Mark Zuckerberg, the youngest billionaire in the world and founder of Facebook—both are Harvard dropouts!

Colleges Attended by Fortune 500 CEOs in 2011

Institution	Total degrees	Undergraduate degrees	MBAs	Other graduate degrees
1. Harvard University	58	11	33	14
2. Columbia University	21	3	9	9
3. University of Pennsylvania	20	6	9	5
4. University of Wisconsin–Madison	17	11	3	3
5. Dartmouth College	16	12	4	0

Harvard's power among lawyers is also nothing to be scoffed at. The Supreme Court is often referred to as an unofficial "Harvard club." In 2012, among nine Supreme Court justices, six had attended Harvard, while the remaining three came from either Yale or Princeton. When President Barack Obama (also a Harvard Law School graduate), appointed Elena Kagan, dean of HLS at the time, as the 112th Supreme Court justice, she became a member of the outstanding total of twenty-three coming from Harvard.

It's no exaggeration to say that the world is run by Harvard graduates. The university continues to be praised as "the best brand in higher education" or simply put, "the best and brightest." I've found a more accurate description would be to call Harvard "the Vatican of all universities." Take, for example, the statues of John Harvard on the main campus and Saint

Which one looks shinier? Right foot of Saint Peter's statue (left), left foot of John Harvard's statue (right).

Peter in Vatican City. John Harvard's left foot and Saint Peter's right are both gleaming and worn from thousands of hopeful touches and kisses of their pilgrims.

With its power and priceless network, it's easy to believe that attending Harvard is the ultimate shortcut to success. As a result of this common idea, it's one of the most competitive schools to attend, with an acceptance rate of 5.3 percent in 2015, lower than any other school except Stanford at 5 percent. No wonder books targeting prospective students, such as the popular *Successful Harvard Application Essays*, quickly become bestsellers. Yet, the application process isn't nearly as bleak for children of Harvard alumni—thanks to Harvard's "Legacy Admission" policy. In 2011, the *Harvard Crimson* reported that the acceptance rate for legacies was about 30 percent—four times higher than non-legacy admissions.

Extreme competition to attend Harvard is not limited to the United States but is a global phenomenon. At the first screening of *Verita$* (the film version of this book), one member of the audience, whose roots are in Africa, recalled that she was raised to strive for Harvard. In South Korea, the desire and pressure to attend Harvard is commonplace. Young students who dream of attending Harvard sacrifice their nights and weekends to attend exclusive preparatory schools that focus on producing Harvard-eligible candidates.

Despite the global worship of Harvard, most people's knowledge of the university delves no deeper than a superficial understanding. How has Harvard become so powerful? What really makes it stand out from other prestigious American universities? To begin to understand the depth and intricacy of Harvard's power, we must explore the university's history, for what Harvard is today is the sum of many yesterdays.

From Religious Fanatics to Guardians of National Defense

In 1636, the Massachusetts General Court established a college across the Charles River from Boston in an area then called New Town (or "Newe

Admission strategy books displayed at Harvard Coop.

Towne"), which would later be renamed Cambridge in honor of the British university that many colonial leaders had attended. Initially, the college was named New College, and it was the country's first institution of higher education. In 1638, John Harvard, a young minister from London and Cambridge University alumnus, died of tuberculosis, leaving half of his estate (about 400 books and 779 pounds) to the college. In 1639, the school was renamed in his honor. During this time, Harvard College was a training school for Puritan ministers.

What is not so commonly understood is how this religious college became the conglomerate university it is today. This process began in the late seventeenth century with the Salem Witch Trials. The history of the Witch Trials is well known, but few people understand Harvard's involvement in the now infamous cycle of fear and punishment. In 1692, a young girl fingered George Burroughs, who graduated from Harvard in 1670 and was a minister in Maine, as a witch. He was then taken to Salem to be tried by a special tribunal. Coincidently, the members of the special court were mainly Harvard graduates, including the Chief Justice of the witch trial, William Stoughton (class of 1650), and two judges, Samuel Sewall (1671) and Nathaniel Saltonstall (1659). Another important figure that influenced the court was Increase Mather, a devoted minister and president of Harvard at that time. His son, Cotton Mather (1678), a Puritan preacher and member of the Harvard Corporation, was also deeply involved and wrote a book, *Wonders of the Invisible World*, giving his account of the Salem Witch Trials.

Salem Witch Trial.

The trials continued for over a year, and of about 185 people who were arrested, some 19 people were executed. In August 1692, Burroughs was executed with four other convicted witches in front of a large crowd that included Cotton Mather. Before being hanged, Burroughs delivered beautifully the Lord's Prayer, which made the crowd hesitate in continuing the execution. Cotton Mather then bellowed before the congregation, "The devil has often been transformed into an angel of light!"[9] Judge Sewall, who later regretted the trial, wrote in his diary "Mr. Mather says they all died by a Righteous Sentence."[10]

The madness of the witch-hunt finally came to an end only after members of high society were accused of being witches themselves. Members of Harvard College began to reflect deeply on the institution's purpose, and a more open-minded, intellectually independent group formed. The Mathers' power diminished, and eventually President Mather, who resided in Boston, resigned from the presidency in 1701, after the General Court passed an order that all presidents of Harvard must live

Harvard Corporation member Cotton Mather defended the Salem Witch Trials.

in Cambridge. In 1708, John Leverett, a judge, took over as the first non-clergyman president, a breakthrough that infuriated Cotton Mather. This was Harvard's first step in moving away from being a divinity school and toward becoming an academic institution.

Though Harvard's leadership still rested mainly in the hands of clergymen, the eighteenth and nineteenth centuries saw profound improvements in diversification of curriculum and students. During this period, Harvard wasn't the only college that diversified; it was a general phenomenon in higher education throughout America. As industrialization intensified, businessmen donated money to Harvard with the wish that their sons could learn more profitable skills than those provided by divinity studies. A group of unsatisfied donors helped establish a specialized school within Harvard for science and technology. In 1865, the year the Civil War ended, a significant change occurred within Harvard's power structure: the Board of Overseers was formed, composed of thirty Harvard graduates, thereby strengthening the influence of alumni in college governance.

During the eighteenth and nineteenth centuries, Harvard became a distinguished rite of passage for young upper-class men in the Boston area, often called "Boston Brahmins." Henry Adams, grandson of John Quincy Adams, the sixth U.S. president and a Boston Brahmin, spoke of this phenomenon in his autobiography: "For generation after generation, Adams and Brookses and Boylstons and Gorhams had gone to Harvard College, and although none of them, as far as known, had done any good there. . . . All went there because their friends went there, and the College was their ideal of social self-respect."[11]

In order to understand the roots of Harvard's prestige, it is important to keep in mind Boston's central role in the founding of the United States. The Boston Tea Party was just one of many momentous events during the

Cotton Mather and the Birth of Yale

The nomination of John Leverett to Harvard president was shocking news to Cotton Mather, who envisioned himself following in his father's footsteps. What did he do? He focused his attention on a fledgling college that opened in Connecticut in 1701. Among twelve founding members of this school, eleven were Harvard graduates. In 1716, the college moved to its current location in New Haven, and Cotton Mather asked a merchant, Elihu Yale, to donate to the college. Yale contributed nine bales of goods, 417 books, and a portrait of King George, which were sold for a substantial amount of money. Mather encouraged the founders of the college to change its name to honor this generous benefactor, who then happily called himself the "godfather" of the new college.

American Revolution that brought Boston, one of the oldest cities in the country, to the forefront of the struggle for independence. During this time, Harvard played a contributing role, as it was here that many revolutionary troops were lodged during the long uprising. Many Harvard men were also important leaders of the revolution, including John Hancock, Samuel Adams, and John Adams. As a result, you can find many Harvard graduates among the signatories of the Declaration of Independence: Samuel Adams, John Adams, John Hancock, Elbridge Gerry, Robert Treat Paine, William Ellery, William Williams, and William Hooper. Harvard also strengthened their ties with political leaders by awarding them honorary degrees, including many Founding Fathers. George Washington (1776), John Adams (1781), Thomas Jefferson (1787), James Monroe (1817), John Quincy Adams (1822), and Andrew Jackson (1833)—six out of the seven first American presidents—received honorary Harvard degrees, illustrating and solidifying Harvard's powerful status.

Until the middle of the nineteenth century, the student body was composed mostly of men from Massachusetts, with some from surrounding New England states. According to social historian Stephan Thernstrom, "Some 82 percent of the students enrolled in the college in 1810 were from the Bay State; in the 1830s the figure was 86 percent. . . . Yale was considerably more successful than Harvard in attracting students from the Midwest, and Princeton had much greater draw in the South. On this count, Harvard was a more provincial institution in the antebellum years than some of the competition."[12]

Before the Civil War, Harvard had been a college for Boston's inner circle, but by the late nineteenth century its student body had rapidly diversified. Charles Eliot, often admired as the greatest president in Harvard history, was the key figure who guided this transformation. Born to an upper-class Bostonian scientist, he believed that "for the safety of Harvard College, and for the welfare of the country, the college [must] draw its material not from Massachusetts or from New England alone; but from the whole country."[13] Governed by Eliot's four decades of leadership (1869–1909), Harvard's population

Harvard President Charles Eliot (1869–1909).

from the Bay State fell from 70 percent to about 50 percent at the end of the century. By 1905, students from other regions accounted for up to 42 percent of enrollments.

Under Eliot's leadership, Harvard transformed itself from a provincial institution into a national university. He invited great scholars from around the country and adopted the "elective system," allowing undergraduates unrestricted choice of study. Eliot reshaped Harvard into the modern university it is today. However, as an upper-class Bostonian, he believed that women's education was unnecessary and even dangerous. He therefore restricted women from entering Harvard, despite severe criticism from feminists. As a delicate gentleman, he also hated tough sports, especially football. He believed football was "a brutal, cheating, demoralizing game" and tried to abolish it at Harvard. Unfortunately his idea wasn't so popular, and Theodore Roosevelt, who had a passion for football, was among those who did not agree. In 1905, President Roosevelt summoned coaches from Harvard, Yale, and Princeton to the White House and encouraged them to reform the sport. They did, by creating what became the National Collegiate Athletic Association (NCAA) and instituting the forward pass as part of the game.

Even though Eliot and Roosevelt had different opinions about sports, they had one important thing in common: they both believed that American universities should serve the national interest. Eliot wrote, "We seek to train doers, achievers, men whose successful careers are much subservient to the public good. We are not interested here in producing languid observers of the world, mere spectators in the game of life, or fastidious critics of other men's labors."[14] Theodore Roosevelt urged college students to enter public service as well, a noble belief eloquently conveyed at a commencement: "Always there has been a harmony of interest between America and Harvard. Every venture of Harvard has been in response to national interest or national need. Harvard became a college because America needed a college. Harvard is what it is today because America wants and needs what Harvard is."[15]

Throughout the twentieth century, the growth of Harvard and the United States were mutually dependent, and as they together went through two world wars, they ended up becoming the leading powers of the world.

The Mythology of a "Left-Liberal" Harvard

A very popular myth about Harvard is that it is the home of American left-liberalism. Senator Joseph McCarthy and Richard Nixon even went so far as to call Harvard "the Kremlin on the Charles," adding to the progressive mystique surrounding the university.

Harvard's liberal reputation is an obstacle that hinders understanding of its true character. While making the documentary film, Verita$, I found that trying to understand Harvard's progressive image was one of my most puzzling tasks, despite my meetings with many of Harvard's progressive professors. In order to understand the university's true character, we must look at the role in which it has played as an institution throughout its long history.

The myth of a "radical" Harvard partly originated during the time of McCarthyism in the 1950s, when an anti-Communist fever swept over the United States. When Harvard came under heavy attack by McCarthy and his followers, many Harvard professors and students pleaded the Fifth Amendment in order not to be forced to testify against colleagues who were suspected of being Communists. Harvard president Nathan Pusey, successor to James Conant, held press conferences and issued statements rebuffing McCarthy's fierce attacks. While some consider Pusey a heroic figure, others also remember his ordering the bloody 1969 police raid on student anti-war activists occupying University Hall.

Harvard's persecution and resistance during the McCarthy Era is a source of great pride for the university. At the 350th anniversary celebration, with Prince Charles along with over twenty thousand people in attendance, student orators frequently referred to Harvard as a haven for dissent, referencing the 1950s. John Trumpbour, a PhD student in the Department of History at the time, (currently research director of the Labor and Worklife Program at HLS) was shocked by the number of scholarly articles and books glorifying the university as a progressive haven. In 1989, he edited the book *How Harvard Rules*, perhaps the most critical book about Harvard available today, regarding the university as a "service station" for the American ruling class.

Dr. Trumpbour analyzed Harvard's reaction to McCarthyism and found it somewhat deceptive. "Whenever McCarthy went after very mainstream establishment people and accused them of being soft on Communism, or of having some kind of leftist affiliation, Harvard would defend those people, and sometimes defend them very strongly. But the reality was, people who were actually socialist or leftist at Harvard—well, Harvard often fed them to the wolves. Harvard cooperated with the FBI. Harvard got rid of people."[16]

Ellen W. Schrecker conducted extensive research on McCarthyism and Harvard's reaction. In her book *No Ivory Tower* she insists, "The academy did not fight McCarthyism. It contributed to it."[17] (McCarthyism and its impact on American universities, including Harvard, will be further analyzed in Chapter 4.)

The simple fact that Harvard men have been monopolizing key positions in the U.S. government for centuries is evidence enough of the mythical nature of Harvard's status as a haven for dissent. For instance, many Harvard men had a strong hand in planning and promoting the Vietnam War, including McGeorge Bundy, Robert McNamara, Samuel Huntington, and Henry Kissinger, to name a few. Not only did Harvardians have prominent roles in the Kennedy and LBJ administrations, but they also made major contributions to the right-wing Reagan administration. Attorney General Edwin Meese openly bragged that the percentage of Harvard people in cabinet and subcabinet positions serving Reagan well exceeded that of JFK and "any Administration in American history."[18]

Though the Kennedy administration is often referred to as left-liberal, Noam Chomsky, MIT professor and well-known author, writes in his book *Necessary Illusions* that he sees the U.S. political system as "one political party, with two factions controlled by shifting segments of the business community."[19] In my interview with him, Professor Chomsky pointed to the myth of Harvard being left-liberal by analyzing what that term actually means. To Chomsky, something considered "left-liberal" in the United States means that they are actually at the center of U.S. imperialism:

> The Kennedy administration, for example, was called left-liberal and it was very closely interconnected with Harvard and MIT, but they were some of the most vicious imperial years in American history. That's when the Vietnam War took off. The war actually began in 1962, overtly when Kennedy sent the U.S. Air Force to bomb South Vietnam.... And it goes right up to the present. I mean, the Obama administration is called left-liberal, but their foreign policy is barely distinguishable from Bush. There is a very narrow spectrum of policy planning. It doesn't really have a right-left dimension very much. In fact, there are times where left-liberal was more extreme than so-called conservative. It's just the state policy spectrum that is extremely narrow. So yes, left-liberal, if you like, may mean people are more critical of programs that failed.[20]

Many people would disagree with this point of view. Harvard is certainly much more liberal than other universities, particularly compared to Yale or conservative universities in the South. Along with conservative faculty members, Harvard also has progressives on its staff. Professor Richard Levins believes that to understand Harvard correctly, one has to grasp its contradictory nature:

> It's an organ of the American ruling class whose mission is to do the intellectual labor that class needs. And they define it very flexibly. In some areas, Harvard really understands the world in order to intervene in it. In other areas, it's justifying the world, and in other areas it's contributing to the world's knowledge through genetics, archaeology, and linguistics, for instance.... So it's this kind of mixture. In

order to be able to carry out this function, it has to allow maximum freedom within the boundaries. . . . The makeup of Harvard is such that it is not going to be focused on revolutionary activities. . . . It's limited and so it's safe.[21]

During our candid meeting, I asked Professor Levins how he maintained his job at Harvard, despite his leftist persuasion and outspoken criticism of the university. He explained that Harvard wouldn't attempt to fire him, though they have other ways of marginalizing him and other radical voices within the university. This made me wonder: why would Harvard go through the trouble of hiring leftist professors in the first place, if they are only going to marginalize them while they're there? After thinking about this question, the answer became obvious: Harvard's pride in the myth of its progressive character. In order to uphold its image of being a haven for academic freedom, they must allow dissidents among their faculty. This makes clear why Harvard hired Professor Levins, who was fired from his position at the University of Puerto Rico for his involvement in their independence movement.

To be a leading academic institution, any university needs progressive scholars for its image as well as to help encourage students to think critically. Because of its superior status and alluring mystique as a sanctuary of academic freedom, Harvard must include leftist and radical thinkers on their faculty. However, despite wanting to maintain the myth, there is a line that they will not cross. Paul Sweezy, an outstanding Marxist economist of the twentieth century, left Harvard because he didn't get tenure. He resigned without hesitation, and founded *Monthly Review* magazine with Leo Huberman. To this day, Harvard still refuses to hire Marxist economists,[22] but to maintain their reputation of openness and critical thought, they've brought in a handful of Marxist biologists. As Professor Levins mildly joked about the relationship of his politics to his scientific field, "They didn't think it mattered."

CHAPTER 2

GOVERNING HARVARD

"We have a system of governance that permits non-consensual and unpopular decisions to be made when necessary. We have learned that not everything is improved by making it more democratic."
—Henry Rosovsky, former dean of Harvard's Faculty of Arts and Sciences and former member of the Harvard Corporation[1]

"The Soviet Union has the Kremlin, the Vatican has the College of Cardinals, and Harvard University has the Corporation."
—Samuel Huntington, Harvard professor of political science[2]

To understand Harvard, where shall we begin? As with any organization, I suggest that we examine its governance. Who makes important decisions? What kinds of people compose the top decision-making body? How do they reach their conclusions? These are key questions we should ask in order to view clearly Harvard's character. We should first look at who chooses the president, a symbolic figure but also a very powerful one.

In 2007, Harvard announced that their new president would be Drew Gilpin Faust, an American historian, after Lawrence Summers ran into deep trouble inside the Harvard community. Founded in 1636, Harvard had chosen only twenty-seven other presidents, and it had finally arrived at a historic moment by naming its first female president. You can imagine what a great fuss the media made about this change. Headlines blared: "Harvard Plans to Name First Female President" (*New York Times*, February 10, 2007), "Harvard Names First Female President" (*Washington Post*, February 12, 2007), and "Harvard Board Names First Woman President" (MSNBC, February 11, 2007).

To me, it is as interesting that Harvard has had only twenty-eight presidents in 371 years as that a female was finally chosen. Think about it. George Washington, the first president of the United States, took office in 1789,

about 150 years after Harvard was founded, and President Obama is the nation's forty-fourth president. So it is easy to see that Harvard's presidents have held office for long periods. Their average term is about 13.4 years. Don't forget that Lawrence Summers, who made a huge contribution, shortened the average by resigning after only five years. Presidents of Harvard hold an imperial seat. Once appointed, no one can force them to quit unless they resign themselves. Who chooses the presidents? The answer is the Harvard Corporation.

Harvard's first female president, Drew Faust.

The Harvard Corporation, the Core of Harvard's Power Structure

Formally known as the President and Fellows of Harvard College, the Harvard Corporation is the university's top governing board. In 1650, the Great and General Court of Massachusetts approved Harvard's charter by establishing the President and Fellows of Harvard College (also known as the Harvard Corporation), making it the oldest corporation in the Western Hemisphere.

For more than three centuries, it comprised seven members: the president, treasurer, and five fellows; but in 2010, Harvard suddenly announced that it would increase its members from seven to thirteen. The chart below shows the structure of Harvard's central administration. As you can see, the Harvard Corporation is the university's top decision-making body.

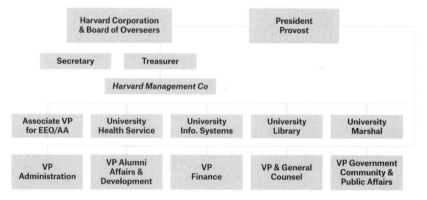

The Harvard Corporation.

Professor Samuel Huntington acknowledged the corporation's absolute power when he referred to it as "our Politburo."[3] Students satirized its operations with the poster shown right.

Another top organization within the above chart is the Board of Overseers. While Harvard Corporation members are sometimes drawn from outside the university, the Board of Overseers, composed of thirty members, is elected solely from the pool of Harvard graduates. The corporation reports to the board about overall affairs of the university, and the board advises and either accepts or denies decisions made by the corporation. In reality, however, the board is a symbolic entity that insiders routinely describe as a device to make Harvard's autocratic regime appear democratic. As Overseer George Leighton, a retired federal judge, summed it up, "The Board of Overseers does not advise on policy. What it does is consent."[4]

Poster satirizing the Harvard Corporation.

Until very recently, the seven members of the Harvard Corporation, including the president, could continue their tenure as long as they wanted. It was impossible for anyone to become a member unless a current member died. When there is a vacancy, the successor is selected in a closed meeting. The corporation's main concerns include finance, budget, and long-term development planning. Their regular biweekly meetings are closed to the public, and they do not disclose meeting locations, agendas, or details of their decision-making process.

It is telling that these "fellows" were exclusively white men until the late 1980s. In 1989, Judith Richards Hope (class of 1964), a Washington lawyer, became the first woman serving in the corporation. The first black man, Conrad K. Harper (class of 1965), of Simpson Thacher & Bartlett, was elected in 2000.[5]

John Trumpbour observed that "the Harvard Corporation's mission is to see that Harvard continues on in its traditions and continues to be a service station for the ruling class."[6] He also points out that it is very much "insulated from public opinion." A good example, according to Dr. Trumpbour, is Henry Rosovsky, a former Harvard dean and the author of *The University: An Owner's Manual*, who "openly bragged that democracy doesn't make everything better and Harvard and the Harvard Corporation, in his mind, was a proof for that."[7]

Who are the Harvard Corporation fellows? One might expect that they are mostly university insiders like deans and professors, but that could not be further from the case. The early fellows were prominent social figures like religious leaders, lawyers, politicians, and eminent scholars. Protestant leaders formed an especially important group in the corporation until long after the Civil War. In this early stage, their most important objectives were to ensure the university's religious mission among the faculty and students, and to raise funds for the management of the college.

Towards the late nineteenth century, as the United States was emerging as the world's economic powerhouse, more and more fellows of the Corporation were replaced by entrepreneurs, financial capitalists, and corporate lawyers. This phenomenon was not limited to Harvard. Clyde W. Barrow studied the impact of corporations on higher education in the United States. In his book *Universities and the Capitalist State*, Barrow found that American universities began to be governed by corporations in the late nineteenth century. After an analysis of jobs held by board members, he noted: "During the first three decades of this [twentieth] century, governing boards at major private universities in the Northeast came firmly under the direction of corporate officials attached to the dominant financial groups."[8] From the late nineteenth century to the early twentieth, the percentage of businessmen and lawyers on university boards of directors more than doubled, jumping from 31.6 percent to 66 percent. During this same time, large donations flowed into universities from big corporations and millionaires.

The following table from the same book illustrates these changes.

Vocations of Trustees at Private Colleges, Universities, and Technical Institutes, 1861-1929 (Percentages)

	1861–1880	1881–1900	1901–1920	1921–1929
Number of cases	147	150	179	144
Number with vocation unidentified	21	21	10	11
Professionals (clergyman, physician, educator, lawyer, judge)	71.5	62	50.3	38.2
Businessmen (journalist, merchant/commerce, mfg./mining, railroad, engineer, banking/finance)	19.1	30.0	38.0	51.4
Agriculturalist	0	0	0	0
Government officials (federal, state/local, military)	7.5	6.6	6.7	4.9
Other	2.0	1.3	5.0	5.6
Total	100.1	99.9	100.0	100.1
Total businessmen and lawyers	31.6	54.7	59.2	66.0

Source: *Universities and the Capitalist State*, p. 36

Entering the second phase of the Industrial Revolution after the Civil War, the United States achieved rapid growth across all major industries, including transportation, banking, mining, steel, finance, newspapers, and communications. As *nouveaux riches* sprouted here and there, the top 1 percent of the American population was estimated to own 51 percent of the entire national wealth in the 1890s. The largest source of operating costs for universities in the early twentieth century was the individual donation. As wealth was amassed more and more by a handful of people, universities increasingly depended upon them.

J.P. Morgan Sr. (left) and Jr. (right).

At that time, two major pillars of the American economy were the J.P. Morgan and Rockefeller families. The former was rooted in finance and the latter in the oil business. Together they practically controlled U.S. industrial production. These two giants became important patrons of Harvard, competitively donating enormous sums of money after J.P. Morgan gave more than a million dollars for the construction of three Harvard Medical School buildings. For more than a century, the two families have continued to have a strong influence on Harvard. Morgan's son, J.P. Morgan Jr. (class of 1889), served on the Board of Overseers, and Morgan's grandson, Henry S. Morgan (class of 1923), also served on the same board for more than four decades from 1935 until he died in 1982. David Rockefeller (class of 1936), John D. Rockefeller's son, served on the Board of Overseers from 1954 to 1966, completing his Harvard career as Chairman of the Board of Overseers from 1966 to 1968.

The strong influence of these two families on Harvard is obvious when we look at Harvard Corporation members. Major Higginson, who served as a corporation member for twenty-six years, was also a board member of J.P. Morgan and the Carnegie Corporation. Robert Bacon, who became a fellow in 1912, was Morgan's partner. Thomas Lamont, another partner of Morgan, also served as a Harvard Corporation fellow. In addition, many fellows of the Harvard Corporation were officers of corporations owned by the Rockefeller family, or members of their advisory boards. Robert

Rubin, a current Harvard Corporation fellow, was a CEO of Goldman Sachs, U.S. secretary of the treasury under President Clinton, and an advisor and executive at Citigroup, which is among the banks that became part of the post–petroleum era foundation of the Rockefeller fortune. As these two families at one point were estimated to have significant ownership stakes in 65 percent of the top two hundred corporations in the United States, it may have been difficult to fill the Harvard Corporation with people unrelated to them.

Whether or not appointed by the Rockefellers and Morgans, Harvard Corporation members are overwhelmingly drawn from business interests. Control of university boards of directors by corporations is currently a standard practice among U.S. universities. This is understandable, since universities need to secure wealthy supporters for its normal and emergency operations. According to John Trumpbour,

> In 1969, the Corporation's members held one corporate chair, three presidencies, and 24 directorships. In 1988, its members possessed five corporate chairs and 34 directorships (though three and fifteen respectively belonged to one man, Robert Stone, who ranks among the greatest of what Richard Rovere refers to as the "interlocking overlappers" of the corporate world). In 1969, the larger Board of Overseers had twelve corporate chairs, five presidencies, and 84 directorships. According to incomplete data (primarily obtained from the University's election brochures), the 1985–86 board had at least seven corporate chairs and 53 directorships.[9]

Why do so many businessmen commit themselves to the management of universities, sacrificing their time to work for nonprofit organizations? Professor Donald Macedo helps us understand the answer to this question:

> As the corporate culture exercises more control over schools, teachers are reduced to the role of imposing "an official truth" predetermined by "a small group of people who analyze, execute, make decisions, and run things in the political, economic and ideological systems." ... Instead students are rewarded to the degree that they become complicit with their own stupidification and become the "so-called good student who repeats, who renounces critical thinking, who adjusts to models, [who] should do nothing other than receive contents that are impregnated with the ideological character vital to the interests of the sacred order."[10]

American businessmen took control of universities because they consider universities as media through which "'an official truth' predetermined by 'a small group of people'" can be transmitted. To them universities are manpower training schools for passive and accommodating intellectuals. As a result of corporate control over universities, universities have certainly lost their character as public institutions. They cannot be free from the demands of specific corporations, their financial backers. A good example of this is the Harvard-Enron scandal in 2002.

The Honeymoon between Harvard and Enron

In 2002, Harvard Watch, a group of Harvard students and graduates, published a shocking report on the intimate relationship between Harvard and Enron. They revealed that Highfields Capital, an investment management firm that handles Harvard's endowments, made $50 million by selling Enron stocks immediately before Enron's declaration of bankruptcy towards the end of 2001. This transaction was extremely timely, so much so that local newspapers made a fuss about Highfields Capital's ability to predict Enron's demise.

It is hard to believe that this success of Highfields Capital was simply due to its exceptional business acumen or luck. Above all, Herbert "Pug" Winokur Jr., the finance committee chairman of Enron at the time, was a member of the Harvard Corporation. Moreover, Winokur had been deeply involved in the management of Harvard's endowment as a director of Harvard Management Company since 1995. Highfields Capital was established by Jonathan Jacobson, the fund manager of Harvard Management Company, using $500 million from Harvard's endowment as seed money. As one of the directors of Harvard Management Company, Winokur approved this deal. In February 2000 Winokur was elected to become a fellow of the Harvard Corporation, whose responsibility was to supervise the Harvard Management Company. It was impossible for the world not to notice these relationships to the incredibly timely sale of Enron stocks by Highfields Capital.

According to the above-mentioned report by Harvard Watch, Winokur was central to the short-lived success of Enron's high-risk business model. Enron leveraged Winokur's corporate finance expertise and government relations experience to advance its deregulatory program. Robert Belfer, a longtime board member of Enron and the largest shareholder of Enron stocks, used his financial resources and personal connections to shape Harvard's research priorities. In 1997 Belfer donated $7.5 million to the Center for Science and International Affairs at Harvard, subsequently renamed the Robert and Renee Belfer Center, for energy-related strategic research.

The relationship between officers of Enron and Harvard was exceptionally intimate. Specifically, Enron had Harvard scholars produce policies that served Enron's interests by funding their research with millions of dollars. Enron was a major contributor to the Harvard Electricity Policy Group (HEPG), a division of the Kennedy School's Center for Business and Government. Predictably, much of the research agenda of the HEPG centers on deregulation of the electricity market. Harvard Business School produced five glowing case studies on Enron, the last of which was published in August 2001, only a few months prior to Enron's collapse. Harvard professors coauthored books with Enron officers and reaped generous financial rewards for their services for Enron.

When the value of Enron stocks plummeted together with the company's collapse in 2001, twenty thousand employees lost most of their savings and pensions. Paul Krugman, the 2008 Nobel Prize–winning economist and *New York Times* columnist, famously said, "In the years ahead Enron, not September 11, will come to be seen as the greater turning point in U.S. society."[11] He believed buildings could be rebuilt, but trust, once lost, could not easily be regained. Even Krugman was subject to controversy, since he had received fifty thousand dollars from Enron as a member of its advisory board.

Of course, Harvard claimed that it was an academic institution and had nothing to do with the whole Enron incident, let alone being responsible for it. However, scholars who received financial support and rewards from Enron and served Enron's interests through their studies cannot be free from responsibilities. Their responsibilities are no lighter than the responsibilities of the officers of Enron. As the scandal grew, Winokur resigned from his position on the Harvard Corporation and Robert Rubin was selected to replace him. However, Rubin had also played an essential role in the legislation favoring Enron during the Clinton presidency, and Citi Group, where Rubin was CEO, was Enron's biggest creditor.

The Enron scandal illustrates well the result of a university's subservient alliance with a specific corporation, but Enron is not the only example of Harvard's suspicious corporate connections. In October 2002, the *Boston Globe* published an article based on another report by Harvard Watch that revealed the circumstances under which Harvard had invested in Harken, an energy company with no positive prospects. When Harvard began investing in Harken, it was a company that had nothing to it other than its connection to George W. Bush, one of its board members before he was elected president. Harvard Management Company began investing in Harken in 1986, immediately after Bush came onto its board. Harvard Management Company saved Harken three times by pouring funds into it from 1989 to 1991, during Bush Sr.'s presidency. During this period, Bush Jr. sold his stocks worth $848,000, two thirds of the Harken stocks he owned. As Harken's financial problems continued, Harvard formed a partnership with Harken in 1990 and poured in another $64.5 million. As a result, Harken's stock price soared, and it was able pay off its twenty-million-dollar debt. In the end, Harvard Management Company lost tens of millions of dollars in the Harken venture. At the time, rumor had it that Harvard had done the Bush family a favor, though of course Harvard Management Company categorically denied the allegation.

Once specific corporations begin to control a university, it is bound to lose its neutrality. Whether or not it is a world-renowned university like Harvard does not matter. Even more alarming, this kind of serious problem is rarely known and even more seldom discussed. That is one reason why organizations like Harvard Watch are a necessity.

"Not My Concern": The Motto of Harvard's President

A new characteristic of Harvard's power structure is its decentralization. Harvard's history of decentralization is not that old. After the Second World War, Harvard continued to receive research funds from the U.S. government and functioned as a strategic research institute. This intimate relationship between Harvard and the government climaxed in the early 1960s, when John F. Kennedy was president. Students began participating in the civil rights movement in the mid-1960s and continued onto the anti-war movement during the 1960s and 1970s, and their confrontation tactics sparked Harvard to change its governing structure.

In 1969, students occupied University Hall to protest Harvard's ROTC program, and Harvard's president Nathan Pusey called in state police to remove the demonstrators, opening up the greatest period of sustained upheaval in Harvard's history. As a result, President Pusey stepped down in 1971.

Derek Bok, Pusey's successor, was a savvy law scholar specializing in labor law. Instead of sending police to attack student demonstrators, Bok showed up with coffee and donuts and struck up conversations with his erstwhile opponents. His goal was to rescue old and decrepit Harvard from its crisis. In order to accomplish this task, he replaced the traditional governing structure with a modernized corporate-style management system. In a few words, he decentralized the university's administrative system. Above all, he separated student affairs from management and enlarged the number of vice presidents from one to five.

Bok decentralized graduate schools as well. With independent tenure, admission, and funding systems, Harvard's graduate schools had been traditionally quite autonomous. These already separate organizations became even more autonomous thanks to decentralization, under which the central administration was entirely relieved of responsibilities for affairs internal to individual graduate schools. As Edward J. Baker, former associate director of the Harvard-Yenching Institute, told me during an interview, "[Harvard]

Harvard president Derek Bok took the initiative in the decentralization of the university structure.

is a very decentralized place. The Harvard saying is 'every tub on its own bottom,' which means every program is supposed to run itself and finance itself."[12]

A good example that testifies to one effect of decentralization was the Safran Affair involving Professors Samuel Huntington and Nadav Safran. As I will discuss in more detail in Chapter 6, as a result of student protests in the late 1960s, Harvard banned secret research in conjunction with the CIA. President Bok was a strong supporter of the new policy, but once the Safran scandal broke out and Professors Huntington and Safran were discovered to have been conducting research in collaboration with the CIA unbeknownst to students and faculty colleagues, President Bok neither enforced this principle nor campaigned for it. Thanks to decentralization, the central administration of the university did not have to take responsibility for whatever happened in any of its units. The decentralized system awarded the university an amnesty.

Robert Weissman, who worked for years as a member of Harvard Watch, wrote an essay, "How Harvard Is Ruled," in which he expounded upon serious problems introduced by Bok's corporate-style governing system. Due to the vertical structure of layers, the responsible party for a certain action becomes obscure, and therefore nobody is willing to take responsibility. In the end, this means that the central administration becomes alienated from all members of Harvard, and especially from students. Weissman argued that this decentralized system has an effect not only on education but also on the way students think. Students are led to passively conform and accept the way the school governs them.[13]

Reluctant Reform

The Harvard Corporation's undemocratic management system has been constantly subject to criticism from both within and outside the school. For example, a select committee of the state legislature began investigating Harvard College in the interests of educational reform in the mid-nineteenth century. Judging that Harvard failed "to answer the just expectations of the people of the State," the committee report called for more vocational training learning "for a specific purpose." Interestingly, "A bill was written to increase membership in the Corporation to fifteen, elected by the legislature for six-year terms."[14] This recommendation suggests that people have been dissatisfied with the mighty power and autocratic system of the Corporation for a long time. Nonetheless, it seems that the state legislature didn't have enough power to overcome Harvard's authority. Action was deferred to the next General Court and eventually dropped quietly away.

A century later, on December 6, 2010, the *Harvard Crimson* ran an article, "Harvard Corporation Announces Historic Overhaul to Governance Structure," which dealt with Harvard's reform of its governing board. The gist of the changes included a near doubling of the board size from seven to thirteen members, limiting their service to a maximum of two six-year terms, and establishing various committees in charge of capital planning and finance, governance, and alumni affairs and development. According to the "Governance Letter from President and Senior Fellow," these changes grew out of "an intensive governance review," "expert outside advice" and "thoughtful input offered by people across the Harvard community." The letter also promised to "take steps to keep the University community better informed about the essence of the Corporation's work, and seek further opportunities to learn from members of the community about their experiences, their ideas, and their aspirations for the University."[15]

Why did Harvard suddenly attempt to reform its governing structure? We cannot help but wonder, especially when we consider Harvard's history of ignoring all kinds of ethical criticisms amid various scandals, from the Harvard-Enron Scandal to criticisms of the university's closed management system. The new structure at the top was a response to the financial crisis of 2008 that shook the world (as I will discuss in Chapter 9).

In the past, the Harvard Management Company had reaped enormous profits through risky investments. Harvard's endowment had dramatically increased every year, and Harvard's fund managers raked in tens of millions of dollars annually from bonuses. However, within a year after the 2008 financial crisis, Harvard's endowment plummeted by $11 billion, almost 30 percent of its entire value. Under these circumstances, Harvard laid off or gave reduced work hours to around a thousand of its personnel and stopped a large-scale construction project underway as a part of its expansion plan. People within and outside the Harvard community strongly protested and criticized the Corporation's obscure and irresponsible management style—and especially its irresponsible actions towards surrounding communities. Some people even argued that Harvard's tax-exempt status should be reconsidered. In this plight, Harvard had no choice but to restructure its management system.

Even after these recent reforms, the size of the Harvard Corporation is much smaller than the boards of most other universities. According to a recent survey by the Association of Governing Boards of Universities and Colleges, the board of private colleges, on average, has twenty-nine members and eight separate committees."[16] It is surprising that a seven-member board had been managing Harvard, one of the world's oldest universities and with the largest endowment of any. Nonetheless, this reform is noteworthy in that it is the first major internal change to this body in more than 360 years of Harvard's history.

CHAPTER 3

THE HARVARD TRADITION: RICH, WHITE, AND MALE

"Educate, and save ourselves and our families and our money from mobs."
—Henry Lee Higginson, Benefactor of Harvard in a fundraising letter, 1886[1]

"I am sorry to have to tell you that in Freshman Halls, where residence is compulsory, we have felt from the beginning the necessity of not including colored men. . . . From the beginning, we have not thought it possible to compel men of different races to reside together."
—Harvard president Abbott Lawrence Lowell (1909–1933) in a letter rejecting a request for a black student to move into the freshmen dormitory[2]

"The Corporation will not receive women as students into the College proper, nor into any school whose discipline requires residence near the school. . . . The world knows next to nothing about the natural mental capacities of the female sex."
—Harvard president Charles Eliot (1869–1909), in his inaugural address[3]

One of my favorite movies from my teens was *Love Story*. I saw it many times when it was aired repeatedly on holidays in South Korea. I'm not sure what made the movie so popular. Was it because it portrayed a bright young couple's tearful love story or because the main characters were Harvard students? However, it left me with the clear impression that Harvard students were generally white. If someone were to ask you to draw a typical Harvard student, you might think of a wealthy Caucasian male wearing a hockey T-shirt.

In the last decade, Harvard has welcomed many other types of students. In April 2006, the *Harvard Gazette* reported that the class of 2010 set new records for economic, gender, and ethnic diversity. Latinos made up 9.8 percent, Native Americans 1.4 percent, African Americans 10.5 percent, and Asian Americans 17.7 percent. Altogether non-white students became nearly 40 percent. William C. Kirby, dean of the Faculty of Arts and Sciences, delivered an impressive message, saying, "Outstanding students from all backgrounds deserve an equal chance at securing a strong education. Harvard will continue to support talented individuals across the socioeconomic spectrum."

Today, Harvard has become a place where students from all around the world are welcomed. As enumerated in the graph below, whites (42 percent) still outnumbered any other ethnicity, and compared to the U.S. population, Asian and Pacific Islanders are far more represented.

Demographics of Harvard's student body

	Undergraduate	Graduate	Professional	U.S. Census
Black/Non-Hispanic	8 percent	3 percent	6 percent	12.1 percent
Asian/Pacific Islander	17 percent	9 percent	12 percent	4.3 percent
White/Non-Hispanic	42 percent	42 percent	43 percent	65.8 percent
Hispanic	7 percent	3 percent	5 percent	14.5 percent
Native American	1 percent	0.2 percent	0.6 percent	0.9 percent
International Students	11 percent	33 percent	22 percent	N/A

Source: Wikipedia, 2011

More than half of the undergraduate student body are women (51.8 percent) as are 48 percent of graduate students and 49 percent of people enrolled in professional courses. This change is remarkable if we consider the three quotes at the beginning of this chapter from very distinguished gentlemen. Henry Lee Higginson donated thirty-one acres to Harvard in the late nineteenth century and later became a fellow of the Corporation. Harvard presidents Abbott Lawrence Lowell (1909-33) and Charles Eliot (1869-1909) were prominent figures who led Harvard for decades. What was Harvard like a century ago?

Of the Rich, by the Rich, for the Rich
Benjamin Franklin, one of the founding fathers of America, once created a character who reflected that Harvard graduates are "as great Blockheads as ever, only more proud and self-conceited."[4] Twentieth-century students who received nearly perfect scores on their SAT's and went through a tough race to be accepted (only a 6 percent acceptance rate), may consider his joke an insult. But if you understand the eighteenth-century atmosphere in which Franklin lived, you would know he wasn't just scoffing.

From the beginning, Harvard was a place of the rich, by the rich, and for the rich. The early graduates of Harvard were all sons of clergymen or ruling elites, and Harvard was stepping stones leading them to become the next social leaders. Henry Lee Higginson's letter, "Educate, and save ourselves and our families and our money from mobs," clearly states Harvard's early character and its goal to reproduce ruling elites. So it is not surprising that Harvard had been very sensitive about the rank of their students.

As John Trumpbour observes,

> Well into the eighteenth century, Harvard's president kept a list iden-
> tifying the social rank of each student, a register printed in the college
> catalog that determined table seating, placement in processions, and
> speaking privileges in class. By the end of that century, the list was
> scuttled, as the president could not handle the mounting complaints
> from student's parents who felt that their family deserved higher
> ranking. In its place, a whole network of finals clubs developed, such
> as Porcellian, A.D., and Fly, which persist to this day, imposing elite
> ranking in a fashion surely as definitive as that of the dons.[5]

Finals clubs, notorious for their exclusive memberships, provide a lucid illustration of Harvard as a university for the rich. Among several social clubs, Porcellian carries the longest history back to 1791. Franklin Roosevelt was refused acceptance there.[6] The distinguished political scientist James MacGregor Burns wrote, "This blow gave him something of an inferiority complex, according to Eleanor Roosevelt; it was the bitterest moment of his life, according to another relative."[7] Even today, when Harvard has more female students than males, these gentlemen clubs still stick to a male-only tradition. Every year, they "punch" new members in an extremely competitive selection process since to become a member means stepping into high society.

Club members are frequently descendants of Harvard alumni who came to Harvard generation after generation. Though all the clubs now emphasize an open policy, the membership can't deny sons of club alumni because much of club revenues come from alumni. One wealthy man was so furious when his son was turned down by the club where he used to be a member that he stormed up with his Rolls-Royce, collected all the goods he had given and joined another club. It appears there are two kinds of Harvard: one is a group of students who worked hard to get in there, and the other was born as nobles and continues to be the ruling elite.

Many people have pointed to Harvard's unfair legacy policy. Professor Victor Wallis, political scientist at Berklee College of Music and Harvard class of 1959, is one of them: "Old Harvard families were admitted regardless of their skills and so on. As critics would put it, it was affirmative action in favor of descendants of Harvard graduates, and they had their separate club life and so on which was independent of the college. They have meals from separate clubs not from the regular houses where most of us eat. And you can sort of recognize them by the elegant way they dressed."[8]

People who associate Harvard with intelligence or genius might feel betrayed. How many legacy students are there? According to a leaflet published by Harvard students during the 1960s, about 20 percent of students at that time were descendants of Harvard alumni, and 40 percent were from prep schools. Today Harvard's acceptance rate is about 6 percent, but legacy admission is almost 30 percent. One recent report says that about 12 to 13 percent of Harvard undergraduates are legacy admissions while Yale remains at less than 10 percent.[9]

Though the ratio of legacy admission is decreasing, it won't disappear so easily. Many people have advocated the policy including former Dean Wilbur J. Bender in an article in *Harvard Today* of February 1958. "I hope and believe that Harvard sons will always have a preference as they do now. This is not just a matter of sentiment or even self-interest. It is based on the belief that in a too rootless world, inheritance and nurture mean something."[10] While his words "inheritance" and "nurture" make lasting impressions, sensible people should come across a dollar sign here. In fact, the legacy policy is not something special at Harvard. Many other colleges welcome legacy students because of their families' fruitful donations. The Ivy League's average acceptance rate hovers between 5 and 20 percent while the legacy rate is over 30 percent.

Harvard's allegiance to the upper class is graphically illustrated in the chart below, which compares 1936 average family income to those whose children went to Harvard. Nearly half of students originated from the top 1.5 percent of high-income families.

Family Income of Harvard Students, 1936

Income	National percent	Harvard percent
$0–2,500	88.0	16.3
$2,500–7,500	10.5	36.3
$7,500–50,000+	1.5	47.3

Source: *Making Harvard Modern*, p. 36

The next chart analyzes fathers of Harvard students in the 1870s, 1903, and 1986. In the 1870s, the offspring of businessmen and professionals overwhelmingly composed Harvard's undergraduate students. During more than a century, class composition didn't change significantly. According to *Harvard Magazine*, 42 percent of undergraduates received scholarships in 1986, meaning poverty wasn't the major issue blocking less wealthy students from enrolling. While the number of students descended from professionals doubled, students from farmers and manual workers decreased.

Occupational Distribution of the Fathers of Harvard Students, 1870–1986 (in percentages)

	Students enrolled, 1870–75	Students enrolled, 1903	Students enrolled, 1986
Professionals	28.6	29.5	59.3
Businessmen	55.7	56.7	31.0
Government workers	4.2	3.0	4.3
Farmers	4.2	3.0	0.5
Manual workers	7.3	7.8	5.0

Source: "Poor but Hopeful Scholar," *Harvard Magazine* (Sept.–Oct. 1986)

Harvard is more diversified today than ever. In 2004, Harvard announced an exceptional scholarship policy providing tuition exemption to students whose families' income is below $40,000. Nonetheless, Harvard's upper-class roots remain firmly planted.

Defend Your Class!

As a university for the rich, Harvard proudly displayed its character during the 1912 Lawrence strike in Massachusetts. On January 1912, about thirty thousand textile workers in Lawrence walked off the job, one of the landmark events in American labor history. Founded in 1845, Lawrence was a center of textile production and became a typical city flooded with immigrants looking for a job. Workers toiled under terrible conditions with low wages. Most were women and children.

According to many sources, about a third of these workers died from tuberculosis caused by dust and fibers. One third of children who started working as teenagers died before becoming adults. As a result of such practices, Massachusetts enacted a new law that reduced the work week from fifty-six to fifty-four hours for women and children. The mill owners responded by cutting wages while forcing workers to manage the same amount of work.

Once outraged workers began to strike, and women workers brought pickets signs, the movement spread throughout the town. The phrase "Bread and Roses" had already been immortalized in a 1911 poem by James Oppenheim, but the statement "We want bread but we want roses, too!" was also attributed to the Lawrence strikers, and soon the strike was dubbed the "Bread and Roses" strike, or the "Strike for Three Loaves." Mill owners and city authorities called out the state militia. Martial law was declared, and many workers and their families were attacked and jailed. Harvard students also mobilized, but their motto was "Defend Your Class!" Those

Left: Children working intensely in the
textile industry.
Above: Bread and Roses Strike.

who volunteered to serve in the Lawrence militia were given academic
credit. Harvard's close collaboration with mill owners is not so surprising
considering the mill owners were valuable supporters of the college.

In 1919 the Boston police went on strike demanding higher pay and
better working conditions. Harvard again encouraged students to join a
special police force to maintain law and order. One hundred and forty-four
college students enlisted and again performed powerful strikebreaking
action. This intervention is well known among contemporary union activists: "Harvard students marched across the Massachusetts Avenue Bridge.
They helped break the strike essentially. They provided strike breakers."[11]

The president of Harvard at that time was Abbott Lawrence Lowell,
a descendent of John Lowell, delegate to the Continental Congress and
federal judge, and the sixth generation of Boston Brahmins to be involved
with Harvard College. Like Lawrence, another textile city was named Lowell,
after Francis Cabot Lowell, a successful businessman and a member of the
great Lowell family, giving us a clue why Harvard exclaimed "Defend Your
Class!"

President Lowell was a typical upper-class white man who spoke of
democracy while discriminating against women, blacks, Jews, and homo-
sexuals without a blink. He also played an important role in the execution
of Sacco and Vanzetti, Italian immigrants and anarchists, convicted for
robbery and murder of men despite weak evidence in the 1920s. When a
judge ordered their execution, worldwide demonstrations and petitions to
stop their execution led the Governor to appoint an advisory committee to
reexamine the case. The members were A. Lawrence Lowell, president of
Harvard, Samuel W. Stratton, president of MIT, and Robert Grant, a retired

Harvard President Abbott Lawrence Lowell.

Harvard President James B. Conant.

judge, but it was so dominated by Lowell that it was called "the Lowell Committee." These learned gentlemen concluded that Sacco and Vanzetti were guilty beyond reasonable doubt, enabling their execution. Though most people today hardly recognize Harvard's role in the bloody execution, at that time Lowell was blamed for polluting the name of Harvard. Novelist John Dos Passos wrote in an open letter, "Are you going to prove by a bloody reprisal that the radical contention that a man holding unpopular ideas cannot get a free trial in our courts is true?"[12] As someone mildly put it, Mr. Lowell was a man who was "blinded by privilege."[13]

It's quite surprising that Harvard chose James Bryant Conant, a forty-year-old chemistry professor at Harvard, as Lowell's successor in 1933. James Conant was the son of a photoengraver and the first one in his family who made it to college. In other words, he was the first Harvard president from the common people. Imagine how shocking the news was to President Lowell. Later, Conant recalled President Lowell's cold attitude when he came to deliver the news of his appointment. Although he wasn't born with a golden ticket, Conant was quite an ambitious man. His power-oriented character is clearly indicated in his diary after he was elected president. "1933 was quite a year for Germany, America and me. Hitler rose to power, Franklin Roosevelt took office, and I became president of Harvard."[14]

Isn't it interesting that the Harvard president saw his rank on a par with the U.S. president and the leader of Germany? Before his wedding, Conant told his future wife about his three ambitions: to become America's leading organic chemist, to serve as president of Harvard, and to hold a cabinet office such as secretary of the interior. Though he didn't make it to secretary of the interior, he became the U.S. ambassador to Germany in 1955.

Conant sought to reduce Harvard's aristocratic image and change it into a meritocratic elite university. He adapted a standard test to select superior students. As other universities modeled themselves after Harvard, the SAT system became a standard entrance exam for colleges. Before World War II, Conant was criticized for his policy discriminating against Jews and his friendly attitude toward the Nazis. During the war, however, he became one of the most powerful Harvard presidents in history as he served on the tiny oversight committee of the Manhattan Project (which developed nuclear weapons) and directed many other high-level government initiatives.

White Anglo-Saxon Protestants

Although most people seem unaware of it, or don't want to remember, Harvard was founded by White Anglo-Saxon Protestants to train Puritan ministers in colonial times. Two centuries passed before Harvard opened their doors to people of color. The first African American who bravely applied was Beverly Williams, who tried to enter the Harvard class of 1851. Williams was the son of a slave from Georgia or Virginia and a ward of the Reverend Parker of the First Baptist Church in Cambridgeport, who taught a son of Harvard president Edward Everett (1846–49). Williams's attempt was very brave considering that the only blacks allowed into the Yard at that time were servants of wealthy students. There were huge protests against his daring venture. Even though the president supported his enrollment, the poor young man died of sudden illness before his dream came true.

In 1865, Harvard admitted a few African American students, including Richard T. Greener, the first black student, and Edwin C.J.T. Howard, who enrolled at the Medical School. Along with George L. Ruffin at the Law School and Robert Tanner Freeman at the Dental School, they became the first black graduates of Harvard. In 1895, W.E.B. Du Bois received a PhD, carving his name as the African American PhD from Harvard. Though they climbed Harvard's high walls, it took a long time for blacks to receive equal hospitality. For instance, black freshmen students were excluded from freshmen halls where all freshmen reside compulsorily, a rule made by President Lowell. For his part, Lowell believed that white men couldn't reside with black men.

No one could say that President Lowell of Harvard was a racist, but his philosophy was made crystal clear when he became vice president of the Immigration Restriction League in 1912.[15] As other great gentlemen of that time, he was concerned that the influx of new immigrants from Southern and Eastern Europe would undermine the well being of Anglo-Saxon Protestants. He was also concerned with the growing number of Jewish students, so he tried to reduce the percentage of Jewish students, causing a huge outcry among Jewish alumni. His view was clear: "Any educational institution that admits an unlimited numbers of Jews will soon have no one else."[16]

At that time, anti-Semitism was a general sentiment among America's upper class. In 1920, when Major Higginson, a Harvard Corporation member, passed away, J.P. Morgan Jr. (1889), an Overseer, sent a letter to President Lowell suggesting that Jews or Catholics should not be members of the Corporation. As Morgan wrote, "The Jew is always a Jew first and an American second, and the Roman Catholic, I fear, too often a Papist first and an American second."[17] This atmosphere was reflected in an article in the *Harvard Crimson* of October 22, 1923. Under the title, "Ku Klux Klan at Harvard Awaits Moment to Strike," the newspaper reported that the two-year-old Harvard KKK branch was "growing more powerful, the Harvard Ku Klux Klan has only been waiting for the favorable moment to show its strength." Imagine Harvard students secretly gathered together

The Harvard Crimson

VOL. LXXXIV. No. 26   CAMBRIDGE, MASS.   OCTOBER 22, 1923   PRICE 5 CENTS

KU KLUX KLAN AT HARVARD AWAITS MOMENT TO STRIKE

"We May Be Inactive but Our Influence is Felt" are Leader's Ominous Words

SEEKING MORE MEMBERS

Indications Point to Good Deal of Activity in Increasing Numbers Before Action

Started two years ago and ever since, month by month, growing more powerful, the Harvard Ku Klux Klan has only been waiting for the favorable moment to show its strength. And now there are indications that the next few weeks will see the largest drive yet for Klan membership. As yet the branch has worked under considerable secrecy but coupled with this drive the Harvard public may expect to see the Klan pursue a more open policy, leading probably to a formal statement of its aims and platform.

The shadow of the Klan lies from West to East across the country. Only recently the Fiery Cross has been seen in Boston. And now Harvard, considered the stronghold of culture and conservatism, is about to try its strength with the boasted omnipotence of the Invisible Empire.

TRADITIONAL POLICY

Following its traditional policy the Crimson refrains from publishing the names of known members of the Harvard branch of the Klan. They will, however, if necessary, be given to authorized persons.

The Harvard Klan was started some two years ago and made its influence felt with a membership drive. At that time a Mr. W—, the organizer of the Chicago chapter and an imperial officer of the Klan, and a Mr. T— were most active in furthering the organization. But the greatest strength and size of the Klan has come only in the past six months.

Klan Opposes Open Door Policy

Whether or not the action of the University last year in decreeing the policy of non-discrimination tended to increase Klan membership is an open question. The plank in the Klan's national platform bearing on the subject is well known, and what part of it the Harvard branch stands for may be only a question of degree. But it is certain that the decision of last spring was a signal for violent demonstrations in meetings of the Harvard Klan. Yet in the final test, the decision was reached to attempt no active participation in the domestic issues of the University.

Such policy has apparently been

pursued during the first few weeks of College. The Klan as such has not interfered with social or religious organizations, and the Harvard public, lulled possibly into a false sense of security, has wondered at the apparent inactivity.

Questioned the other day concerning the plans of the organization, a prominent member hesitated to admit this inactivity. "The Harvard Klan," he said, "is inactive. But it is very far from being disorganized, nor can I say that even now its influence is unfelt. And the remarks and actions of associate members fully bear out his statement.

KU KLUX KLAN WILL STRIKE WHEN READY

Like all organizations the Klan has sought for a representative Harvard membership. While few prominent undergraduates have openly declared their allegiance, yet from the very nature of the organization it is impossible to tell what man's friends or acquaintances may belong or may be aspiring to membership. The national platform, to which the Harvard branch subscribes, appeals at once to men of the most advanced and most conservative political opinions. Nor can the type be defined until the Klan chooses to abandon its present temporary inactivity.

What the reasons are for the present apparent stagnation is more difficult to ascertain. The Klan's activities in Oklahoma have raised adverse criticism from the public, criticism which, as some have suggested, a relatively small chapter might be unwilling to encounter in the year's first demonstration. Others interested in the Klan have suggested that there may be division in the Harvard branch itself. To many Harvard may appear so much 100 per cent American that education by the Klan is futile. While more despairing members may see so little Americanism in the University, so much unpatriotism, such a mass of political, racial, religious, and intellectual filth, that the task of making it pure would be too Herculean for even the "white wings" of the Invisible Empire.

Coeducation may not appear as a plank of the platform to be published by the Klan, yet it has lately looked with no aversion on the scheme of founding a branch of the Kamelia (the female of the Klan) at Radcliffe. This latter plan holds innumerable possibilities for furthering the principles of the Klan.

But what the definite policy of the Harvard Klan may be can only be ascertained from their more open appeal for members, which the University can expectantly await within the next few weeks.

Article on the Harvard Ku Klux Klan in the *Harvard Crimson*.

with white peaked hoods crying and cursing non-WASP's. Among libraries of books singing Harvard's praises, none describe this shameful dimension.

Recent attempts have been made to uncover and rectify Harvard's racism. In the winter of 2011, a Harvard research team (composed of a historian with more than thirty graduate and undergraduate students) published "Harvard and Slavery: Seeking a Forgotten History." Its findings included that "three Harvard presidents owned slaves; that slaves worked on campus as early as 1639; that among the first residents of Wadsworth House (built in 1726) were two slaves, Titus and Venus; that slave labor often underwrote the success of Harvard's early private benefactors; and that the connection between College donations and slave-related industries persisted until the Civil War."[18]

Some might say that was long ago, that Harvard is a different place now as evidenced by diversification of its student body. While there is truth to that, it is important to remember that recent changes didn't happen by themselves. Numerous people worked hard to open Harvard's exclusive entrance policy. Professor Jonathan Beckwith at Harvard Medical School was one of them. Back in 1968, when Martin Luther King was killed, he and a friend realized they should do something. "When we looked into it, we found that of the 150 medical students at Harvard, they only admitted one black student every two years. So, it is like essentially a half African American student per year. So we went to the Dean and faculty and proposed they should bring more African American students. And the argument we should use was . . . you know Harvard is training the future leaders of the society, and this is clearly changing in society by the civil rights movement. African Americans are going to become more important in society, so if Harvard wants to be there and in a way to be controlling people, they should let more African Americans come. And they said that's a good idea. It worked."[19]

Charles V. Willie, the first tenured African American professor at the Graduate School of Education in the 1970s, also witnessed Harvard's reforms. With support from President Derek Bok, he and his colleague planned a breakfast meeting with deans. They invited one dean at a time so they could determine the actual situation of each department. Many deans said, "We can't find anybody," but Professor Willie and his colleague persuaded them by saying, "Because our association is very diversified, we will help you to find [good students]."[20] Through these efforts, Harvard's solid wall holding out people of color was finally broken down.

Harvard and Eugenics

Over the past half a century ago, America has gone through tumultuous changes brought about by the civil rights movement. Today, many immigrants still confront desperate situations. As an economic downturn has intensified, the immigration issue is shaking the country. Starting with Arizona, several states passed harsh anti-immigrant laws allowing police unreasonable searches and arbitrary arrests. As has often been said, history repeats itself. This recent conflict is a repetition of the "Eugenics movement" that swept over this country in the early twentieth century. Although Harvard continues to reform itself, its involvement with the eugenics movement is quite different than its present discourse.

What is eugenics? Beginning with Francis Galton, a cousin of Charles Darwin and an anthropologist in nineteenth-century England, it involved a strong belief that class and racial differences are determined by genetics. Eugenicists believed the human race could be improved genetically, and for that reason they insisted people with "bad genes" shouldn't have children. Advocated widely in the United States, eugenicist logic spread to the world as conservative scientists used science to justify their racist arguments. Harvard wasn't an exception. In fact, Harvard professors were heralds leading this phenomenon. Jonathan R. Beckwith, a geneticist at Harvard Medical School, once wrote an essay pointing out that Harvard was one major source providing theories of rationalizing inequality of race, class, and sex.

Louis Agassiz, a prominent nineteenth-century Harvard zoologist, claimed that the Negro brain was imperfect just like a "seven-month-old fetus." He also believed that "the skull structure of the black infant closed earlier than that of the white infant," therefore, "if the Negro learned too much, the brain would swell and the skull wall would burst."[21] Many other professors at Harvard also put a great deal of effort into proving white superiority, and their tireless effort blossomed through the spread of the eugenics hypothesis in Germany. Professor Richard Levins of Harvard's School of Public Health ascribed historical motives: "The owning class had to justify slavery and so they began using racist arguments, evolutionary arguments. After Darwin, they claimed that the tropics produce lazy, inferior people, but where the temperature is challenging, they produce superior people."[22]

After Harvard biology professors Edward East and William Castle claimed in the 1910s that marriages between blacks and whites would yield inferior children, their eugenicist logic was used to support the passage of miscegenation laws in thirty-four states, prohibiting marriage between different races. William McDougall, department chair of psychology, advocated the replacement of democracy by a caste system based upon biological capacity, with legal restrictions upon breeding by lower castes and intermarriage between the castes. Professor Nathaniel Hirsch purported to demonstrate the genetic inferiority of immigrant classes. Anthropologist Ernest Hooton raised a possibility of "criminal career based on the racial heredity of the individual" in a book published in 1935. Anthropology professor Carleton Coon concluded that blacks were at an earlier evolutionary stage of development than whites. His evidence was widely used; even a Ku Klux Klan newspaper quoted him in support of racial discrimination.[23]

What made eugenics so popular? Professor Beckwith pointed out the influx of immigrants and economic slumps at the time were two key factors that generated the phenomenon. "There was more and more immigrants coming into the country and many people didn't like that. There were economic problems at times that would generate that feeling. So there were social and environmental reasons fostered. But at the same time, professors like Harvard professors were writing textbooks which had sections on eugenics, so the ideas were spreading into the society."[24]

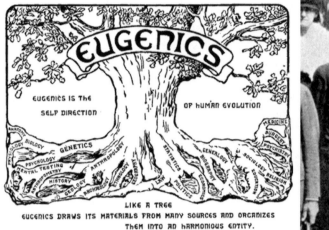

Logo for the 1921 Second International Congress of Eugenics (left) and Charles Davenport, the father of American eugenics and a prominent Harvard biologist.

Eugenics spread quickly among American elites. In 1912, the First International Congress of Eugenics was held at the University of London. Charles Eliot, president of Harvard from 1869 to 1909, served as U.S. vice president. That year, president Lowell, Eliot's successor, became a vice president of the Immigration Restriction League.

Often called the father of American eugenics, Charles Davenport was a prominent biologist from Harvard. In 1911, Davenport wrote a textbook *Heredity in Relation to Eugenics* in which he emphasized family heredity. "One family will be characterized by political activity, another by scholarship, another by financial success, another by professional success, another by insanity in some members with or without brilliancy in others, another by imbecility and epilepsy, another by larceny and sexual immorality, another by suicide, another by mechanical ability, or vocal talent, or ability in literary expression."[25] Davenport believed that a continuing influx of immigration from southeastern Europe would make America "rapidly become darker in pigmentation, smaller in stature, more mercurial, more attached to music and art, more given to crimes of larceny, kidnapping, assault, murder, rape and sex-immorality."[26] His book concluded that, "In other words, immigrants are desirable who are of 'good blood'; undesirable who are of 'bad blood.'"[27]

In 1898, Davenport became director of Cold Spring Harbor Laboratory, where he launched the Eugenics Record Office (ERO) in 1910. Cold Spring Harbor was a center for eugenics and human heredity research whose first mission was to determine the most unfit Americans. It was clear the goal of eugenicists was to purify American blood. Who were prime targets? "Ten groups were eventually identified as 'socially unfit' and targeted for 'elimination.' First, the feebleminded; second, the pauper class; third, the inebriate class or alcoholics; fourth, criminals of all descriptions including petty criminals and those jailed for nonpayment of fines; fifth, epileptics; sixth, the insane; seventh, the constitutionally weak class; eighth, those predisposed to specific diseases; ninth, the deformed; tenth, those with defective sense organs, that is, the deaf, blind and mute."[28]

These categories made me tremble with fear because I have epilepsy. Therefore, I'm in category five of those to be eliminated by eugenic measures. How many people became targets for this eugenic crusade? "Prioritizing those in custodial care—from poor houses to hospitals to prisons—the unfit totaled close to a million." An additional three million people were "equally defective, but not under the state's care." Finally, Davenport focused on the so-called borderline, some seven million people who "are of such inferior blood, and are so interwoven in kinship with those still more defective, that they are totally unfitted to become parents of useful citizens." All in all, "The estimated first wave alone totaled nearly eleven million Americans, or more than 10 percent of the existing population."[29]

Eugenicists' plans to eliminate 10 percent of the population were supported by members of wealthy economic circles, who joined the movement by supporting eugenics research. For example, the ERO was financed by Mary Harriman, widow of railroad tycoon E.H. Harriman, the Rockefeller family and the Carnegie Institution. Davenport's annual salary was $3,500 plus travel expenses, a quite large amount of money in those days.

Eugenics had a huge impact on national public policy. In 1924, restrictive immigration laws were passed based on the alarms raised by eugenicists. The number of immigrants from southeast Europe dropped drastically. Moreover, beginning with Indiana in 1907, twenty-four states passed forced sterilization laws by the end of the 1920s.[30] Targets for sterilization were not only mentally retarded or physically deformed people but also African American women, some of whom were sterilized against their will,

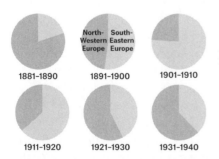

Changes in the ratio of Northwestern European to Southeastern European immigrants (left) around the time of the 1924 immigration laws, which President Coolidge signed (right).

often without their consent, while they were in a hospital for other reasons. Sometimes sterilization took place in prisons targeting criminality. Over sixty-five thousand people were sterilized in the United States.

American eugenicist theory, practice, and legislation quickly spread to Europe and particularly prospered in Nazi Germany. Hitler was a zealous supporter of American eugenics. He sent a letter of appreciation to American Eugenics Society executive secretary Leon Whitney and Madison Grant after reading Grant's book, *The Passing of the Great Race*, thanking him for a wonderful book. Hitler called Grant's book "his Bible" and promised he would reproduce the American eugenicist program in Germany.[31] Not at all secret at the time, this dimension of Nazism's underpinnings has been often neglected. Professor Richard Levins at Harvard's School of Public Health reminds us of the relationship between Nazi scholars and American eugenics:

> The Nazi scholars used American sources to justify their own social Darwinism. There were books circulating here *The Decline of the West* [via Germany], *The Passing of the Great Race* [via the USA], so it was eugenics in a very racist sense and there was eugenics more individualized trying to select good people within the superior race. The Nazis picked up on both of these, particularly Himmler and the German medical profession. So for the German doctors, Hitler did not force racism on them. If anything, they were pushing Hitler to be more racist and eugenicist, and they relied on support from the United States, from conservative American scientists, who gave them respectability.[32]

In 1907, after Indiana became the first state to legislate sterilization, it became a model for Germany. In 1923, a German physician urged the government to copy U.S. sterilization laws and its implementation. "What we racial hygienists promote is not at all new or unheard of. In a cultured nation of the first order, in the United States of America, that which we strive toward was introduced and tested long ago. It is all so clear and simple."[33]

In 1933, as Hitler came to power, he began to construct a "pure" state modeled on the United States. American eugenicists were thrilled. Their scientific theory, advocated for decades, would finally be tested systematically under the German state's control. "American eugenicists were eager to assist. As they followed the day-to-day progress of the Third Reich, American eugenicists clearly understood their continuing role."[34] Along with American scholars' continuing support, the Rockefeller Foundation also funded Nazi racial studies. These close relationships continued until the late 1930s. After World War II, many Nazi scientists claimed their innocence at the Nuremberg trials since their experimental research on concentration camp prisoners followed American examples. They pointed to the work of Richard P. Strong, a U.S. Army Colonel who did experimental research on Philippine prisoners in the early twentieth century. Strong infected prisoners in the Philippines with cholera to study the disease, killing most of them. While the U.S. Army classified his research "top secret," Dr. Strong became a professor at Harvard Medical School in 1913.

Eugenics was quickly erased among peoples' memory as the shock caused by the Holocaust and antipathy over Nazi crimes required it to disappear from view. Eugenics evaporated from textbooks. Professor Jonathan Beckwith, who enrolled Harvard in the 1950s, attested that he never heard of eugenics while he was an undergraduate. It is quite different with scientists who were involved in the Manhattan Project and later tried to control nuclear weapon after realizing that they had created a very dangerous weapon.

Eugenics demonstrates the grave danger of elites using "knowledge" to cover ideology. Its history is a warning that science, often believed to be objective and based on fact, can be widely applied for destruction of people labeled ideologically inferior. Scientists can't be free from the biases of their own social class, national outlook, or big corporations who fund their research. Beckwith warns us that the danger posed by genetic research and "scientific" ideas can be especially perilous because they persist for decades. "If somebody publishes a scientific paper or an article and gets a lot of attention in the media, people criticize it but that doesn't get into the media. Then through things like television shows, movies, and school text books, suddenly the idea becomes a truth for the culture in which that particular argument is made."[35]

Harvard's Nazi Connection

Harvard's relationship to the Nazis was not just obsessive scientists who wanted to "purify" the human race. In 2004, historian Stephen H. Norwood published a chapter titled "Legitimating Nazism: Harvard University and the Hitler Regime, 1933–1937," analyzing Harvard's cooperation with Hitler's regime during the 1930s. Though President Conant was publicly praised as an anti-Nazi hero, Norwood's research clarified that Conant actually was silent about Nazi crimes.

In May 1934, the Nazi warship *Karlsruhe* arrived in Boston harbor. Both the Massachusetts governor and Boston mayor welcomed it at an official reception attended by many Harvard men. At its 1934 commencement party, Harvard welcomed Ernst Hanfstaengl, a close friend of Adolf Hitler. A graduate of Harvard's class of 1909, Hanfstaengl was a wealthy businessman born to a rich German father and American mother. A talented pianist, he composed several songs for the Harvard football team.

Harvard crowd at Yale Bowl in 1914 giving what later became the Nazi "Sieg heil" salute.

He claimed that it was he who introduced "the stiff-armed Nazi salute and *Sieg Heil* chant, modeled after a gesture and a shout he used as a Harvard football cheerleader."[36]

In 1922, he met Hitler, whom he thought would save "Germany and civilization," as he said to a friend. He became one of Hitler's earliest supporters. In 1923, after Hitler's Beer Hall Putsch failed, Hitler took refuge at Hanfstaengl's country home, where he was subsequently arrested. It is said that Hanfstaengl's wife deterred Hitler from killing himself when police came to arrest him.

Along with his fabulous Harvard diploma, Hanfstaengl's wealth and connections were valuable assets for Hitler. Hanfstaengl introduced Hitler to Munich high society, helping to polish his image in addition to providing financial support. He became the chief of the Nazi party's foreign press. In 1934, Hanfstaengl was invited to Harvard's twenty-fifth reunion class of 1909. Harvard welcomed their successful alumnus, with the *Harvard Crimson* proposing he be named a vice marshal of his class as a sign of "honor appropriate to his high position in the government of a friendly country."[37] Because of complaints from Jewish alumni and anti-Nazi student groups, however, Hanfstaengl's proposed honorific position was unrealized.

According to Norwood, Hanfstaengl's visit was quite a scandal. Upon his arrival in New York, 1,500 protestors shouting anti-Nazi slogans

Hanfstaengl, Hitler, and Göring, Berlin, June 21, 1932.

confronted him. Heywood Broun, a well-known *New York World Telegram* columnist, wrote that there were "hundreds of thousands of people [in New York] who have relatives and friends . . . suffering at this very moment under the heavy hand of Hitler."[38] The *Baltimore Sun* also reported his visit and denounced the proposal for his honorary graduation role. Despite the public outcry, Harvard administrators and scholars warmly greeting Hanfstaengl upon his arrival in Cambridge. The Nazi official was kept busy being entertained by Harvard men—he was invited to many parties, had fun enjoying horse races at a country club, and received tea at President Conant's house. At the same time, campus and city police were busy tearing down anti-Nazi stickers and arresting protestors. At the commencement, President Conant's remarks were interrupted by two young women chanting "Down with Hitler!" Immediately, the police arrested them. Soon, protests spread to Harvard Square, and seven more people were arrested and charged with harsh crimes. As the *Boston Post* noted, "A record of three centuries of peaceful and orderly exercises centering around commencement at Harvard was broken."[39]

Originally Hanfstaengl offered Harvard University a $1,000 scholarship to provide for a Harvard student to study in Germany for a year, but given the protests and public anger, President Conant rejected the offer. Nonetheless, Harvard's warm welcome for Hanfstaengl had an impact on others. "The Harvard administration's friendly reception of Hanfstaengl at the June commencement provided a rationale for Yale University President

James Rowland Angell's decision to welcome a delegation of Italian fascist students to his campus in October 1934. The *Yale Daily News* rushed to President Angell's support, justifying his decision by 'cit[ing] President Conant's hospitality to Ernst F.S. Hanfstaengl last June.' The *Harvard Crimson* ran a news story entitled 'Yale Follows Harvard's Lead Greeting Italians.'"[40]

The next year, in March of 1935, the Harvard administration allowed the swastika emblem to be displayed in Memorial Church (Appleton Chapel), near a tablet honoring four Harvard men who were killed fighting for Germany in World War I. Permitting the swastika in its chapel was a clear sign that Harvard acknowledged the legitimacy of the Third Reich.

Although Conant had turned down the Nazi scholarship offer, Harvard and the Nazis continued to exchange students with each other. In June 1936, Harvard sent a delegate to the University of Heidelberg's 550th anniversary, as they did the next year for the 200th anniversary of Georg-August University in Goettingen. Several British universities (such as Oxford and Cambridge) had already refused to attend these ceremonies to protest Nazi persecution of faculty members and suppression of academic freedom.

Harvard portrayed its delegation as "purely academic," but the celebration in Heidelberg featured a speech by high-ranking Nazis, including Joseph Goebbels, Nazi propaganda minister. Harvard representative George Birkhoff, dean of the faculty of the College Arts and Sciences, was accompanied by Josef Goebbels, Alfred Rosenberg, Nazi racial theorist, Education Minister Rust, Ernst Hanfstaengl, and SS chief Heinrich Himmler. Two Harvard professors, Kirsopp Lake and Reginald Aldworth Daly, were awarded honorary degrees.

Considering Harvard's reputation today, their collaboration is quite surprising. Why did Harvard continue their tight relationship? First of all, I can find the answer in president Conant's anti-Semitism. Like his predecessor, President Lowell, who expressed his anti-Semitism freely, Conant also continued to limit enrollment of Jewish students. More importantly, I think its ties to the Nazis were based on Harvard's innate respect for power. In the 1930s, the Nazis were still gaining power and few people anticipated their defeat. The simple fact that the Rockefeller Foundation poured money to Nazi scholars unsparingly was one clear indication that they had no doubt of Hitler's success.

Harvard wasn't alone in this parade of Nazi supporters. *Currency Wars* by Song Hongbing is a sensational book that exposed a group of private banks controlling Western countries and predicted the 2008 financial crisis. The author revealed a shocking relationship between Hitler and Wall Street. Between 1924 and 1931, Wall Street loaned 138 billion Marks to Germany. At the same time, the war indemnity Germany provided was only 86 billion

Scientists belonging to "Operation Paperclip."

Marks. With capital support from the United States, Germany was able to reconstitute their military.[41]

After the war, the U.S. government relied upon Nazi war criminals in Europe to suppress Communists. They secretly brought Nazi scientists to America to develop advanced weapons. "Operation Paperclip" was but one program propelled by the OSS, the predecessor of the CIA. The core of this program was to recruit Nazi scientists. When President Truman ordered members of the Nazi Party or active supporters of Nazi militarism to be excluded from the program, the agency created false records for many scientists, and these "bleached" Nazi members were granted the green light to work in the United States. About five hundred scientists were brought to White Sands Proving Ground in New Mexico, Fort Bliss, Texas and Huntsville, Alabama to develop missile and ballistic missile technology that became crucial to the foundation of NASA and the U.S. long-range missile program. In November 2010, the *New York Times* published "Nazis Were Given 'Safe Haven' in U.S., Report Says," an article that recounted this secret history and exposed many surprising facts. For instance, Arthur L. Rudolph, who was honored by NASA and often called the father of the Saturn V rocket, was a Nazi scientist who ran the Mittelwerk munitions factory. Wernher von Braun, "the father of rocket science" who directed NASA's space program in the 1960s, was a leading Nazi scientist who developed rocket technology in Nazi Germany.

Harvard wasn't alone in this Nazi-recycling phenomenon. The Russia Research Center at Harvard, the front line against Communism, brought Nicholas Poppe, an employee of the Wannsee Institute (the notorious SS think tank), into the United States and advocated for him to receive a Harvard position. Poppe claimed to have been promised a job at Harvard, "half of my salary coming from the Far Eastern Department and the other half from the Center for Russian studies."[42] But despite support from some key Harvard faculty, he didn't get an appointment at Harvard and later settled at the University of Washington.

No Place for Women at Harvard

From its origins, Harvard was a university for men, by men, and of men. Even decades after the first wave of feminism had won the right to vote in 1920, Harvard refused to admit women. At that time it was commonly assumed that women's brains were too small to execute complicated intellectual work. So it might be unfair to single out Harvard as particularly harsh to women. Although Harvard questioned women's capacities, it never denied their donations.

From the start, women were important benefactors of Harvard. Lady Mowlson (Anne Radcliffe) was one of the earliest female philanthropists, for whom Radcliffe, the women's educational institute that opened in 1879, was named. As early as 1732, Dorothy Saltonstall donated money for poor scholars. Generous female contributions continued and to help Harvard survive financial difficulties. In the middle of the nineteenth century, a new wave of female supporters desired to enroll at the university that their ancestors had helped. Rather than remaining just generous benefactors, they had dreams to attend Harvard, which were considered a dangerous potential disruption of the social order by most of the gentlemen leading society. Subsequently, Harvard's history involved brutal quarrels as women, blacks, and minorities tried to climb over Harvard's high threshold while the white establishment did all they could to obstruct them.

Many women who tried to enroll at Harvard drank a bitter cup of disappointment. In 1848, Harriot K. Hunt, who had practiced medicine in Boston for fifteen years, applied to Harvard Medical School but failed because of student protests. Three years later, after students passed resolutions opposing her being allowed to attend lectures, she wrote "The class at Harvard in 1851, have purchased for themselves a notoriety they will not covet in years to come." In 1879, a $10,000 fund was offered to the Medical School on the condition of women's admission, but it was turned down. For more than a century, protests and furious arguments continued in connection with women's acceptance into Harvard. This struggle wasn't limited to the Harvard Medical School; the dispute over coeducation brought huge debates within the community.

Charles Eliot, who took office as the president of Harvard in 1869, firmly believed coeducation was impossible. His philosophy was made crystal clear in his inaugural address: "The Corporation will not receive woman as students into the College proper, nor into any school whose discipline requires residence near the school. The difficulties involved in a common residence of hundreds of young men and women of immature character and marriageable age are very grave. The necessary police regulations are exceedingly burdensome. . . . The world knows next to nothing about the natural mental capacities of the female sex."[43]

Louis Agassiz, a nineteenth-century
Harvard zoologist who claimed Africans
were biologically inferior.

Helen Keller, a Radcliffe graduate
and socialist activist who fought for
women's voting rights and labor rights.

As a sophisticated scientist, Eliot dodged the mystery of women's mental capacities, but if you read his words carefully, you can see he was just worried about male students being disturbed by females. Although many feminists criticized his narrowmindedness, Eliot wasn't alone. It was common sense at that time that women were intellectually inferior, that if women received too much education, it would harm their health and create problems for them to have children.

In 1879, the Harvard Annex, a private non-degree program for women taught by Harvard professors, opened. It was welcomed both by women who were thirsty for knowledge and Harvard professors who would receive extra bonuses for repeating the same lectures. Though the Annex successfully enrolled two hundred students within fifteen years, Eliot and the Corporation remained opposed to a women's department at Harvard. In 1894, the Commonwealth of Massachusetts chartered the Annex as Radcliffe College. Elizabeth Cary Agassiz, the widow of prominent Professor Louis Agassiz, became the first president. As it became one of the most prestigious higher educational institutions for women, Radcliffe produced many distinguished women such as Helen Keller and Gertrude Stein.

Between 1837 and 1889, seven liberal arts colleges for women, the so-called "seven sisters," were founded in the northeastern United States: Mount Holyoke College, Vassar, Smith, Wellesley, Bryn Mawr, Barnard, and Radcliffe. At the same time as women's desire for higher education was undeniable, in 1920, after years of demands, women finally obtained suffrage, changing their social status dramatically. In 1919, Harvard appointed

The former Radcliffe academic campus.

Significant Dates in Radcliffe History

1879	The Harvard Annex was established
1894	The Annex was chartered as Radcliffe College
1943	Because of the war, Radcliffe students were allowed into Harvard classrooms
1963	Harvard's Graduate School of Arts and Sciences was opened to women
1970	The first joint Harvard and Radcliffe commencement was held
1975	Limits on the number of women student were abolished
1977	Radcliffe and Harvard signed a partnership agreement
1999	Radcliffe and Harvard officially merged

its first female professor, Alice Hamilton, an assistant professor in industrial medicine at Harvard Medical School. The medical school made three conditions for Hamilton's appointment: not to use the Harvard Club, no access to faculty football tickets, and not to march in commencement parades or appear on the commencement stage with university leadership.[44] Hamilton accepted these demands and became the first female faculty member at Harvard. In 1935, when she reached retirement age, Harvard lost its sole female professor and became once again an exclusively male haunt.

Women were still not allowed to attend classes in Harvard Yard, so Harvard professors used to teach the same material to Radcliffe women after they taught the boys in the yard. This strange tradition continued until World War II, when classes were merged only because there were not enough professors since many had joined the war. Beginning in 1943,

Radcliffe students began to take classes in Harvard Yard, and by 1947, most classes became coeducational. In 1948, a historian, Helen Maud Cam, became the first tenured female professor at Harvard.

Until the late 1960s, there remained very few female tenured professors. Margaret Gullette, Radcliffe Class of 1962, remembered that she had no opportunity to study with female professors. "There were no women. I was never taught by a woman when I was an undergraduate. [There was] nobody. There was only one woman faculty member who was a full time senior

Alice Hamilton, Harvard's first woman professor.

faculty person, and she was in astronomy, and I just didn't take astronomy."[45] Harvard's male-oriented atmosphere had deep impact on the students. With great honesty, Margaret Gullette told me a bitter anecdote. One day in a writing class, a professor gave students an assignment to write "I wish I were a . . ." While some students wittily wrote, "I wish I were a polar bear," she wrote, "I wish I were a man."[46]

In the 1960s, as the civil rights and anti-war movements reached their culmination, feminism unfolded dramatically, producing huge changes in women's lives and stirring up Harvard as well. In 1963, Harvard's Graduate School of Arts and Sciences was opened to women, and Radcliffe students received Harvard diplomas. Nonetheless, the number of male faculty far outnumbered female faculty. The following chart comparing the number of male and female teachers ("officers") at Harvard in the late 1960s clearly demonstrates the imbalance of Harvard's employment policy.

Over the years, Harvard has made dramatic changes. In 1977, Harvard and Radcliffe signed an agreement to merge the two institutions, and twenty-two years later, they officially became one. Today, more than half of undergraduates are females. To keep pace with these changes, Harvard has tried to hire more female professors. According to Harvard's official records, between 2011 and 2012, some 22 percent of professors were women, as were 33 percent of assistants and associates.[47] Considering there were only three women tenured professors in the middle of the 1950s, that is rapid progress.

In 2001, Lawrence Summers became president. During five years of his presidency, the number of tenured female faculty decreased visibly. In 2004, Harvard offered thirty-two tenured positions, but only four were

Harvard University Officers, 1968–69

	Total	Male	Female	Female percent of Total
Corporation	7	7	0	0.0
Board of Overseers	30	30	0	0.0
Officers of instruction				
University professors	5	5	0	0.0
Professors	580	577	3	0.5
Associate professors	151	143	8	5.3
Assistant professors	401	384	17	4.2
Research professors and assistant research professors	3	3	0	0.0

Source: *How Harvard Rules Women*, by Harvard students, 1970

women. The following year, Summers delivered a remarkable speech in which he explained that innate differences might explain the reason women are less successful in science and math careers. Reactions to his remarks (and to his poor treatment of African American faculty) were so intense that he was compelled to resign. As Harvard tried to clean up the mess Summers left, he was replaced by Drew Gilpin Faust, the first female president in Harvard's history. According to the March 12, 2010, *New York Times* article "Women Making Gains on Faculty at Harvard," various new programs were created to support women in science and research careers as well as to hire more tenured women professors. Harvard financially supported childcare.

While there is still a long way to go, Harvard is changing. Looking at it today, it is hard to imagine that it was a place exclusively for rich, white males—which it was less than a century ago. Can we today imagine a Harvard professor who advocates eliminating ten percent of the American population? What about Harvard students secretly gathered with white peaked hoods, crying "burn Negroes!"

It is not as easy as it used to be to enroll at Harvard just because you were born with a golden ticket. No more discrimination or being forbidden entering into a library because your chromosome is XX. These changes didn't happen automatically but because people struggled and fought continually from inside and outside Harvard. The future of Harvard depends upon what kinds of universities we dream and dare to create.

CHAPTER 4

PENTAGON UNIVERSITY

"The best thing that ever happened to Harvard was World
War II."
—Professor George Goethals[1]

"We are committed in a larger sense to developing the
connection between our university and the Armed Services
in a wide variety of ways, because one of the characteristics
of the middle of the 20th century is that we are in a period
which is not peace and not war, a period in which the
techniques of academic learning, both in the Social Sciences
and in the Natural Sciences, are more closely connected than
ever before with those of the National Defense. A university
which does not try to develop to a maximal degree the
interest, cooperation and understanding between its staff
members and those of the National Defense forces is not
doing its full job."
—McGeorge Bundy, 1955 in a presentation to a ROTC panel[2]

Everyone has a decisive moment in life. In Harvard's case, World War II
was a huge turning point. By achieving a glorious victory in the devastating
war, America obtained absolute wealth and power, and this triumph brought
enormous changes to all American universities, including Harvard.

Professor Noam Chomsky carefully reminds us that before World War II,
the United States was still a kind of cultural backwater. For instance, people who
wanted to study philosophy or physics went to Germany or England. People
who wanted to be writers went to Paris because these were the centers of the
world. And it was the same in international affairs. Before the war, although
U.S. territories had expanded to the Philippines and the United States controlled most of the Western Hemisphere, the major player in world affairs was
Britain. The United States was still secondary. The world war changed all that:

During the Second World War, the other countries' industry was
either destroyed or severely harmed, but the U.S. grew enormously.

Industrial production almost tripled during the Second World War. By the end of the war, the U.S. had a position of power with no historical precedent. It literally had half the world's wealth and incomparable security. And the American elite understood this. They knew they are replacing the old traditional imperial power that the U.S. is going to be the global power.[3]

The ascendance of the United States was wholly reflected in the academic world. Americans, who were "against the prewar sense of inferiority, when the United States had, culturally speaking, a subordinate relationship with Europe,"[4] didn't want to give deference to incompetent Europe anymore. Instead of European culture which was considered a total failure, studying the Soviet Union or China would be much more productive to keep pace with a new world order. As the United States suddenly emerged as the most powerful country in history, Americans were swept away by reckless patriotism, a feverish impulse that intensified as they stepped into a new battle, the Cold War.

Harvard During World War II

In order to understand how Harvard was changed by World War II, we should begin by looking into Harvard's activities during the war. As we saw in Chapter 3, Harvard had continued a close relationship with Germany until the late 1930s. So it should not be surprising that the majority of Harvard men didn't want to be involved in the war, or rather, they wanted to cooperate with Germany—whom they thought was more likely to win. Even well-known World War II hero John F. Kennedy, wrote an anonymous article in the *Harvard Crimson* urging President Roosevelt to negotiate with Hitler since England would be defeated. "It would save us from a probable reenactment—only on a more terrible scale—of the 1917 debacle."[5] Kennedy wasn't the only one who didn't want to be wasted as a human shield on the battlefields. According to a Harvard Student Union poll of over eighteen hundred undergraduates, 95 percent opposed the United States joining the war, and 78 percent were opposed even if it meant that England and France would be defeated.[6]

In late September 1939, after Germany invaded Poland, Harvard President James Conant, who previously had said very little about the war, changed his standpoint. "I believe that if these countries are defeated by a totalitarian power, the hope of free institutions as a basis of modern civilization will be jeopardized," he wrote in an open letter. The next year in May, he spoke over nationwide radio: "I believe the United States should take every action possible to insure the defeat of Hitler." Conant recommended supplying weapons and airplanes to France and England. Harvard

Navy Supply School students marching through Harvard Yard, 1943.

students, however, were not persuaded. The editors of the *Crimson* criticized his speech, and the senior orator at the 1940 commencement claimed, "America must not again be dragged into the anarchy that is Europe." This mood continued until 1941 with the attack on Pearl Harbor. The attack on American soil quickly united students. The *Crimson* editors wrote, "We realize that we are the ones who will be manning the ships and the guns and facing the bombs and destruction of the enemy. We know after it is all over, it will be some of us who will have our names engraved on the college's bronze memorial."[7]

Another factor behind this sudden transformation was Ensign Philip R. Gazecki (class of 1941) having been killed at Pearl Harbor—the first Harvard casualty in World War II. Within a few days, the faculty introduced compulsory training programs for undergraduates and soon, the navy and army began to occupy university facilities. As a result, more Harvard men became casualties during World War II than in any other war. Altogether, 697 students were killed, almost double the number during World War I (373). If we compare this number to the 18 Korean War fatalities, it's almost forty times more.

Professors were also massively drawn into the war. Many Harvard professors volunteered for the newly formed Office of Strategic Services (OSS), providing a central role in gathering information and analysis. The influx into the military caused a sudden decrease in teaching staff on the campus, unintentionally providing an opportunity for Radcliffe students to attend classes in Harvard Yard. During the war, many scholars joined intelligence agencies and established relationships that continued once the war was over.

Among many Harvard men contributing to the war, the most outstanding was President Conant. Through the Second World War, he engraved his name in history. Though he had maintained a good relationship with Nazis and supported academic interchanges with Nazi scholars during the 1930s, once he changed his viewpoint, he immediately became a strong anti-Hitler leader. In 1940, he was appointed to the National Defense Research Committee (NDRC), later becoming its chairman, and directed development of bombs, fuels, gases, chemical warfare, and the Manhattan Project, which created the first atomic bomb. He worked closely with General Leslie Groves and Dr. J. Robert Oppenheimer and observed the first atomic bomb test at Alamogordo, New Mexico, on July 16, 1945. Most importantly, he was a member of the eight-person interim committee who advised President Truman to drop atomic bombs on Japan. At that time, committee members had various opinions about targets and the effects of bombing. Below is a portion of notes of the meeting on May 31, 1945:

> After much discussion concerning various types of targets and the effects to be produced, the Secretary [i.e., Secretary of War Henry Stimson] expressed the conclusion, on which there was a general agreement, that we could not give the Japanese any warning; that we could not concentrate on a civilian area; but that we should seek to make a profound psychological impression on as many of the inhabitants as possible. At the suggestion of Dr. Conant (Director of the National Defense Research Committee) the Secretary agreed that the most desirable target would be a vital war plant employing a large number of workers and closely surrounded by workers' houses.[8]

To think of the president of Harvard calling for targeting workers' houses to maximize the effect of the atomic bomb is quite chilling. The effect of his suggestion is now part of the sorrowful historical record of humanity. The United States dropped two atomic bombs in Japan: the first one, "Little Boy," on Hiroshima on August 6, 1945, and the second, "Fat Man," on Nagasaki three days later. The effects were overwhelming. On the day of the blast in Hiroshima, between 70,000 to 80,000 people, or 30 percent of the city's entire population, were killed by the explosion and firestorm. Within the next few months, 90,000 to 166,000 people died in Hiroshima and 60,000 to 80,000 in Nagasaki, mostly civilians. The necessity of using the atomic bomb is still in question. Historian Howard Zinn, who served as a bombardier in Europe during the war, later insisted that bombing Japan was not necessary because they were defeated and ready to surrender before the bombs were dropped.[9]

After the war, President Conant received a heart-warming reception from the Harvard community as he joined the 1946 commencement. A *Boston Globe* article helps us taste this atmosphere. "The alumni head introduced the President of Harvard by the name all Americans have come to know and respect for his value in an epoch of national emergency: 'Conant of Harvard.'"[10]

James Conant, the first Harvard president not from an elite background, had become a preeminent war hero. With other Cold War warriors such as Paul Nitze, a Harvard professor who became a key policy planner, Conant was often "uncritically praised for promoting a massive conventional arms buildup to forestall the resort to nuclear war."[11] It seems, however, that the legendary warrior tired of developing weapons of mass destruction. In fact, he strongly opposed the development of a new bomb, fifty to hundred times more powerful than the Hiroshima weapon, known as the H-bomb.

American Universities after the War

"In terms of military research, the universities became extraordinarily important. . . . For all these reasons, the expansion in higher education after World War II was dramatic, and higher education became one of the central forces of capitalist production."

—George Katsiaficas, from the documentary film
Verita$: Everybody Loves Harvard

The Second World War turned American universities upside down. A primary cause of this change was the Servicemen's Readjustment Act, also known as the GI Bill of Rights, enacted on June 22, 1944. Its official purpose was to provide a wide spectrum of benefits for returning veterans, but the real goal was to prevent massive unemployment and negative situations as millions of young men were returning to society. Including low-cost mortgages, loans to start a business, the bill provided free education with living expenses in addition to one year of unemployment compensation. Anyone who had been on duty at least ninety days during the war—combat was not

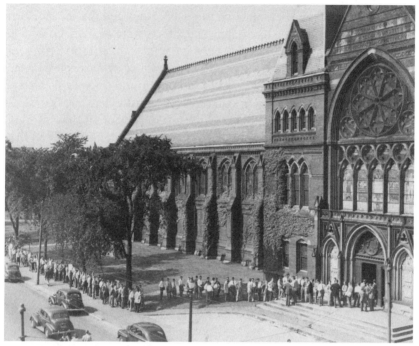

Registration day at Memorial Hall, 1946.

required—and had not been dishonorably discharged could apply for the benefits. The result of the law exceeded expectations.

By 1956, about 2.2 million veterans had used the education benefits to attend colleges or universities while an additional 6.6 million received some kind of training program. Before the war, higher education was considered a privilege for the rich, but after the war, the door was wide open. People who had been thirsty for learning flocked into colleges. This phenomenon led to the extraordinary growth of American universities.

The GI Bill disarmed Harvard's exclusive entrance policy as well. Under the GI Bill, people could go to Harvard for free. Thousands of veterans, who could never before dream of attending Harvard, crowded into the campus, setting a new record for admissions every semester. Before the war, the college's student body never exceeded 3,500. In the fall of 1946 alone, almost 9,500 veterans enrolled in the college, ten graduate schools, and professional schools. By 1947, enrollment reached 14,000. The wartime victory was clearly a triumph for Harvard as well. Not only were more Jews and Catholics admitted, but President Conant and other faculty members busily developed new guidelines for general education, dividing various fields of learning and demanding certain courses to be taken by undergraduates. Needless to say, Harvard's innovations became the role model for higher education in America—as well as in the rest of the world.

Students were packed for registration.

Wartime collaboration among universities, government, and industries was maintained during the Cold War, intensifying the military's impact on American universities. One of the most significant domestic effects of the Second World War was a shift in the relationship between universities and the government. Before the war, there was little if any research directed by the state. The United States Naval Observatory, founded in 1830, was one of the oldest scientific institutions supported by the government. During the Civil War, President Lincoln founded the National Academy of Science, to mobilize elite scientists for the government. Following in this tradition of government using academics to strengthen the country, President Woodrow Wilson also founded the National Research Council during World War I to make good use of scientific and technical personnel. Before World War II, however, federal and state funding for university research was mainly for agricultural research and constituted a small portion of total research expenditures. For instance, "the total federal funding for research and development in 1940 was a mere $74 million, of which agriculture accounted for 40 percent."[12]

The huge success of the Manhattan Project changed the role of universities. Planners realized the importance of science for the security and prosperity of the country and believed that government should support large-scale science projects. As universities hosted the military's development of advanced weapons, enormous sums of money flowed onto campuses. The following graph illustrates this dynamic. As can be seen, the influx of money from the government suddenly increased right after the war and soared dramatically every year until the 1970s.

As a leading institution that helped to create these changes, Harvard gladly accepted its intimate partnership with the government. Why not? Massive amounts of public funding surged into Harvard under the name of national security. By 1965, about a third of university spending was from money provided by the government. As President Conant gently reported, "At the moment not inconsiderable amounts of government money are being spent in the universities to support research, thanks to the vision of certain leaders of the Navy and Army."[13]

As a result of the Second World War, the status of Harvard reached new heights. The victory of the United States was also a victory for Harvard. Prominent political leaders vied to visit its commencement to improve their status. In 1943, while still in the middle of combat, Winston Churchill made a special visit to Harvard, pledging that England would march side by side with the United States until victory. In 1946, World War II hero General Dwight David Eisenhower, who later became the thirty-fourth president of the United States, attended Harvard's commencement and received an honorary degree. The next year, Secretary of State George Marshall used the occasion to announce the "Marshall Plan." (The Marshall Plan, also known as the European Recovery Program, was the American aid program for Europe to restore their economies as well as to restrain Soviet Communism.) Marshall's speech was less than twelve minutes long, and

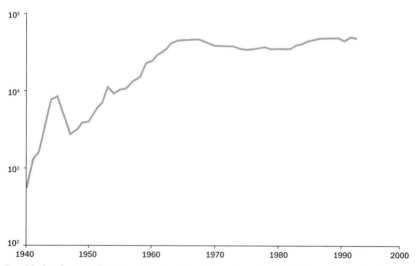

Total federal expenditures on research and development in millions of constant (1983) dollars.

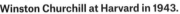

Winston Churchill at Harvard in 1943.   **Secretary of State George Marshall at Harvard in 1947.**

most of the people didn't understand its significance at that time, but it was probably the most important commencement speech in Harvard's history. That Marshall chose Harvard to announce such a significant policy well illustrates the tight relationship between Harvard and the government.

As wartime tension continued during the Cold War, competition intensified between the United States and the Soviet Union to develop advanced weapons. Under the name of National Security, American universities became increasingly militarized. When the Soviet Union successfully launched Sputnik 1, the first artificial Earth satellite, in 1957, American ruling elites panicked at the thought that the Soviets were ahead of the United States. Sputnik's shock triggered a new space race. In 1958, the National Aeronautics and Space Administration (NASA) was established, accelerating all sorts of new space programs.

Along with the hard sciences, social sciences were also utilized for military purposes, particularly in foreign countries. According to Professor Richard Levins, American leaders realized that soft science could be used by the military. In one early instance, a friend of Professor Levins who was researching lizards in Panama was told that the government would support his research, and the only thing they wanted from him was to correct the maps of rivers. In other words, any research conducted in strategic countries now has military use and such distortion was justified under the name of national security. Professor Noam Chomsky emphasized that the U.S. government strategically used the Cold War tension to strengthen the system of control:

> The Cold War propaganda—you know, the Russians are coming—was used for domestic control. . . . If you take a look at the actual events of the Cold War, that's very little to do with Russia and the United States. They have to do with intervention, subversion, aggression, terror, and so on within the domains of the two powers. For the United States,

that's most of the world. . . . It's kind of interesting to see what happened when the Soviet Union collapsed. It's a very telling moment about the Cold War. What happened to NATO? I mean, NATO was sold and funded as a military organization necessary to protect Western Europe from Russian hordes. In 1990 no more Russian hordes. If you believed the propaganda, you should have said okay, NATO will disappear. It didn't, it expanded. It expanded to the East in violation of promises to Gorbachev, in fact. By now, it is a global intervention system under largely U.S. control.[14]

The Cold War altered the trajectory of American intellectuals. Just as we saw in the case of President Conant, a new kind of intelligentsia emerged, exercising fabulous capacity in policymaking and seeing themselves in the front ranks of history. As Theodore Draper described, "A new breed of politicized intellectuals appeared—the foreign affairs intellectuals."[15] Harvard professors performed jobs faithfully during the Cold War. Paul Nitze, who helped to shape defense policy, was one of many Harvard men whose association with the government served the expanding American empire. Distinguished Harvard historian William Langer, head of the Research and Analysis branch of the OSS during World War II, put a great deal of effort into enhancing the purview of the intelligence community. In the early 1950s, he was called upon by CIA Director Walter Bedell Smith, and asked to improve the new agency's research division. Historian John Ranelagh praised their work, "The achievement of Langer and Smith in reorganizing the CIA's analytical and estimating procedures was one of the most important in the Agency's history." President Harry Truman commented that through Smith and Langer's work the CIA became "an efficient and permanent arm of the Government's national security structure."[16] The CIA website has also noted Professor Langer's contribution in this transition, but Langer was just one of many connections between Harvard and the federal government. As President Conant reported, "Numerous members of the university staff are heavily involved as consultants in highly confidential scientific matters connected with the armed forces. Indeed many professors here and elsewhere find themselves perplexed as to how to divide their time between calls from the government and their responsibilities as scholars and teachers."[17]

Of course, Harvard wasn't alone in this parade. It was a general phenomenon among American universities who competed for the funds and prestige of federal research grants. The raging wind of the Cold War polluted the academic world, and scholars who accepted their holy duty to serve the empire received ample rewards. "A lot of American intellectuals at big universities at that time wanted to be used by the government. They wanted to be advisors of different kinds. That was their dream. Even if just for a year or two, after they came back, they would have a lot of status. Even those who were not directly advising, their writing was mostly to support the state ideology and state policies."[18] For these people, the Cold War period may have been remembered as a beautiful time, "Oh, the good old days!"

But for conscientious scholars, the Cold War was associated with grief and resentment. Many progressive intellectuals were swept away by the anti-Communist witch-hunt. The academic world was deeply and morally wounded. For these people, the Cold War epoch would be remembered as the dark ages of politics, education, and ideology. Anti-Communist fervor peaked from 1949 to 1954 as so-called McCarthyism turned America upside down.

McCarthyism and Harvard

During the Second World War, when the United States was allied with the Soviet Union, anti-Communism became muted. By the early 1940s, the Communist Party of the United States (CPUSA) had about seventy-five thousand members. But when the war ended, as the Soviet Union set up Communist regimes across Central and Eastern Europe, the temporary truce was over.

In the early 1950s, Joseph McCarthy, Republican U.S. Senator of Wisconsin, declared that he had a piece of paper, which contained a list of 205 Communists who were still working for the State Department. That was the opening salvo of the McCarthy era. Though he couldn't prove that allegation, he continued with irresponsible statements that the press rushed to turn into headlines. As hunting Communists became a popular sport, McCarthy became one of most important politicians in Washington.

What were the reasons for this fever sweeping the country? There were several social and political events that accelerated McCarthyism: the unexpected detonation of an atomic bomb by the Soviet Union on August 29, 1949, the declaration of the People's Republic of China (PRC) in October 1949, and the outbreak of the Korean War on June 25, 1950. The American people were tired from World War II, so to persuade them to fight another war, McCarthy was just the media spectacle needed by the U.S. government to spread extreme anti-Communist zeal. After extensive research on McCarthyism and its impact on American universities, Professor Ellen W. Schrecker pointed out that he was, in fact, just one of many faithful performers. "McCarthy, though the most flamboyant politician identified with the anticommunist crusade, was hardly its most influential practitioner. That honor belongs to J. Edgar Hoover. In fact, if we had known in the 1950s what the Freedom of Information Act has taught us since the 1970s, I think we would probably be talking about Hooverism."[19]

Joseph McCarthy.   **J. Edgar Hoover.**

Numerous people fingered by McCarthy were summoned to the House Un-American Activities Committee (HUAC), an investigative arm of the House of Representatives. Alger Hiss was one of them. A State Department officer who had deep effect on early policy-making for the Korean Peninsula and a 1929 graduate of Harvard Law School, Hiss was accused of being a Soviet spy and convicted of perjury in 1950. In addition to Hiss, many more Harvard graduates who had been members of Communist circles while in the college were summoned in a row which granted Harvard the unwelcomed nickname "the Kremlin on the Charles."

Several Harvard graduates were subpoenaed to appear before the congressional committee and pressured to testify against those who had been in Communist cells while at Harvard. Cold War ideology compelled intellectuals to become informants for survival. Wendell Hinkle Furry, associate professor of physics at Harvard whose name was revealed during a hearing, refused to join this dog-eat-dog game and declined to answer any inquiries related to Communist activities. Furry employed the Fifth Amendment, and as other Harvard men followed his strategy, McCarthy crusaders became furious. Under pressure to fire Furry, the Harvard Corporation summoned him to hear his story and make a final decision. Here is a portion of what the Harvard Corporation's careful deliberations produced:

> We deplore the use of the Fifth Amendment by one of our faculty. . . . In the first place we think full and candid testimony by all teachers would disclose that there is little Communist activity today in education institutions. But more important, the use of the Fifth Amendment

Alger Hiss, a Harvard graduate, imprisoned for spying for the Soviet Union.

is in our view entirely inconsistent with the candor to be expected of one devoted to the pursuit of truth.[20]

Although the Corporation didn't fire Furry, it put him on three years' probation. They also announced that Harvard would keep two other non-tenured teachers who had used the Fifth Amendment—Helen Deane Markham, assistant professor at the Medical School and Leon J. Kamin, a teaching fellow—but they broke that promise as their contracts were never renewed. Many other institutions also set up investigative committees and performed house cleanings, but Professor Ellen Schrecker believed "Harvard's was more hypocritical," because people like Furry who were prominent were saved while vulnerable junior faculties were dismissed once their spotlight was off.[21]

Though Harvard carries great pride in having defended academic freedom during the McCarthy period, its covert cooperation with the FBI—the real commander of the witch hunt—was perceivable in cases like that of Sigmund Diamond. During 1953–54, Dr. Diamond was offered a five-year appointment to an administrative job with some teaching work. One day, two FBI agents with a recording machine visited him and demanded that he reveal his past political associates. After they left with empty hands since he refused to answer, he was summoned by McGeorge Bundy, then dean of the Faculty of Arts and Sciences (FAS) who worked closely with the CIA and FBI. Bundy was a great-nephew of President A. Lawrence Lowell and a graduate

McGeorge Bundy.

of Yale, where he was a member of the Skull and Bones secret society. His pedigree was already valued as he became associate professor at Harvard with only a bachelor's degree. During their meeting, Dr. Diamond made it clear that he had once been a Communist Party member but was not anymore.

Bundy wasn't satisfied. As Diamond later recalled, "Bundy told me that this was not good enough, but that he would present my appointment to the Harvard Corporation if I would talk about others as well. He urged me to talk about the matter with Harvard faculty members whom I knew, and he scheduled another appointment with me. Both the first and second conversations were recorded on a disk, which revolved on a machine in a plain sight."22

As we can imagine, Dr. Diamond didn't get the promised prestigious Harvard position. He later wrote a book, *Compromised Campus*, that exposed mutual cooperation between universities and the intelligence community during 1945–55.

When the Soviet Union succeeded in manufacturing atomic bombs, fear swept America, and the witch-hunt intensified. The realization that the magic technology of atomic bombs, which had brought preeminent world power to the United States, went over to the "enemy" was shocking news. Crusaders insisted that spies working in the U.S. government had delivered decisive technical information to the Soviets. The Communist victory in China and the outbreak of the Korean War made the anti-Communist crusaders ever more desperate. Their allegations of an atomic spy game became more plausible. The climax of the early Cold War panic came when Ethel Rosenberg and Julius Rosenberg were convicted of conspiracy to pass information about the atomic bomb and executed in 1953.

American universities marched obediently to the patriotic hymns that resounded in the media. In 1949, the University of California attached a loyalty oath to employment contracts, as did many other universities. In 1953, the Association of American Universities issued a statement, "The Rights and Responsibilities of Universities and Their Faculties," in which the group declared its opposition to Communism. In their view, a Communist Party membership "extinguishes the right to a university position." Altogether

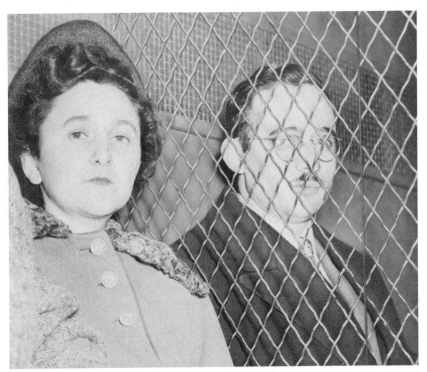

Ethel and Julius Rosenberg.

thirty-seven administrations endorsed the statement, including the heads of Harvard, Yale, Columbia, Princeton, and MIT. The signatories declared, "the modern American university is an association of individual scholars," and "they are united in loyalty to the ideal of learning, to the moral code, to the country, and to its form of government." Nor did they neglect to add that, "free enterprise is as essential to intellectual as to economic progress."[23]

Years later, Ellen Schrecker confessed that she had once signed a loyalty oath when she was hired as a teaching assistant in graduate school. At the time, she felt a few qualms, but nobody was making a big deal of it, so she signed. A few years later, a braver and more politically aware colleague refused to sign. There was something of a flap, and the oath was finally rescinded. But the teacher who protested was denied tenure.[24] In her book *No Ivory Tower*, Schrecker wrote,

> Marxism and its practitioners were marginalized, if not completely banished from the academy. Open criticism of the political status quo disappeared. . . . [T]he full extent to which American scholars censored themselves is hard to gauge. There is no sure way to measure the books that were not written, the courses that were not taught, and the research that was never undertaken.[25]

McCarthyism had a huge impact on Harvard, causing the unexpected departure of President Conant, a hero of World War II who had achieved a glorious victory for Harvard. Though Conant was a firm anti-Communist, McCarthy's fierce sword was now targeting universities after he finished housecleaning at the State Department and Hollywood. As Harvard was known as "The Kremlin on the Charles," Harvard wasn't safe from political pressure. The FBI targeted Conant and conducted an exhaustive investigation of him. When newly appointed Secretary of State John Foster Dulles requested a security clearance for Conant, FBI director J. Edgar Hoover ordered twenty-three FBI field officers to "conduct a thorough investigation as to the character, loyalty, reputation, association, and qualifications of Conant."[26]

It wasn't clear why Conant became a target. He didn't remove several faculty members who had been members of the Communist Party and he opposed development of the H-bomb, a stance that gave courage to Oppenheimer to stand against it as well. Clearly Conant wasn't happy about the situation. In his 1953 annual report, he wrote:

> I would not be party to the appointment of a Communist to any position in a school, college, or university. There are no known adherents to the Party on our staff, and I do not believe there are any disguised Communists either. But even if there were, the damage that would be done to the spirit of this academic community by an investigation by the University aimed at finding a crypto-Communist would be far greater than any conceivable harm such a person could do.[27]

Practically speaking, that report was Conant's farewell to Harvard. In January 1953, he announced his acceptance of a position offered to him by newly elected President Eisenhower as U.S. high commissioner to Germany. Conant's surprising decision shocked the community. Harvard was in the crosshairs of the anti-Communist crusade, and several Harvard graduates had been summoned to appear before congressional committees. Few people could understand Conant's decision, including Professor McGeorge Bundy, for whom "It seemed ten steps down for the president of Harvard to merely run Germany."[28]

After Conant's sudden departure, the Corporation rushed to find a replacement who would be as strong a leader as Conant. Several inside and outside men were recommended, including McGeorge Bundy, a thirty-three-year old associate professor and David Rockefeller, the patriarch of the Rockefeller family. The Corporation made an unexpected choice, naming Nathan Pusey, president of Lawrence College in Appleton, Wisconsin, the hometown of Senator Joseph McCarthy. No one could believe it was just a coincidence. As McCarthy put it, "Harvard's loss is Wisconsin's gain."[29]

Pusey was the first Harvard president with origins outside the eastern United States. He was a pleasant man but uncompromising in his principles. McCarthy called Pusey "a rabid anti-anti-Communist" and continued to target Harvard, but each time he did, Pusey either held a press conference or issued a statement snubbing him.[30]

McCarthy's incomparable power and political domination reached its end when he attacked the U.S. Army. In 1954, his investigative hearing on the Army was televised and watched by some twenty million people, many of whom real-

President Pusey, the successor of James Conant.

ized that he was just a blowhard with possible con-man proclivities. As the Korean War was concluded with an Armistice Agreement, one of the chief causes of the crusade was removed, and its mouthpiece was no more needed. It was time for a change. On December 2, 1954, the Senate voted to impeach Senator McCarthy by a vote of sixty-seven to twenty-two, and a few years later the addle-brained man died of alcoholism.

The man may have died but McCarthyism had a lasting impact on the academic world. Professor Richard Levins pointed out that after the McCarthy era, political repression still continued systematically:

> There is a difference between the political repression of the McCarthy period and then later on. During the McCarthy period, many academic professors defended their colleagues and the expulsion of people was pressured from the outside. . . . Later on, it was much less intervention from the government but more of it coming within the department deciding somebody isn't qualified as an economist because they do Marxist economics. . . . So the discrimination came within the academic departments through regular procedures, and they imagined they were being objective . . . nowadays certain kinds of research are regarded as respectable and others they wouldn't even consider looking at.[31]

Pentagon University

Under the justification of protecting Western Civilization, American universities became militarized throughout the 1950s. As the American ruling elite understood the importance of academic support to fight and achieve a victory against Communism, they founded several research institutions at universities to execute their needs. The Center for International Studies (CIS) was founded at MIT in 1952, and the Center for International Affairs (CFIA) at Harvard opened in 1958. These quickly became major spokes in the Cold War research hub. Though the CIS was based at MIT, many Harvard scholars were deeply involved in founding it, a close relationship only revealed in a confidential document Harvard students discovered when they occupied the University administrative building in 1969 in the midst of the anti-war movement: "Much of the initiative for the establishment of the Center came from members of the Harvard Faculty. It has been conceived of from the beginning as in all substantive respects a cooperative enterprise serving the interests of the entire Cambridge community."[32]

The memo also included several important names of the advisory board.

Advisory Board

Paul Buck	from Harvard University,
Edward S. Mason	Harvard University
Julius A. Stratton	MIT
John E. Burchard	MIT
Henry M. Wriston	Brown University
Advisory Board on Soviet Bloc Studies	
Charles Bohlen	U.S. Department of State
Allen Dulles	CIA
Philip E. Mosely	Columbia University
Leslie G. Stevens	Vice admiral, U.S. Navy retired

Source: *How Harvard Rules,* by Harvard students, 1969

This list speaks for itself. As we can see, the CIS was a typical Cold War research institute combining academics, the State Department, the CIA, and the military. Today, the CIS website describes its goal as "to support and promote international research and education at MIT," but its founding came in the aftermath of secret Project Troy, a covert initiative to solve the problem of the Soviets jamming Voice of America (VOA). Its purview later extended to developing the contents of VOA during the Korean War. From its beginning, the CIS was a military operation funded by the CIA.

MIT has long been a center for developing advanced weapons systems, thereby functioning as the Pentagon's attached lab. In his article "The Cold War and the University," Noam Chomsky described MIT as a "virtually Pentagon university." He recalled, "aside from two military labs that it ran (by the Pentagon), about 90 percent of the budget came from the Pentagon."[33] Its close association with the CIA was overt until the 1960s.

By the time student movements questioned the military's role because of the Vietnam War, CIS funding became more clandestine. Professor George Katsiaficas, a student activist at MIT during the anti-war era, recalls that when East Cambridge was developed in the 1960s, the Portuguese neighborhood was remodeled to build Kendall Square. The first tenant to move into the first high-rise building was the CIA. Now we can understand why anti-war students used to call MIT the "Pentagon on the Charles."

Harvard's Center for International Affairs (CFIA) was established in 1958 as an upgraded version of CIS. Often described as the "the CIA at Harvard," the CFIA has performed significant service to American foreign policy. Gentlemen who were involved in establishing the CFIA include several distinguished names: McGeorge Bundy, the dean of FAS and later National Security Advisor (1961–66); Henry Kissinger, political scientist at Harvard and later Secretary of State (1973–77); Don Price, Ford Foundation vice president and the dean of the Kennedy School (1958–77); James Perkins, vice president of the Carnegie Corporation (1950–63) and president of Cornell University (1963–69); Dean Rusk, president of the Rockefeller Foundation (1952–60) and later Secretary of State (1961–69); and Robert Bowie, a cofounder and the first director of CFIA and later the CIA chief National Intelligence Officer (1977–79).

Because of its close association with government intelligence agencies, the center was targeted by student activists during the anti-war movement. When students occupied the building, some confidential documents were released exposing it as a nest for secret CIA affairs. To me, the way they named it the "CFIA" sounds so similar to the "CIA" that it couldn't be a coincidence. Dr. Trumpbour, the editor of How Harvard Rules, jested that the American journalist Andrew Kopkind used to say that the "F" in CFIA is there to distinguish it from the CIA. In an interview for my documentary, one interviewee mildly joked that people at CFIA always stressed the "F" because they wanted to make sure people did not think that they are the CIA.

These institutes are clear evidence confirming universities as subcontractors of the government. Understanding these institutes' tasks could be a useful barometer for comprehending universities' roles during and after the Cold War. What is the universities' mission? How does their service to the government affirm their goals?

Noam Chomsky analyzes two major dimensions: "First of all, personnel, significantly all administrations, I mean, the whole political class comes from the elite universities: Harvard, Yale, Princeton, and basically a couple of others like MIT. So, partly personnel, but I think primarily ideology. You have to construct a doctrinal system, which inculcates young people with the doctrines that undergird the Cold War imperial system."[34]

Chomsky often describes intellectuals as "experts in legitimation."[35] Whenever needed, they have provided circumlocutional rhetoric to justify American foreign policy. Harvard professors were forefront in this divine job as they enjoyed the most prestigious university's name. A prime example would be Samuel Huntington, political scientist at Harvard who promoted "Forced Draft Urbanization" to justify massive bombing of South Vietnam as a means of fast "modernization." Though Harvard has produced numerous masters of justification promoting destructive U.S. foreign policy, it has a fairly progressive image and great self-confidence in its defense of academic freedom. But if we look back at its history, it's obvious these are just comforting mythologies.

Professor Katsiaficas pointed out that many professors who served the empire justified their action under the name of academic freedom. As an example, he pointed to Professor Ithiel de Sola Pool, a prominent political scientist at MIT. During the Vietnam War, Pool conducted war research—as did many other MIT professors. One of Pool's research projects was analyzing enemy motivation using interrogation records of captured Viet Cong suspects, which were kept inside file cabinets in his office. It was obviously applied research oriented to torture and killing other human beings, not pure research. Student activists challenged him but Pool's answer was that he had a right to do whatever research he wanted to do. Katsiaficas criticizes this academic argument because what Pool meant was that he could do research to kill people if he wanted. At this point, it is natural to remember those psychologists who more recently have provided illegal interrogation skills to torture people in Iraq, Afghanistan, and many other places and to ask where they got the idea. They might share some values with professor Pool, but academic freedom doesn't mean freedom from consequences. It rather carries a heavy burden of responsibility. More importantly, Katsiaficas pointed out the concept of academic freedom had been intentionally misused.

> Academic freedom when it was originally developed in Europe was to protect the rights of dissident people who disagreed with the church, who disagreed with the government, to speak up without sanctions. It was never intended to protect the rights of war makers to make weapons of massive destruction or to harm other people. It was always intended for professors and the university community to be a place of free speech in order to have free debate. . . . I think Harvard today and MIT and large universities hide behind the veil of academic freedom to mask the fact that they are prostituting universities to big government and to the military. The purpose of academic freedom was to protect the dissident voices not to protect corporate, church,

government, and military leaders so that they could use the resources of universities for evil purposes.[36]

Professor Ngo Vinh Long also indicated an important contradiction: those scholars who worked closely with the government often pretended that they were only neutral. But if their research was used for supporting government policy or ideology, it couldn't be neutral. Likewise, in a situation like the Vietnam War, when the majority of government planners were supporting the war, if you didn't say anything in your position, you were supporting the war too. Many Harvard and MIT professors involved in war research during the Vietnam War excused themselves, saying that I wasn't even there, but if their research contributed to the war, they were already involved in the war. Whether or not they fired the bullets was not so important.

Someone might ask a question in return why academics and universities shouldn't keep in step closely with the state when the government is supporting them. The answer is apparent. When universities are controlled by mammoth powers like the state, they lose their original function that is cultivating righteous citizens who would develop a healthy society. Developing destructive massive weapons and promoting militaristic foreign policies that resulted in millions of innocent civilians' death are certainly not something we expect from higher education. But looking back, that was what Harvard was doing in the name of national security. Professor Richard Levins noted that as the government became a financial resource for universities, it deeply corrupted scientific world.

> In order to work for the government or industry, you have to not question. Another thing is it narrows the horizons of science to those things that have practical values for rulers, either as intellectual domination or physical domination through the military. So it has general all-around corrupting influences. For instance, from scientific study of how rumors can be propagated, the CIA manuals tell you about how to organize riots. So science is being subordinated to the mechanisms of rule. That corruption is also discouraging young people from going into science. When they see the careerism and competition, science used to be a community of knowledge, but now people keep secrets from each other. Increasingly students make a decision should they go into business school or science according to the expectation which would pay better. . . . So it has corrupting influence on science as a community, it makes more and more corners of our lives into commodities because part of scientific engineering is asking how to commercialize something.[37]

Area Studies: A New Management Strategy

"The area study programs developed in American universities in the
years after the war were manned, directed, or stimulated by graduates of the OSS."[38]

—McGeorge Bundy

Alongside founding several institutes dealing with international affairs, the
expansion of area studies was another fruitful product of the Cold War.
After the war, the demand for foreign affairs experts increased, and the field
of international studies grew drastically. Before World War II, "the number
of centers of international studies could be counted on both hands. By 1968,
there were 191, 95 of which were concentrated at twelve universities."[39] As
their goal was not purely academic but rather political, area studies programs were quite different from traditional ones composed of experts: historians, sociologists, economists, political scientists, and more. As John
Trumpbour described, area studies programs were "extension schools for
the State Department," executing a delivery service in effective analysis and
disciplined trainees to manage the globe.

McGeorge Bundy was frank about it. As you can see in his quote
above, he openly bragged that many of the scholars who devoutly worked
to enlarge area studies were actually former OSS agents, the predecessor
of the CIA. Formed during World War II as a wartime intelligence agency
to fight against totalitarianism, its membership included many prominent
figures such as Ralph Bunche, 1950 Nobel Peace Prize recipient; Arthur
Goldberg, ambassador to the United Nations; Saul K. Padover, political
scientist; Arthur Schlesinger Jr., historian and special assistant to Kennedy;
Bruce Sundlun, the governor of Rhode Island (1991–1995); and John Ford,
famous film director. According to JFK–LBJ advisor Roger Hilsman, when
the OSS was set up in 1941, the basic idea behind was "the novel and
almost impish thought that scholars could in some respects take the place
of spies."[40] Professor Chomsky analyzed the expansion of area studies as
a new management strategy over colonized countries:

> After the Second World War, the United States was becoming the
> counterpart to the colonial administrator. The U.S. did it differently
> from traditional empires. It didn't send administrators to run the
> countries. It did it in a more indirect way but still had that kind of
> influence. First we have people on the ground, but we also have some
> kind of comprehension of how to deal with the leadership of these
> countries, which meant having area studies programs.[41]

Before World War II, the field of international studies was still in the
wilderness even at a place like Harvard. Paul Buck, who became the director

of Harvard University Library in 1959, once noted: "In 1903 not a single Harvard thesis dealt with anything beyond the limits of Classical Antiquity, Western Europe, and the United States"[42] With a very few exceptions, for most Harvard scholars, the word "world" meant the Western World, and others didn't exist yet or were a subject for conquest. The Second World War and the rise of the Soviet Union as the powerful counterpart generated a strong sense of urgency developing international studies as a base of foreign affairs.

There was an interesting shift indicating how area studies came to be used in political ways. In 1943, the Committee on World Regions of the Social Science Research Council (SSRC) drafted a report titled "World Regions in the Social Sciences," considering the outlook of Area Studies. They chose two major areas permanently interesting to the United States: the Far East (China and Japan) and Latin America. By the end of 1945, when Harvard's committee made its report, the priority areas had shifted. While Japan and Latin America were removed from the priority areas, the Soviet Union and China became the main targets. "The selection of the Soviet Union and China for regional study reflects various considerations. For an indefinite period, knowledge and understanding of Soviet Russia will probably be the most important single concern of our foreign policy. . . . Harvard can provide, from its existing resources, a strong team for work on Soviet Russia."[43]

As asserted in the report, Harvard majestically founded the Russian Research Center in 1948. It was a huge collaboration between Harvard and the CIA funded by the Carnegie Corporation with a total sum of $750,000 during the first five years. Harvard historian William Langer, the head of the OSS research and analysis branch during the wartime, became the Director there in 1954 after his return from Washington, DC, where he had reorganized the CIA analysis system. In his words, the Russian Research Center was a "front for anti-Communist propaganda and activity,"[44] and its programs were full of military staff and its research was financed by military contracts. The situation was not so different in other area studies centers. In 1954, Harvard's Center for Middle Eastern Studies (CMES) was founded, the first of its kind in

Harvard historian William Langer (Courtesy of the Boston Public Library, Print Department).

the Unites States, and Langer became the first director there. Another prominent Harvard historian, John K. Fairbank, who served in the OSS in China, founded the East Asian Research Center in 1955, now called the Fairbank Center for Chinese Studies.

During the early Cold War period, area studies expanded dramatically at American universities. Abundant support from corporate philanthropies was aggressively pursued to reconstruct the field of international studies. The Rockefeller and Carnegie Foundations played dominant roles in the initial period, contributing $34 million between 1945 and 1948. The Carnegie Corporation funded Harvard's Russian Research Center while another leading Soviet study center in Columbia was financed by the Rockefeller Foundation. After 1950, the Ford Foundation joined in the parade, contributing plentiful funds for all or the major part of eighty-three centers.

This fruitful collusion between universities, government, and corporations aided the rise of the United States as a new global empire. Corporations, experiencing difficulty to find managerial staff in priority areas, poured money into area studies. In 1943, a committee on area studies at Columbia University reported: "The comment of a high officer in one of the great oil companies to the effect that for the Far East his company will have to recruit entirely new staff since he does not believe it would be possible to send back to Asia men who had lived there in the era when white superiority and arrogance were the accepted thing."[45]

The great demand from oil companies poured money into academic circles, and universities provided a training ground for recruits to mammoth corporations. Harvard joyfully joined in this parade by founding the Harvard Center for Middle Eastern Studies in 1954 under Langer's guidance. So it's not so surprising that in 1962–63 the annual report of the Center for Middle Eastern Studies reported that its "strongest feature of the financing of the Center over the nine academic years of its existence has been consistent support of the corporations with operations in the Middle East ... American Independent Oil Company ... Gulf Oil ... Socony Mobil Oil Company ... SOCAL, SOHIO, Texaco, Inc., Westinghouse ..."[46]

The successful launch of Sputnik on October 4, 1957, and the ensuing crisis also contributed to growth of area studies. With the growing urgency of supporting education, the National Defense Education Act (NDEA) was signed in 1958. Under Title VI of NDEA, area studies received plenty of money for more than twenty years. In conclusion, area studies performed decisive roles in degrading American universities into intelligence agencies whose mission was to pursue foreign policy. As French historian Jean B. Duroselle criticized, "A study of an area which treated its subject in the absolute and failed to regard it as essentially an element in the human universe, would be pure verbiage, without any scientific value. . . . It is finally possible to imagine—and it would not be such a very extravagant flight of fancy—area studies being commissioned by the Defense Ministry or the Foreign Affairs Ministry of this or that country, with a militarist or imperialist aim."[47]

Area studies prospered with complete support from government and corporations but soon became entangled in a huge scandal in the 1960s caused by Project Camelot, a social science research project propelled by the Special Operations Research Office (SORO) of American University and financed by the U.S. Army in 1964. The goal of the project was "to determine the feasibility of developing a general social systems model which would make it possible to predict and influence politically significant aspects of social change in the developing nations of the world."[48] In other words, its main mission was to study more effective ways of counterinsurgency and to anticipate the appearance of possible rebellions.

The ambitious project fell apart because of an unexpected obstacle. SORO hired Hugo Nutini, a Chilean-born professor of anthropology, to search for cooperative scholars who would conduct such studies in Chile, the first test site of Camelot. While Nutini contacted Chilean professors, Johan Galtung, a Norwegian sociologist in Santiago, received an invitation to SORO's seminar indicating the U.S. Army as the sponsor of the study. Soon the hidden fact that the U.S. military was behind the project was exposed through the media, bringing a huge discussion in Chile. The United States couldn't avoid heavy criticism that it was using scholars for its counterinsurgency program. After congressional hearings in 1965, the entire project was cancelled.

The scandal provided an opportunity to reflect on the function of area studies, which led to an ethical awaking among some academics. Also many governments became more aware of American scholars conducting research in their countries and kept distance from them. The surging anti-war movement helped to bring attention as well. As its sudden expansion was due to the quick boost of the empire, its crisis was natural with the turmoil of the Vietnam War. The country was swept away by the historical waves of anti-war movement. The so-called 1968 Revolution challenged American universities—militarized to fulfill the Cold War needs—to devise new ways to finance research.

The Kennedy Mythology

> "And so, my fellow Americans: ask not what your country can do for you—ask what you can do for your country."
> —John F. Kennedy, inaugural address, January 20, 1961[49]

John F. Kennedy, the youngest president elected to the office in American history, is an icon of American liberalism and of Harvard. In his inauguration

Cartoon satirizing Kennedy-Harvard connection.

address, often praised as one of the great speeches in history, he vigorously asked the American people to question what they could do for the country instead of whining. His speech, every single word, was full of pride and fulfillment as the absolute power of the empire reached its peak. I couldn't imagine any newly elected Korean president or those of any other countries would make such a demand, but if they did, they would be impeached the very next day. Gore Vidal, who knew JFK well, considered the president's desire that "we shall pay any price, bear any burden" to be muscular Mussolini talk, but many U.S. intellectuals found it awe-inspiring.

As a devoted graduate of Harvard, Kennedy shared some characteristics with his alma mater: charming, smart, strong, and worshipped. Kennedy called in many Harvard men into his administration: McGeorge Bundy, as the National Security Advisor to the president, Robert McNamara (MBA 1939) as secretary of defense, C. Douglas Dillon (1931), an Overseer, as new secretary of the treasury, and Robert Kennedy (1948), a beloved younger brother, as attorney general. Besides the above men, Archibald Cox

(1934) served as solicitor general, David Bell as director of budget, Abram Chayes (1943) as legal advisor to the State Department, Professor John K. Galbraith as ambassador to India, Professor Edwin Reischauer as ambassador to Japan, and Professor Arthur Schlesinger Jr. as special assistant to the president. As numerous Harvard men were summoned to the White House, there was a cynical joke saying that only squirrels were left in Harvard Yard since scholars were called to Washington. With the inauguration of the Kennedy administration, Harvard was full of pride and self-respect. As one Harvard graduate recalled, it was "the center of the universe."[50]

Many scholars who didn't get appointed to Kennedy's administration were also involved in advisory boards, and therefore busy coming and going between Boston and Washington, DC. Professor Chomsky remembers the very close connection between Washington and Cambridge scholars. According to his memory, in the morning Harvard and MIT faculty went down on the same shuttle and in the evening, they'd come back with pride that they had lunch with Jackie or advised Jack. [51]

As holders of major positions in the Cabinet, Harvard men led American foreign policy through historic events such as the Cuban Missile Crisis and the Vietnam War. After serious embarrassment from the failure of the Bay of Pigs Invasion,[52] Kennedy quickly recovered his popularity through the Cuban Missile Crisis, the hottest moment in the Cold War. As the crisis ended with Soviet Union's withdrawal of nuclear weapons from Cuba, Kennedy rose up as a superhero who saved the world from another destructive nuclear war. Throughout the globe, it has been praised as one

The author interviewing Noam Chomsky in his office at MIT in 2010.

of the defining moments in his presidency. For instance, whenever the 2010 crisis of North Korea's nuclear weapons became an issue, the conservative South Korean media cried out to let the Cuban Missile Crisis be a good lesson to ourselves. Though the saga of the great man may continue, we should reexamine if the worship of Kennedy is just.

First, let's remember that before the Soviet Union located nuclear missiles in Cuba, the United States set up missiles in Turkey that could reach almost anywhere in the Soviet Union. In other words, the United States provoked the Soviets, though hardly anyone recognized it—including Kennedy. He rather chose to shock the world by imposing a U.S. naval blockade of Cuba to turn back Soviet ships. People around the world were afraid of the threat of world war. Cities checked air raid sirens and children at school practiced taking shelter from bombs. Finally the crisis was ended when the Soviet Union agreed in secret negotiations to remove its nuclear weapons from Cuba in exchange for U.S. removal of its nuclear weapons from Turkey. Simply praising Kennedy as a man of action would be a distortion of history. Here is a perfect example of Kennedy's unabashed mind from "Documentation: White House Tapes and Minutes of the Cuban Missile Crisis."

> Bundy: "I would think one thing that I would still cling to is that he's [Khrushchev] not likely to give Fidel Castro nuclear weapons. I don't believe that has happened or is likely to happen."
> JFK: "Why does he put these in there though?"
> Bundy: "Soviet-controlled nuclear warheads . . ."
> JFK: "That's right, but what is the advantage of that? It's just as if we suddenly began to put a number of MRBM's [medium range ballistic missiles] in Turkey. Now that'd be goddam dangerous, I would think."
> Bundy?: "Well, we did, Mr. President."
> Johnson" "We did it. We . . ."
> JFK: "Yeah, but that was five years ago."[53]

So according to Kennedy's principle, if the United States positions nuclear missiles, it is okay because it is only for peace; but if others do so, it is a serious threat to humanity. If a leader of another nation asserted this principle, many members of the world community might exclaim, What an absurd and shameless imperialistic mind! The brilliant Harvard men's move was also far from intelligent. Then Secretary of Defense McNamara proposed a powerful air strike, "associated with it potential casualties of Cubans, not of U.S. citizens, but potential casualties of Cubans in, at least in the hundreds, more likely in the low thousands," and Robert F. Kennedy, still beloved as a peace icon, suggested that there might be a way to "sink the *Maine* again or something."[54]

U.S. military plane spraying Agent Orange in Vietnam.

Even if Kennedy and his administration take credit for settling the Cuban Missile Crisis, the myth of Kennedy and the Vietnam War should also be reconsidered. Many people widely accept the idea that Kennedy was a secret dove who desperately tried to stop the escalation of the Vietnam War and that his assassination threw away a chance to end war. On the contrary, JFK never stopped supporting the war. In the early stage of the Vietnam War, Kennedy propelled three major strategies in Vietnam: the Green Berets, Agent Orange, and Strategic Hamlets.

The United States Army Special Forces, also known as Green Berets, was created in 1952 as an elite force in an attempt to boost pro-American regimes and later conduct a counterinsurgency program in South Vietnam. In May 1961, Kennedy sent four hundred American Green Berets as special advisors to South Vietnam to train South Vietnamese soldiers. By the time he was assassinated in November 1963, there were more than sixteen thousand U.S. military advisers in Vietnam. Agent Orange was the euphemism for chemical warfare carried out by the U.S. military in Vietnam from 1961 to 1971. As a result of the program, an estimated four hundred thousand people were killed or maimed and five hundred thousand children born with birth defects. To defoliate forests to deprive guerrillas of cover and force rural people from their homelands, the U.S. military sprayed nearly twenty million gallons of one of the world's deadliest chemicals in Vietnam, eastern Laos, and parts of Cambodia. Though it is the worst chemical warfare in humanity—far beyond Saddam Hussein's—people hardly recognize it. When they do, they forget that it was authorized by Kennedy, the liberal dove. Strategic Hamlets involved massive population removal in an effort to separate South Vietnamese people from guerrillas. Millions of people were relocated into barbed wire enclosed concentration camps in another ruthless program propelled by Kennedy. The transfer was often accompanied by brutal violence as Kennedy sent the U.S. Air Force to bomb rural areas in South Vietnam, where more than 80 percent of population lived. People had to witness their homes burning in front of their eyes. To those people, the portrait of Kennedy as a peace-loving dove who tried to stop the Vietnam War would be an insult.

In his book *Rethinking Camelot: JFK, the Vietnam War, and U.S. Political Culture*, Professor Chomsky questioned the common mythology of Kennedy, which characterizes him as a peace-loving hero who would have withdrawn from Vietnam—an image supported by prominent figures such as director Oliver Stone, Arthur Schlesinger, and others. Based on secret documents opened to the public in the 1990s, Chomsky argues that Kennedy's intention on Vietnam had been always firm. Chomsky's research of official documents revealed that Kennedy favored escalation of the war, while Pentagon officials advised against it. Chomsky also paid attention to intellectuals' reaction before and after the 1968 Tet Offensive, a wake-up call for most Americans, which brought the miserable realization that the United States was far from winning, causing the country massively to turn against the war.

> It is quite interesting to see the reaction of educated intellectuals' shifting policy. For example many people had written memoirs of the Kennedy years: Arthur Schlesinger, Sorensen, and others. They all rewrote their memoirs. They didn't reedit them. They just published different books. In the early books, Kennedy was a hawk who had no intention of any peaceful settlement of Vietnam. He wanted to win. He knew he was popular. Let's win and get out of it as soon as possible. In the post-Tet period, he was reconstructed as a secret dove who was far from the military and courageously attempted to extricate us from Vietnam. It is an astonishing shift.[55]

Chomsky stated that most of the myths about Kennedy are based on memories after the Tet reversal. As the war became unpopular, even the business world turned against it. The portrayal of Camelot, the castle of legendary King Arthur here indicating Washington during the Kennedy presidency, reveals a longing to frame JFK's heroism in the middle of social crisis.

From East to West, it is natural to be generous to the deceased. After JFK was assassinated on November 22, 1963, before he finished the third year of his term, it became more difficult to criticize his role in Vietnam. With his tragic death, JFK is remembered as a brave hero and is still admired as one on the greatest presidents in American history. His myth is quite similar to Harvard's, so by reevaluating Kennedy, we take a step to uncover Harvard's true character, which is also concealed by numerous fantasies.

CHAPTER 5

HARVARD AND FOREIGN POLICY

"A kind of internationalist interventionism long ago came to be a leading idea in Harvard's conception of foreign affairs."
—Colin Campbell, journalist[1]

As we have discussed in the previous chapter, numerous scholars have contributed to U.S. foreign policy decisions. More than any other university, Harvard has provided the largest number of influential men to the pool of foreign policy decision-makers. Every administration has had its team of Harvard men. Eisenhower had his Kistiakowsky, Kennedy his Bundy, and Nixon his Kissinger.

McGeorge Bundy was deeply involved in U.S. intervention in the early stages of the Vietnam War. Henry Kissinger, first as Nixon's National Security Advisor and then as his Secretary of State, prolonged the Vietnam War by sabotaging the 1968 Paris Peace negotiations. Additionally, he played a key role in secret bombing campaigns in Laos and Cambodia, killing hundreds of thousands of innocent people. He was also deeply involved in civil wars, coups d'état, and assassinations worldwide, and actively supported Pinochet's military junta that ousted democratically elected President Allende in Chile. We will look into Kissinger's checkered career in more detail in the next chapter. Zbigniew Brzezinski, national security advisor to President Carter, strongly urged the United States to become involved in the 1977–78 Somalia-Ethiopia border conflict and exacerbated the situation.

Some might argue that these were examples of only a few power-hungry individuals who happen to be Harvard graduates. But as Colin Campbell's article in the *New York Times* suggests, there is nothing new about these recent events. To fully grasp the scope of this hidden history, we need to know who makes American foreign policy decisions and how they do it.

The Council on Foreign Relations: Compass for American Foreign Policy

There are many influential civilian groups diligently working on American foreign policy decisions. The most notable among them is the Council on Foreign Relations (CFR). Based in New York City, the CFR is one of the most powerful elite American organizations. It is no exaggeration to say that the CFR is where the preponderance of ideas behind American foreign policies is born. According to Sung Hung Bing, the author of *Currency Wars*, all American presidential candidates except for three since World War II belonged to this organization. Since its establishment in 1921, the U.S. secretary of the treasury was appointed almost exclusively out of the pool of the Council's members. It has also produced fourteen secretaries of the state, eleven secretaries of defense, and nine directors of the CIA. According to *How Harvard Rules*, "of the first 82 names on a list proposed by JFK for staffing his State Department, 63 were members of the Council."[2]

Although the media rarely discusses the CFR, it has openly acknowledged its influence. *Newsweek* called the CFR the "foreign policy establishment of the U.S." and the *New York Times* suggested that it "has made substantial contributions to the basic concepts of American foreign policy."[3] People argue that the domination of major government posts by the CFR is a key reason why American foreign policy remains stable despite changes in party affiliation in U.S. administrations.

Research reports published by the CFR often become compasses that guide America's foreign policy direction. It is said that officials in the State Department may establish a new policy or change existing ones after reading these reports. It is not surprising, then, that influential figures at some level regard the CFR as the "real State Department." As John Trumpbour clarified in an interview: "Some people have called the Council on Foreign Relations 'the real State Department' because many times, as John McCloy said, when he was high commissioner to Germany after World War II, whenever we need a man, we will look down the membership rolls of the Council on Foreign Relations to pick people."[4]

Who are the members of this council? McGeorge Bundy, Henry Kissinger, and Zbigniew Brzezinski—former National Security Advisors and Harvard graduates—were all members. According to the CFR's own website, its membership ranges from high officials, renowned scholars, journalists, and lawyers to renowned specialists belonging to NGOs. The honor of getting on this member list is not awarded to just anybody. No matter how smart or wealthy one is, one has to be recommended by a current member to be admitted.

The CFR was established soon after the end of World War I when the governing elite faced conflicting opinions regarding America's foreign policy direction. After the war, President Wilson proposed to establish an international organization in order to handle international relationships and to maintain order among the world's nations. The result of this was the establishment of the League of Nations under U.S. leadership. But many in the Senate favored isolationism or limited international cooperation, which led to a failure to ratify the Treaty of Versailles. A few influential people who were not happy about this development initiated the establishment of the CFR. Former Secretary of State Elihu Root became its first honorary president, and John W. Davis, a Wall Street lawyer and 1924 Democratic Party presidential candidate, its president. Interestingly, a key subgroup of this council was composed mostly of capitalists concerned with international relations such as bankers, oilmen, and corporate lawyers. Again, according to John Trumpbour, "the CFR has membership heavily weighted towards the most internationalist wing of the capitalist Establishment: the banks (eight members each from Chase Manhattan and J.P. Morgan and Co., seven members each from First National City and Chemical Bank), the oil companies (seven members from Mobil, six from Exxon), corporate law firms (eight members from Sullivan and Cromwell), and, in particular, the Rockefeller group of financial interests."[5]

These core members of the CFR who took the initiative in establish-ing and expanding the organiza-tion were Harvard graduates. It is said that a number of gentlemen gathered together and discussed this matter while leisurely chatting at the Harvard Club in New York. Among them were Archibald Cary Coolidge, historian and the first editor-in-chief of the CFR's organ *Foreign Affairs*, and Edwin Gay, the first dean of Harvard Business School and the person who pro-posed the publication of *Foreign Affairs*.

Archibald Cary Coolidge, the first Russian historian at Harvard,

Archibald Cary Coolidge, the first editor-in-chief of *Foreign Affairs*, published by the Council on Foreign Relations.

had been an active member of Inquiry, an advisory group for President Wilson in 1917. Wilson had launched this group composed of about a hundred fifty scholars in order to prepare for the peace agreement after World War I. This is generally considered the first U.S. government attempt at mobilizing scholars for the establishment of long-term foreign policies. A select group of scholars belonging to this team took the initiative of founding the CFR. More than a third of the Inquiry team were either Harvard graduates or professors. According to Dr. Trumpbour, Coolidge "considered Theodore Roosevelt, William Howard Taft, Charles Evans Hughes, Henry Cabot Lodge, and Herbert Hoover to be among his circle of friends, and he liked to brag to his students that the State Department doorman knew him by name."[6]

Edwin Gay worked in the War Industries Board during World War I and was well versed in the publishing world. From 1920 to 1923 he was the president of the *New York Evening Post*, owned by Thomas Lamont, the CEO of J.P. Morgan. Believing that a journal would be the best tool for the education of the public, he recommended Coolidge as the first editor-in-chief of *Foreign Affairs*.

Since the publication of its inaugural issue on September 15, 1922, *Foreign Affairs* has been an essential reference that marked new milestones in every stage of U.S. foreign policy decision-making. In particular, "The Sources of Soviet Conduct," an article by George Kennan in the July 1947 issue, is considered a monumental article that laid the groundwork for the Cold War. Then a policy advisor at the Department of State, Kennan advocated a strong containment policy against the USSR, defining it not as a partner but a rival. Because he published this article under the pseudonym "X," the article has since been referred to as the "X" article.

Early leaders of the CFR shared one noticeable characteristic: they were all aware of the emergence of the United States as the new superpower succeeding the British Empire. Edwin Gay, for example, reportedly said: "When I think of the British Empire as our inheritance I think simply of the natural right of succession. That ultimate succession is inevitable."[7]

George Kennan, who published an article on the containment policy against the USSR in *Foreign Affairs*.

Dr. Trumpbour points out that the ruling elite in the United States from the late nineteenth to the early twentieth century rather instinctively sensed that they would become the next global leader. The United States began to clearly emerge as a new imperial power after it won the Spanish-American War of 1898 fought over Cuba: "In many ways they said we will be the successor to the British Empire. That is our natural right. They studied a lot of the classics at Harvard where they learned about Greece and Rome. And sometimes they said, 'The British are like Athens in Greece and we are like Rome, and we will be the Roman Empire to follow them next.'"[8]

Progressive thinkers have long pointed out that American imperialism is similar to its Roman precursor. In his book *The Assassination of Julius Caesar: A People's History of Ancient Rome*, progressive thinker Michael Parenti explains the power struggle between conservative and reformist forces as the reason why Roman aristocrats assassinated Caesar. He also implicitly likens U.S. imperialism to Roman imperialism by quoting conservative economist Joseph Schumpeter:

> . . . that policy which pretends to aspire to peace but unerringly generates war, the policy of continual preparation for war, the policy of meddlesome interventionism. There was no corner of the known world where some interest was not alleged to be in danger or under actual attack. If the interests were not Roman, they were those of Rome's allies; and if Rome had no allies, then allies would be invented. When it was utterly impossible to contrive such an interest—why, then it was the national honor that had been insulted. The fight was always invested with an aura of legality. Rome was always being attacked by evil-minded neighbors, always fighting for a breathing space. The whole world was pervaded by a host of enemies, and it was manifestly Rome's duty to guard against their indubitably aggressive designs.[9]

Professor George Katsiaficas also points out that there are two significant differences between the governing structures of Greece and Rome. First, while the ruling elite in Greece, which was composed of city-states, fought among themselves, the ruling elite in Rome was united under the banner of the Roman Empire. Like the Roman ruling elite, the contemporary American ruling elite has been putting forward a united front for the sake of their empire's interest. Professor Chomsky confirms this: "The United States has essentially a one-party system and the ruling party is the business party."[10]

The second difference between the governing structures of Greece and Rome has something to do with their way of governing their colonies. While Greeks enslaved their colonies after conquering them, Romans adopted an assimilation policy, making an alliance with their colonial subjects and awarding leaders with Roman citizenship. In other words, Romans absorbed them into their empire as its loyal members. This is somewhat similar to the institution of American citizenship. As "all roads led to Rome" in the past, all roads now lead to the United States—at least for people of talent. Of course, the American empire is different from its Roman predecessor in that it overwhelms other countries through politics, economy, and culture rather than through territorial rule. Nevertheless, it is obvious that the institution of citizenship has been foundational to the growth of the American empire.

All in all, Rome and America resemble each other considerably. As Rome established colonies all over the Mediterranean through its military power, the United States has been building military bases all over the world. English, like Latin, is the modern lingua franca. As Roman culture blossomed all across its territories, American popular culture, symbolized by Hollywood, Starbucks, Coca-Cola, and McDonald's, has conquered the world. Could some of this resemblance between Rome and the United States be a result of the American ruling elite's conscious effort to model itself after Rome?

The intimate relationship between the CFR and Harvard University continued throughout the twentieth century and is still ongoing. In particular, most major scholars of international relations at Harvard University have been CFR members. According to a 1973 investigation, "twelve out of 30 of Harvard's Board of Overseers belonged to the CFR in 1973. In 1986, six out of 30 were members." The same source also reports, "a survey of the directors of the CFR from 1922–1972 indicates that at least 24 percent were officers, or staff members at Harvard. The latter figures do not even include the sizable Harvard alumni at the CFR."[11] One could even mistake the CFR as a sort of social club of Harvard men.

Currently, the CFR is a huge organization with over forty-three hundred members. The proportion of Harvard men is not as large as it was before. Still, the relationship between the CFR and Harvard is exceptional. For example, Robert Rubin, one of the most influential fellows of the Harvard Corporation, is currently the co-chair of the CFR. Former Harvard president Lawrence Summers has been a member. During Summers's presidency, all seven fellows of the Harvard Corporation were CFR members.

It is essential to understand the CFR in order to understand international relations under the leadership of the United States. For example, it was the CFR that drafted the models for restructuring the world order centered on American capitalism, which eventually led to the postwar creation of the IMF, the World Bank, and the UN.

Imperial Ambition and the "Grand Area"
In late 1939, a week after Germany invaded Poland, the CFR launched a research project centered on restructuring the world order with the United

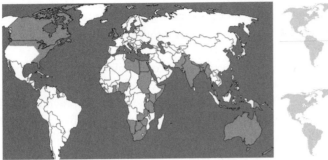

The U.S. drew up plans to control 1) the former British Empire, 2) the Western Hemisphere, and 3) the Far East before the end of World War II.

States at its center. This was dubbed the "War and Peace Studies" project. Its purpose was to develop a concrete vision of the economic and political objectives of the United States as the rising new global leader after World War II. It is noteworthy that the date of this launch preceded the Japanese attack on the Pearl Harbor by two years. The CFR had already set its global ambition in motion even before U.S. participation in the war.

This project was composed of four areas: economy and finance, security and armaments, territory, and politics. More than a hundred people participated in this project. They met several hundred times in New York and delivered 682 memoranda to the Department of State. The entire operation was conducted in a strictly confidential manner. Geographer Isaiah Bowman at the time justified the hushed-up modus operandi: "The matter is strictly confidential because the whole plan would be 'ditched' if it became generally known that the State Department is working in collaboration with any outside group." Memoranda were distributed to relevant governmental departments. The Rockefeller Foundation funded the project with nearly $350,000.[12]

Professor Chomsky directs our attention to the concept of the "Grand Area," the foundation for American imperialist strategies:

> Even before the United States entered the war, planners and analysts concluded that in the postwar world it would seek "to hold unquestioned power," acting to ensure the "limitation of any exercise of sovereignty" by states that might interfere with its global designs. They outlined "an integrated policy to achieve military and economic supremacy for the United States" in a "Grand Area" to include at a minimum the Western Hemisphere, the former British empire, and the Far East, later extended to as much of Eurasia as possible when it became clear that Germany would be defeated.[13]

It is interesting that Europe was excluded from this "Grand Area." In the early stages of the war, the "Grand Area" was supposed to be a non-German world. As mentioned in Chapter 3, at that time the American elite was convinced that Germany would win the war, so they envisioned a Germany-centered Europe.[14]

The essence of the "Grand Area" was to establish a global control system centered on the United States. A number of Harvard men participated in this grave project. Notable among them was Isaiah Bowman, the leader of the "War and Peace Studies" project and a founding member of the CFR. Additionally, other Harvard alum who participated included economist Alvin Hansen and historians William Langer and Crane Brinton.

Professor Chomsky notes that most recommendations by this project had indeed been carried out. This is not surprising, if we consider that many of its participants later became high governmental officials. Allen Dulles, a participant in this project and a Princeton graduate, served as the director of the CIA from 1953 to 1961, and his brother was also an important member of the CFR, served as secretary of state under President Eisenhower from 1953 to 1959.

In a letter to Hamilton Fish Armstrong, Isaiah Bowman, a central member of the CFR, openly acknowledged postwar U.S. global ambition: "The measure of our victory will be the measure of our domination after victory."[15] The plans of Bowman and other CFR members later materialized into the UN and the Bretton Woods System.

The Carter Administration within the Palms of the Trilateral Commission

Besides the CFR, there was another significant civilian foreign relations lobby organization: the Trilateral Commission. Established in 1973, the Trilateral Commission was from the outset inseparable from the CFR. The Trilateral Commission was established under the strong leadership of David Rockefeller, the chairman of the CFR. David Rockefeller (Harvard class of 1936), a descendent of the Rockefeller oil family, consistently exerted strong influence on U.S. foreign policies.

The Trilateral Commission's mission was to foster closer cooperation among three areas, North America, Western Europe, and Japan. In the beginning, about sixty renowned politicians, businessmen, and scholars of these three areas participated as representatives. The number of its members continued to increase to 240 members in 1982, and as of August 2011 has reached 390 members (Europe 170, North America 120, and Asia 100).[16] Present-day members include such politicians as Paul A. Volcker, former chairman of the Federal Reserve; Otto Lambsdorff, former chairman of the Free Democratic Party of Germany; Henry Kissinger, former U.S. secretary of state; Bill Clinton, former U.S. president; and prominent businessmen from SONY, AT&T, Pepsi-Cola, and Chase Manhattan Bank.

Zbigniew Brzezinski, a leader of the Trilateral Commission (left) and President Jimmy Carter, a member (right).

Harvard political scientist Zbigniew Brzezinski came up with the idea of this commission and played a leading role in its establishment. At the time, many members of the ruling elite felt threatened by several developments. The American economy stagnated during the 1970s after the global insurgency of 1968, a large-scale worldwide resistance movement centered on Europe, America, and Japan during the late 1960s. The Trilateral Commission was established with these dynamics in mind.

The Crisis of Democracy was published by the Trilateral Commission in 1975, a comprehensive report informed by the sense of crisis deeply felt within the elite circles. The book was a collection of lectures held by the commission and delivered by French sociologist Michel Crozier, American political scientist Samuel Huntington, and Japanese sociologist Joji Watanuki. According to these scholars, in certain politically tumultuous regions, governments were overloaded with civilian participants. They diagnosed that "the crisis of democracy" stemmed from "an excess of democracy" and advocated "to restore the prestige and authority of central government institutions." From their perspective, true democracy could be recovered only when people become more docile and indifferent.

Members of the Trilateral Commission became key members of the Carter administration in 1977. President Carter was himself a member after Zbigniew Brzezinski, its core member, recommended that Carter, then the governor of Georgia, be accepted as a member. Supported by David Rockefeller, the founding funder of the Trilateral Commission, Carter eventually became president. After Carter was elected, Brzezinski naturally became Carter's U.S. national security advisor, allowing him to have direct influence on U.S. foreign policies. Twenty-five out of sixty-five U.S.

members of the Trilateral Commission were appointed to major government positions. Professor Chomsky notes that a civilian organization had rarely influenced an administration to this level. He also points out that this introduction of "trilateralism" reflected the awareness by the ruling elite that the world now needed to go beyond the "Grand Area":

> The new "trilateralism" reflects the realization that the international system now requires "a truly common management," as the Commission reports indicate. The trilateral powers must order their internal relations and face both the Russian bloc, now conceded to be beyond the reach of Grand Area planning, and the Third World.
>
> In this collective management, the United States will continue to play the decisive role. As Kissinger has explained, other powers have only "regional interests" while the United States must be "concerned more with the overall framework of order than with the management of every regional enterprise."[17]

In the end, it is fair to say that the Trilateral Commission was a variation of the Grand Area project adapted to a different situation and that their objectives and nature were essentially the same. The Trilateral Commission did not weaken the influence of the CFR at all. This conclusion is strongly supported by Dr. Trumpbour's analysis that 84 percent of Trilateral Commission members who held key positions in the Carter administration were also members of the CFR.[18]

Although President Carter is widely known as a symbol of human rights, he did not always side with people trying to obtain it. For example, he approved of the armed suppression of the Gwangju Uprising in May 1980. Professor George Katsiaficas describes the decision-making process among Carter administration members:

> In the midst of the Gwangju Uprising, on May 22, 1980, at 4 p.m., an extraordinary meeting took place at the White House to discuss Korea with Secretary of State Edmund Muskie, Deputy Secretary of State Warren Christopher, Assistant Secretary of State for East Asian and Pacific Affairs Richard Holbrooke, National Security Advisor Zbigniew Brzezinski, CIA director Stansfield Turner, Defense Secretary Harold Brown, and former Seoul CIA Station Chief Donald Gregg in attendance. They agreed on the need to suppress the Gwangju Uprising and simultaneously decided to sanction the June 1980 visit to Seoul by John Moore, president of the Export-import Bank (Ex-Im Bank) of the United States, so that he could arrange U.S. financing of mammoth ROK contracts for U.S. nuclear power plants and expansion of the Seoul subway system.[19]

Members of the Carter administration agreed that the most urgent matter was "the restoration of security and order in South Korea while deferring pressure for political liberalization."[20] The American ruling elite's primary concern was the adaptation of the South Korean economy to the neoliberal market economic system in order to maximize American economic gains. President Carter was quite explicit about this point, telling CNN television on May 31 that security interests must sometimes override human rights concerns.[21]

On the surface, Carter emphasized the human rights of certain Third-World countries. In particular, he voiced strong concerns about the human rights oppression by the Shah of Iran (reign: 1941–79), which the United States had formerly tolerated. This offended many Americans, turning them decidedly against President Carter and costing him his reelection. Even David Rockefeller, a strong supporter of Carter in the first election bid, was known to have expressed his displeasure.[22]

The honeymoon between the Shah of Iran and the governing U.S. elite had lasted for decades after the Iranian coup of 1953, which was manipulated by the CIA to prevent Iranian oil nationalization. Harvard had even invited the Shah to its campus and awarded him an honorary degree in 1968. In the late 1970s, when human rights abuses and massacres were at their height in Iran, the United States did not curtail its support of the Shah.

The Shah's pro-American stance helped to spread anti-American sentiments in Iran, resulting in the Iranian hostage crisis in 1979. Having failed to rescue the hostages, Carter also stumbled in his reelection campaign, and this ushered in the Reagan administration. Barbara Honegger, who had worked for Reagan's election campaign, later alleged in her book *October Surprise* that the Reagan-Bush campaign team had conspired to make sure that Iran did not release the hostages until after the U.S. election in exchange for arms.

The Committee on the Present Danger, the Foundation of the Reagan Administration

Another important civilian foreign policy lobbying group was the Committee on the Present Danger (CPD). The CPD had been formed three times and exercised a particularly powerful influence during the Eisenhower, Reagan, and George W. Bush administrations. It was first founded in 1950 by politicians, businessmen, and scholars in favor of an expansive national security budget against Communist powers like the USSR and China. Its core members included Paul Nitze (Harvard class of 1928), who drafted the top-secret U.S. National Security Council NSC-68 policy paper, and James Conant, then president of Harvard.

Hawkish Democrats and nationalist Republicans revived the CPD in 1976 after Jimmy Carter was elected president. Eugene Rostow, former

Paul Nitze, a core member of the Committee on the Present Danger.

under secretary of state under President Johnson and professor at Yale University, Paul Nitze, and Harvard historian Richard Pipes led this revival. Harvard historian Oscar Handlin and *Commentary* editor Norman Podhoretz were also members. They spent the four Carter administration years lobbying, particularly against détente, using various means including publishing papers advocating hawkish policies towards the USSR.

If the Trilateral Commission was the cornerstone of the Carter administration, the CPD was the foundation of the Reagan administration. A substantial number of CPD members were appointed to high positions related to foreign relations and national security. According to Dr. Trumpbour, "Out of a preliminary survey of 90 Reagan advisors, cabinet and sub-cabinet appointments, thirty-two belonged to the CPD including Reagan himself, thirty-one to the CFR, and only twelve to the Trilateral Commission."[23]

The CPD advocated reinforcing combat troops and escalating U.S. intervention to staunch the spread of Communism.[24] To support its argument, it exaggerated the threat of the USSR. Richard Pipes, who had called for U.S. nuclear superiority during the Carter administration, became a member of the National Security Council in charge of East European and Soviet Affairs during Reagan's presidency. He argued that Reagan was too soft on Communism and that he needed to be reeducated about the aggressive nature of Russians. He went so far as to deny Gorbachev's reform effort itself.

Richard Pipes wrote a piece in the late 1980s denying that Gorbachev was bringing true change to the Soviet Union. He said it was a ruse designed to trick the West into believing the Soviet Union was changing so that we would be weakened and would stop spending so much money on the military.[25]

Hawkish Republicans and Democrats launched the third CPD in 2004 to address the War on Terror. Former CIA director R. James Woolsey Jr. served as its head, and Senator Jon Kyl and Senator Joseph Lieberman, Al Gore's 2004 presidential campaign running mate, were honorary co-chairs.

According to its mission statement, the CPD sought to "educate free people about the threat that militant Islamism poses to the United States and the free world; to counsel against the appeasement of terrorists and the states that sponsor them; to support policies to confront this menace; and to encourage the development of civil society and democracy in regions from which the terrorists emanate."[26] Former CIA Director James Woolsey went so far as to say that the United States was engaged in World War IV. In the address to a group of UCLA students, Woolsey described the Cold War as the third world war and said, "This fourth world war, I think, will last considerably longer than either World Wars I or II did for us. Hopefully not the full four-plus decades of the Cold War."[27] The notable members listed on the CPD website include neocons and associates of the American Enterprise Institute, the Heritage Foundation, the Hoover Institution, the Manhattan Institute, and Freedom House.

Organizations for Imperial Consensus-Building

What are the functions of these civilian-lobbying organizations? Dr. Trumpbour suggests that the CFR, the Trilateral Commission, and the CPD "provide three major functions for the ruling class by fostering 1) ideological consensus, 2) elite recruitment, and 3) cohesion among Establishment institutions."[28]

Regarding fostering an ideological consensus, Henry Kissinger succinctly summarized the elite's position: "You need an establishment. Society needs it. You can't have all these constant assaults on national policy so that every time you change presidents you end up changing direction."[29] According to Kissinger, the United States needed a small pressure group to guarantee its interests and to prevent changes in its basic foreign policy themes. Naturally, this leads to the question: whose interests does this minority pressure group represent? The answer to this question is clear when we consider the funders and members of this group—mostly high officials, Wall Street businessmen, and elite professors.

Elite recruitment is a fundamental function of these organizations. Successive administrations have appointed their members to important governmental posts. As a result, membership in these organizations has functioned as a dividing line between insiders and outsiders. For example, if you are a member of the CFR, you have that much more chance to be included in that select gentlemen's group. Twentieth-century U.S. political history confirms this, as does John McCloy's remark: "Whenever we needed a man we thumbed through the roll of Council members and put through a call to New York."[30]

Lastly, we should pay attention to how at key historical moments these groups have played significant roles in formulating the long-range goals of U.S. foreign policy. University regional research institutes and international relations institutes have information about policymaking centered on specific agenda and short-term tasks. Prestigious foreign policy organizations have played the role of managing and moderating rifts among numerous elite organizations. As Roman elites united to build an enormous empire, American elites must also have been clearly aware of their need to control and manage various opinions among themselves. Civilian elite groups have taken charge of this role.

It is noteworthy that members of these organizations were related not only to elite educational institutions including Harvard but also to the CIA and large corporations that financially supported them. For example, McGeorge Bundy, a CFR member, was a Harvard dean and deeply involved in the establishment of the Center for International Affairs at Harvard. Additionally, he was the national security advisor to President Kennedy and the president of the Ford Foundation, a major funder of regional studies. McGeorge Bundy is typical of the intimate relations among Harvard, the U.S. government, and large corporations.

Although these are civilian organizations, the CFR, the Trilateral Commission, and the CPD have been intricately entwined with the government and have wielded incredible influence on U.S. foreign policy. The three organizations were established in different periods and have had different names and objectives. But they are the same civilian U.S. foreign policy groups controlled by the U.S. ruling elite, epitomized by Harvard and the Ivy League establishment.

CHAPTER 6

HARVARD IN CRISIS: THE ANTI-WAR MOVEMENT

"There is a time when the operation of the machine became so odious, makes you so sick at heart, that you can't take part; you can't even passively take part, and you've got to put your bodies upon the gears and upon the wheels, upon the levers, upon all the apparatus, and you've got to make it stop. And you've got to indicate to the people who run it, to the people who own it, that unless you're free, the machine will be prevented from working at all!"
—Mario Savio, a key member of the Berkeley Free Speech Movement

After World War II, the Cold War had two kinds of influence on higher education. First, the accelerating arms race between the United States and the USSR contributed to the expansion of American universities. Second, the federal government sponsored university research institutes and, as a result, a subservient partnership was formed between the federal government and universities. Universities accepted these changes as an inevitable consequence in the joint effort to defeat Communism, and, subsequently, universities ended up at the forefront of ideological warfare.

It was not only governmental officials but also university intellectuals who believed that universities should become pillars for national security. Clark Kerr defined the role of universities in his 1963 book *The Uses of the University*: "Intellect has also become an instrument of national purpose, a component part of the "military industrial complex." In the war of the ideological worlds, a great deal depends on the use of this instrument. . . . Thus it only pays to produce knowledge if through production it can be put into use better and faster."[1]

According to Kerr, the university's mission was to produce knowledge that could meet national needs. He then argued that in order to meet this requirement, we needed a "multiversity" rather than a "university." His attitude was typical of the American ruling elite's superficial understanding of knowledge and scholarship.

Harvard scholars greatly contributed to dissemination of this type of thinking from their posts in government and educational institutions. Thanks to the widespread social hysteria of the time, epitomized by 1950s McCarthyism, this trend in nationalistic education settled in as unavoidable reality. Oppression and various forms of restrictions became commonplace in the American university setting. However, unlike the previous Great-Depression and World War II–era generation, the younger generation of this period, raised in times of abundance and freedom, resisted. Students began to take an interest in reform and various social issues including racial/gender equality, poverty, and war. This wave of students' awareness joined forces with the civil rights movement that had begun heating up during the 1950s and the anti-war movement of the 1960s. The combined forces of these movements thoroughly shook the status quo.

"I Have a Dream"

On November 4, 2008, the first African American president in U.S. history was elected. Barack Obama's election was an epochal event in the several-hundred-year narrative of African American suffering and discrimination.

Even after the abolition of slavery in the mid-nineteenth century, African Americans continued to endure heavy discrimination and second-class citizenship. Their social status turned a decisive corner only during World War II when almost a million African Americans went to war and fought side by side with their white American counterparts. Even then, the transition was far from seamless. African Americans had to fight against not only enemy fire but also widely prevalent military racial discrimination. Thanks to these events, however, their social standing began to change after the war. The average African American household income increased due to the wartime economic boom. Average African American income more than doubled during two decades between 1940 and 1960. African Americans experienced unprecedented highs in gainful employment. By and large, the financial and economic situation of African Americans was improving.

However, as their financial situation improved, the African American desire for equality in other aspects of life increased accordingly. As African Americans gained voting rights in the northern states, the race/equality question became a rising hot-button political issue. The National Association for the Advancement of Colored People (NAACP), founded in 1909, and the Congress of Racial Equality (CORE), organized in 1942, became important centers for the African American civil rights movement.

In the 1950s, two landmark events in the history of American civil rights occurred one after another. The first event was the wildly controversial

Brown v. Board of Education, in which the Supreme Court declared unconstitutional state laws separating public schools by race. This decision overturned the *Plessy v. Ferguson* decision of 1896, which allowed state-sponsored segregation. This ruling, although limited to public schools, was a major victory of the civil rights movement.

Rosa Parks and Dr. Martin Luther King Jr.

The second event was in 1955 when Rosa Parks refused to obey a bus driver's order to give up her seat to a white passenger. Her defiance prompted the Montgomery Bus Boycott and the formation of the Montgomery Improvement Association, the president of which was none other than Dr. Martin Luther King Jr. African American residents of Montgomery continued the boycott for 381 days until the city repealed its law requiring segregation on public buses. This followed the Supreme Court ruling in *Browder v. Gayle* in which this form of segregation was deemed unconstitutional. Thus the Montgomery Bus Boycott was meaningful in two ways: it set a precedent for a successfully organized protest by African Americans, and it introduced Dr. Martin Luther King Jr. to the world as a dynamic civil rights movement leader.

Following these two deeply influential incidents, James Farmer, the national director of CORE, organized "Freedom Rides" in 1961. The Freedom Rides consisted of mixed race/gender groups journeying through the Deep South to contest segregation on interstate buses. The first trip south ended with participants returning home severely beaten and injured after making it to Alabama. Undeterred, the Student Nonviolent Coordinating Committee (SNCC) immediately sent students to the South again to restart the Freedom Rides. Although they met with various obstacles and severe violence, they were able to draw national media attention, further invigorating the African American civil rights movement.

Another landmark event for the movement was the March for Jobs and Freedom in Washington in 1963. Tired of waiting for respectful treatment and equal opportunities, a record-breaking two hundred thousand African Americans gathered in front of the Lincoln Memorial on August 28, 1963. This march, generally considered one of the most successful political rallies in modern history, was broadcast to television sets all over the country. In front of a nationally televised audience, Martin Luther King

Jr. delivered his historic "I Have a Dream" speech, advocating hope and racial harmony. This rally reached its peak when Reverend King met with President Kennedy at the White House. A direct result of this meeting was the 1964 Civil Rights Act, which outlawed major forms of discrimination against racial, ethnic, national, and religious minorities and women.

The civil rights movement spread to university campuses. Students born after World War II grew up in more racially tolerant environments. They believed racism was against American values. Consisting largely of white student activists and civil rights–oriented SNCC members, Students for a Democratic Society (SDS) was formed in 1959 and subsequently became a new center for student movement.

Burning Campuses

In the 1960s, a series of major upheavals rocked the Western world, threatening global capitalism at its foundation. There was the Cuban Revolution in 1959. Algeria achieved independence from France after a fierce eight-year-long struggle. Social movements against capitalist contradictions and oppression erupted all over Western European countries as well. The New Left movement opposing both conservatism and the conventional left (hence the name "New Left") swept across Europe and America. Students were at the forefront of these revolutionary movements.

Student struggles were something as expected as the cycle of death and rebirth in nature, but the 1960s movements went beyond mere rebellion. Students were disillusioned by the subservience of universities to governments and corporations, by overt racism, and by unjust and inhumane wars. In June 1962, fifty-nine representatives from various student movement organizations gathered in Port Huron in Michigan to work on a political vision statement. After a few days' discussion, they adopted a statement drafted by Tom Hayden, then the field secretary of Students for a Democratic Society (SDS) and the editor-in-chief of a student newspaper at the University of Michigan. This manifesto was called the Port Huron Statement. With the drafting of this statement, SDS emerged as one of the leading organizations of the New Left.

The spark that set the 1960s American student movement ablaze was the Free Speech Movement (FSM), a student protest that took place at the University of California, Berkeley campus during the 1964–65 academic year. As students' participation in the civil rights movement grew, the university administration banned all political activities on campus. Thousands of students immediately protested, occupying school buildings and demanding the repeal of these restrictions. Although prevented from reaching its goals due to ruthless police intervention, the FSM served as a great opportunity for students to express their doubts about their university's

Tom Hayden at the 30th Commemoration of the May 18 Uprising in Gwangju, Korea.

role in serving the status quo. The FSM remained an inspiration for student protests throughout the late 1960s, and it became a turning point for the most radical student movements in American history.

As the U.S. government began a large-scale deployment of troops to Vietnam after the Gulf of Tonkin Incident in 1965, the student movement began focusing on the war. Students and intellectuals organized "teach-ins" at campuses across the country to educate fellow students about the unjustifiable nature of the war and U.S. involvement in Vietnam. Professor Ngo Vinh Long, the first Vietnamese to enter Harvard University, participated in teach-ins and was especially committed to educating his audience about the desperate situation in Vietnam. His participation played a crucial role in the growth of the anti-war movement. Twenty-five thousand people turned out at Washington rallies organized by SDS, confirming the organization's political base.

As the U.S. government expanded the draft in 1966, the anti-war movement intensified even more. Students and youth had to fight even harder not to be sent to war. According to historian Howard Zinn, "Young men began to refuse to register for the draft or to refuse induction if called. Students signed petitions headed We Won't Go. Over a half million men resisted the draft. About 200,000 were prosecuted, 3,000 became fugitives. There were too many cases to pursue and most were dropped. Finally, 8,750 men were convicted of draft evasion."[2] As resistance to the draft continued, President Nixon was compelled to abolish it in 1973.

Ngo Vinh Long, University of Maine professor and activist against the Vietnam War.

College students including Harvard students had been exempt from the draft until they graduated. Although students preferred not to participate in the war, they also didn't find it fair to be given the privilege of exemption because they were college students. Probably for this reason, some students resisted even more fiercely.

Truth Exposed

Until the mid-1960s, SDS at Harvard consisted of only around twenty members. John Kennedy's election had ushered in the Harvard age. Numerous Harvard men were appointed to influential governmental posts, much to the pride of the Harvard community. Within Harvard, the prevailing sentiment was "We are the center of the universe." A great many Harvard students at that time were legacy students. Until the late 1960s, when the anti-war movement took a dramatic leap, only a very small number of Harvard students participated in the student movement, and students generally tended to have a very low level of political awareness. For example, when SDS distributed pamphlets listing and clarifying lies propagated by the president and the government in general, many Harvard students refuted it by saying, "You may have a point about some policies, but the president of the United States never lies."[3]

Harvard's tight-knit community believed that U.S.-style liberal democracy and a market economy were the final destinations of human civilization. Students took a U.S.-centered world order for granted. Had it not been for the Vietnam War, most of them may not have ever known where Vietnam

A teach-in at which students were educated about the truth of the Vietnam War (left) and a demonstration in Washington, DC (right).

or Indochina was located on the world map. The civil rights movement and the Vietnam War forced Harvard students to confront the violence and hypocrisy of the university system and to ask fundamental questions as to the right way for them to live.

In 1964, SNCC organized a voter registration drive billed "Freedom Summer" that spanned the entire South. Harvard and Radcliffe student participants returned to report that Harvard University was the largest shareholder in Middle South Utilities, a holding company that owned Mississippi Power and Light and contributed significantly to racist state policies. Students petitioned the Harvard Corporation to declare its opposition to the racist activities supported by its investments and to use its influence to force an end to these practices. Students also requested that Harvard withdraw 10 percent of its $10 million investment to use as bail for students who had been jailed working for civil rights in Mississippi. The Harvard Corporation declined to act on these requests.[4]

In December 1964, Harvard SDS organized a march in support of Berkeley's Free Speech Movement. In 1965, they also organized demonstrations against the Vietnam War, Harvard's investment in South Africa (Harvard was a staunch supporter of apartheid at the time), and its wide-scale gentrification practices. These activities provoked Harvard students to question their university—what it taught, where it invested its endowment funds, and the exact nature of the contractual relationship it had with the government. Harvard SDS membership grew from about twenty members in the early 1960s to twelve hundred members in 1968. Their fight shook the triumphant Harvard world to its foundations.

Samuel Huntington and Henry Kissinger: War Criminals

One of the most important concerns of students during the anti-war era was the practical reality of university research in service of war. Students believed in the neutrality of educational institutions, objecting to the intimate relationship between government and universities. This intimate relationship was, of course, not limited to only Harvard, but prevalent in most universities. As the war dragged on, more and more scholars were mobilized to assist U.S. operations in Vietnam.

Historian Ngo Vinh Long observes this close relationship between universities and government during the Vietnam War in government contracted research at the University of Tennessee. The purpose of that specific research was to identify the causes of the American failure in the Vietnam War and to propose possible solutions. Researchers concluded that deeply rooted Vietnamese nationalism was the cause of America's failures and that this nationalism originated from people's indoctrination in Vietnamese history, culture, and national heroes. The research suggested that Americans should introduce education focusing on science and technology rather than history and culture as well as tests requiring multiple choice or short answers rather than essay writing. The researchers also recommended that Americans could defeat Vietnamese Communists by introducing pornographic movies and magazines so that Vietnamese youth would use less brain and more "lower body."[5]

Many universities conducted research of a similar kind, as universities ultimately became research bases to study how to defeat Vietnamese guerrilla warfare. Numerous scholars participated in these types of studies, raking in advisor's fees and research funds. For example, Ithiel de Sola Pool, renowned social scientist and MIT Center for International Studies research director, earned $18,000 for his supervision of the secret "Chieu Hoi" project and $32,000 for another Vietnam War–related project. Also, the Simulmatic Corporation, which Pool took part in establishing, analyzed Viet Cong POWs and exiles in a $2.5 million project funded by the Pentagon and the CIA. Professor George Katsiaficas, an MIT student at that time, debated Pool noting that Professor Pool kept interrogation files of Viet Cong POWs in his office, "research" that he used to analyze "enemy" motivations.

Harvard University was where much essential Vietnam War research was conducted and where most of the critical policies on the war were produced. Indeed, many of the politicians, officials, and scholars from Harvard were key protagonists of the Vietnam War. Harvard hero President Kennedy, Secretary of Defense McNamara, and National Security Advisor McGeorge Bundy were central players who contributed to the expansion of the war in its early stage. Harvard scholars also poured a great deal of their talents and energy into rationalizing the reasons for war. Harvard political scientist

65

A sarcastic cartoon about Harvard scholars making money from war research.

Samuel Huntington, for one, was an especially clear example of this. More governmental official than scholar, Huntington served as the White House Coordinator of Security Planning for the National Security Council and worked on numerous research projects in collaboration with the CIA.

Best known today for his book *The Clash of Civilizations*, Huntington made his political character clear in his proposal to concentrate the entire rural population of South Vietnam as a means to isolate the Viet Cong. According to Huntington, the United States was having a difficult time in Vietnam because half of South Vietnamese population lived in rural areas (often Viet Cong bases) and therefore it was imperative that the United States drive them out. Huntington advocated a forced migration policy that was actually attempted in vain during the Kennedy administration under the name: "strategic hamlet program." Huntington also argued that this forced migration would promote urbanization and modernization and aid Vietnamese democracy as a result.

American intellectuals have long had a history of justifying American political, economic, and military intervention in the Third World under the banner of liberal democracy. This long history is why Noam Chomsky called intellectuals "professional justifiers." Yet, Huntington's sophistic argument that "the American sponsored urban revolution undercut the VC rural revolution" put him on top in this history of professional justification:

> In an absent-minded way the United States in Viet Nam may well have stumbled upon the answer to "wars of national liberation." The effective response lies neither in the quest for conventional military

victory nor in the esoteric doctrines and gimmicks of counter-insur-
gency warfare. It is instead only through forced-draft urbanization
and modernization that rapidly brings the country in question out
of the phase in which a rural revolutionary movement can hope to
generate sufficient strength to come to power.[6]

The essence of this "forced-draft urbanization and modernization"
program consisted of comparing guerrillas to fish and the general population to the sea: empty the sea so that the fish could not swim. But the idea
of massive forced migration of millions of people largely through saturation
bombing is, no doubt, a criminal notion.[7] Professor Ngo Vinh Long, who
knew Professor Huntington personally, testified that Huntington's understanding of Vietnam was extremely simplistic. Huntington believed that if
America forced urbanization and provided food and goods, revolutionary
forces would immediately collapse: "He [Huntington] called this the Honda
Revolution. He said, 'If you provide Viet Cong cadres with Honda [motorcy-
cles], then they would turn against revolution.' So I talked with him. I said,
'Sam, has it ever entered your head that a revolutionary can ride a Honda
and still be a revolutionary?'"[8]

Complying with Huntington's recommendation, the American military indiscriminately bombed Vietnamese villages and drove millions of
Vietnamese farmers out of their ancestral homes. A B-52 bomber can drop
about twenty-five thousand pounds, which can devastate everything within
a half-mile radius. Eight B-52s delivering this kind of payload have the same
destructive power as one Hiroshima atomic bomb. The American military
dropped about seven million tons of explosive material during the Vietnam
War, about three times more than the bomb tonnage used during the entire
Second World War. An estimated 1.5 million South Vietnamese civilians
were killed during these bombings. It is no wonder anti-war activist students called him "a mad dog." Michael Ansara, one of the Harvard SDS
leaders at that time, described Huntington:

> He's (Samuel Huntington) got more blood on his hands than the
> people who actually had to go and do the dirty work. The people who
> think it up, who design the programs, who create the rationales, these
> are not ideas divorced from their consequences. . . . If you justified
> certain policies, you have to take responsibilities for them. . . . The
> fact that you can sit in Cambridge and come to the table with your
> hands clean is an illusion. You have moral responsibility for what you
> have set in motion.[9]

Speaking of Harvard men criminally involved in the Vietnam War,
we cannot fail to mention Henry Kissinger, national security advisor and

Samuel Huntington.

Henry Kissinger.

secretary of state under President Nixon. When people describe him, they often call him Harvard's most successful government official. Who is Kissinger, though? As a professor at Harvard in the 1950s, he secretly read fellow professors' letters and volunteered to deliver information he gathered to the FBI, according to documents released via the Freedom of Information Act. He was a Cold War scholar deeply engaged in an intimate relationship with government intelligence agencies.

In late 1968, Kissinger greatly hindered President Johnson's efforts to conclude peace negotiations in Paris in order to assist Nixon's election. The Johnson administration had been working on negotiations for months to help Democrats win the election, but their efforts were for naught when three days before the election, South Vietnamese leaders rejected them. As is well known today, this rejection was largely the product of behind-the-scenes operations by the Nixon camp: Nixon had promised better terms to the South Vietnamese government in exchange for rejecting the Johnson administration's proposals. A telegram sent from the Republican camp to South Vietnam read: "Hold on, we are gonna win."[10]

As a result of Kissinger and the Nixon administration's intervention, the war continued until the 1973 Paris Peace Accord was finally reached five years later, an agreement that offered the exact same terms as the ones proposed by the Johnson administration. During those years, more than twenty thousand more American troops died, and countless Vietnamese, Cambodians, and Laotians were killed or victimized.[11]

As national security advisor, Kissinger ordered massive bombings in Laos and Cambodia, claiming that these two neutral countries were also North Vietnamese camps. During this bombing campaign, the number of civilian casualties in Cambodia amounted to 600,000, and in Laos 350,000.[12] Chomsky notes that at that time Kissinger ordered the American military to simply bomb everything that moved: a massacre order.[13] In *The*

Trial of Henry Kissinger, journalist Christopher Hitchens discusses how Kissinger was involved in war crimes, massacres, assassinations, and kidnappings all over the world.

One might with some revulsion call it a "menu" of bombardment, since the code names for the raids were "Breakfast," "Lunch," "Snack," "Dinner," and "Dessert." The raids were flown by B-52 bombers which, it is important to note at the outset, fly at an altitude too high to be observed from the ground and carry immense tonnages of high explosive: they give no warning of approach and are incapable of accuracy or discrimination because of both their altitude and the mass of their shells. Between March 18, 1969, and May 1970, 3,630 such raids were flown across the Cambodian frontier. The bombing campaign began as it was to go on—with full knowledge of its effect on civilians and with flagrant deceit by Mr. Kissinger in this precise respect.[14]

Professor George Katsiaficas also points out that Kissinger's policies sent hundreds of thousands of people to their deaths in Indochina and that soldiers who carried out his order suffered massive psychological trauma. He asserts, "Kissinger was one of the worst war criminals in the twentieth century. When the true history of the twentieth century is written, his name will be inscribed next to the most bloodthirsty tyrants and butchers of this epoch."[15]

After the peace treaty of 1973, Henry Kissinger received the Nobel Peace Prize for his contribution to the Paris Peace Accords. North Vietnamese negotiator Le Duc Tho was also given the honor, but he declined to accept. Retired from politics in the late 1970s, Kissinger still exercises a powerful influence on the American political scene as a foreign policy consultant.

Samuel Huntington and Henry Kissinger are examples of the destructive capacity of human beings wearing the mask of "academic freedom" without love for fellow human beings or the importance of justice. Can we call them intellectuals at all, knowing that they used their superficial knowledge to serve the elite? Perhaps it is more accurate to say that they are knowledge technicians volunteering to submit themselves to capital and power. In "The Responsibility of Intellectuals," Chomsky argues that the responsibility of intellectuals is to delve as deeply as possibly into the truth of critical issues and to let the appropriate people know these truths. He also advised in an interview that when we evaluate intellectuals we have to pay attention to their morals as well as their intellectual qualities.[16]

Of course, Huntington and Kissinger are just the tip of the iceberg when counting the many scholars who have triumphantly served the American empire. But what also matters is that these scholars have been largely free from the legal and moral responsibilities of the policies they created or justified. When Huntington died in 2008, major media outlets created fervor over the passing of a great intellectual. A fellow Harvard professor praised him with the words: "Sam was the kind of scholar that made Harvard a great university." We also need to remember that he was the kind of scholar who made Harvard a blight on those experiencing the true horrors of the Vietnam War.

The Anti-war Movement, a Driving Force for Change

The Vietnam War shook American society to its very roots. As the war raged thousands of miles away, a cultural and social civil war broke out within America itself. Many students fought against racism, bureaucracy, war, nuclear armament, and gender discrimination and oppression. 1968, the year of the global revolution, was a particularly important year not only in U.S. student movement history, but also modern history in general. A wide range of critical events occurred in 1968. On January 30, lunar New Year's Day, joint Viet Cong and North Vietnamese forces launched a devastating large-scale military offensive against South Vietnam, the United States, and their allies in what has become known as the Tet Offensive. Through waves of surprise attacks, the Viet Cong and North Vietnam occupied a host of major South Vietnamese cities and even the U.S. embassy itself. When news of this joint offensive was broadcast across America, it was clear that claims of imminent victory by President Johnson and his administration were not real. Public opinion rapidly turned against the war. Johnson announced his decision not to seek reelection on March 31. When Martin Luther King Jr. was assassinated on April 4, angry crowds rioted in more than a hundred cities across the country.

Following the fervor of these critical historical events, student demonstrations gained serious momentum. On April 23, 1968, Columbia University students occupied university buildings throughout the campus after they discovered links between the university and the ongoing Vietnam War, as well as the university's planned expansion into surrounding neighborhoods. Due to the university's purchase of neighborhood real estate, the area's rents were skyrocketing and working families were being driven out. The April 23 Columbia sit-in lasted almost a week before it came to an end when the NYPD violently quashed it and arrested hundreds of students. On June 5, presidential candidate Robert Kennedy, younger brother of the late president John F. Kennedy and anti-war candidate favored by student activists, was assassinated. The two assassinations—of Martin Luther King Jr. and Robert Kennedy—sent tremendous shock waves through the population. Students' fights intensified and demonstrators began to attack research institutes with close ties to intelligence agencies in order to halt university research for the Department of Defense and the CIA.

In the midst of these crucial political and social developments, Harvard University made the anachronistic gesture of conferring an honorary degree

Harvard's Center for International Studies (CFIA) was attacked by student activists in 1970.

on the Shah of Iran. Harvard's President Pusey praised the Shah as "a twentieth century ruler who has found in power a constructive instrument to advance social and economic revolution in an ancient land."[17] Eleven years later, this same Shah would be ousted from his post and seek exile in 1979 during the Iranian Revolution.

Despite a relative unwillingness to change, Harvard University would finally enter its own revolutionary phase in 1969 after a succession of critical events. First, there was the Secretary of Defense Robert McNamara's visit to the Harvard Kennedy School in November 1966. The spokesperson for SDS requested that McNamara participate in a debate with students on the topic of the Vietnam War. McNamara immediately declined. Following his refusal, students protested outside the lecture hall during McNamara's lecture. Afterwards, students surprised McNamara and surrounded his car. Eventually McNamara agreed to take a few questions with Harvard SDS co-president Michael Ansara leading the debate atop McNamara's car.

The debate took a turn for the worse when, at one point, a student asked if he knew the number of civilian casualties in the Vietnam War. McNamara answered he didn't, this despite his reputation for having an in-depth knowledge of the numbers related to his policies. When Ansara pressed him by saying, "How could you not know when so many people are dying because of your policies?" the crowd began heckling him with accusations of being a "liar" and "murderer." Furious and incensed, McNamara shot back, "I acted like you when I was in school. But there are two big differences. First, I was polite, and second, I was tougher than you. And I'm tougher than you now." Eventually, the police had to help McNamara escape the crowd through a three-hundred-yard underground tunnel. Although student activists were elated with that action, Harvard was embarrassed. Dean Monroe sent McNamara an official letter of apology with two thousand student signatures.[18]

Student activists also paid attention to Dow Chemical Company's campus recruitment. Students barricaded a recruiter from Dow Chemical for seven hours in the Mallinckrodt Lab, protesting the company's role in producing napalms and defoliants for the Vietnam War. Many students sympathized with this protest against their university's hosting a company like Dow Chemical.

Poster demanding the abolition of ROTC.

Afterwards, students focused on three issues: the abolition of ROTC, abandoning the university's plan to randomly expand to neighborhoods, and withdrawing endowment funds from investment in apartheid-supporting South Africa. The issue of ROTC emerged as one of the most important issues in relation to the Vietnam War. ROTC was first introduced to Harvard during World War I through Harvard president Abbot Lawrence Lowell. Michael Ansara explains why student activists paid attention to ROTC at that time: "It was another symbolic way in which the university was saying, 'We support what our government is doing and we are going to materially help it by training officers.' So it was a very symbolic way we could say the university is involved in the war. We were saying, no ROTC on the campuses."

As negative opinions on the Vietnam War were becoming increasingly widespread, Harvard faculty also began to support the cause of abolishing ROTC. On February 4, 1969, Harvard faculty voted to downgrade the status of ROTC to an extracurricular activity, citing academic standards on coursework as a reason. This vote also denied ROTC teaching staff the status of faculty. Although the Harvard Corporation was willing to accept this decision, President Pusey strongly opposed it. On March 25, about a month after the vote, President Pusey appeared before the Student-Faculty Advisory Council and said: "I think it's important that ROTC be kept here. I personally feel it's terribly important for the United States of America that college people go into the military. . . . The current notion that the military-industrial complex is an evil thing does not correspond to reality."[19]

There was an important reason why President Pusey had this opinion. During his tenure between 1953 and 1963, annual federal funding for Harvard research increased from $8 million to over $30 million, about one third of the university's operating budget. The federal government was the single largest source of Harvard's income.[20] People complained and criticized that Harvard sold its independence and scholarly freedom

Michael Ansara.

for money. In the end, President Pusey's anachronistic attitude helped to bring about both the first sit-in in Harvard's history and his own demise as the president.

The First Occupation

On April 9, 1969, dozens of Harvard students took over administrative offices in University Hall. When Harvard students had gathered the previous day to discuss their future strategies, opinions ran the gamut from the occupation of University Hall to wait-and-see and to a strike. The conclusion was to withhold decision for the time being and to wait and see. After the meeting, students marched to the official presidential residence and demonstrated, shouting slogans like "ROTC Must Go!" The next day, a more radical group of students associated with Labor-Student Alliance and Progressive Labor Party took over University Hall, believing that other students would support their decision once they took action. Although Michael Ansara had already graduated from Harvard, he rushed to University Hall when he heard the news and joined the occupation.

> Inside University Hall was in the spirit of those times—a crazy, idealistic, exciting, invigorating experience, because all these students had taken over the administration offices, and what they did was to make a university. All of a sudden, ideas of all kinds were being discussed and debated. What does this mean? What should the university do? What should the university be? What does it mean to really be dedicated to ideas? What does it mean to have a moral life? All these kids were just debating it freely hour after hour after hour.[21]

Inside University Hall a few students proposed looking into university administration files. As the university was not the private property of the administrators, this was a natural decision. Looking through university files, students were greatly surprised. Everything that Harvard had denied turned out to be true. According to the secret files students discovered, Harvard had been receiving funds from the U.S. Army, Navy, and Air Force, as well as various intelligence agencies. Harvard *was* a secret research base for the CIA. Harvard had disgraced itself by becoming a research institute subservient to the U.S. government and lying to cover it up.

Perhaps worried about these secret documents, President Pusey rushed to call in city and state police. Around 3 a.m. on April 10, the second day of occupation, Boston and Cambridge police began moving towards Harvard. A little before 5 a.m., the police round up began. Most policemen at that time came from blue-collar backgrounds. Many of their friends and colleagues were dying in Vietnam. To most of them, the political struggles of Harvard students who enjoyed all kinds of privileges seemed like child's play. Many police were known to detest students. Students

Harvard students violently taken out of the University Hall.

decided to hold onto their nonviolent principles and to calmly face the riot police with their arms chained together.

Police operations were violent and merciless. They threw students down the stairs, dragged them, beat them with clubs, and maced them. It was a bloody scene filled with cries and shrieks. The following testifies to the details of that day.

> It was all over in twenty minutes. One hundred and ninety-six persons were arrested and taken in vans and buses to the Third District County Court in East Cambridge for booking and arraignment. Forty-eight injuries required medical care, including two concussions and a fractured skull. The Cambridge police billed Harvard $5,007 for overtime police expenses on April 10, but the Boston police were a bargain at $1,226.[22]

It was reported that President Pusey watched police operations through binoculars. But he was not the only person who witnessed it. From freshmen dormitories that surrounded University Hall, a significant number of resident students also witnessed the events. Even those who did not support the takeover were outraged after witnessing the elite institution's hypocrisy in exercising violence while preaching peace. Although police violence at Harvard was on a much smaller scale than that in Vietnam or even Columbia University a year previously, it attracted a significant degree of media attention because it was an event at Harvard.

Within a few hours after the strike's violent suppression, students had gathered en masse, eventually resulting in a general student strike.

The shootings at Kent State University on May 4, 1970.

This strike was completely different, however, from the kinds led by SDS. Students voluntarily formed leadership based on dorms and schools. This voluntary, full-scale student movement was a forerunner of the enormous changes that were about to occur in Harvard.

Counterattack

This full-scale, voluntary student strike was not limited to Harvard. There were student strikes and occupations in universities nationwide. On April 30, 1970, President Nixon announced to the country that the United States had no choice but to attack Cambodia in order to cut off supplies to the Viet Cong. Although Nixon had won the 1968 election with the promise to end the Vietnam War, he was actually expanding the war into Vietnam's neighboring nations. People were enraged, and the anti-war sentiment reached its peak.

On May 4, the Ohio National Guard shot unarmed college students at Kent State University, killing four students and wounding nine others. All four of those killed were white. This unprecedented turn of events sent shock waves throughout the entire country. Ten days later, police at Jackson State University killed two black students under similar circumstances. Students were enraged and a resistance movement swept through the entire country. Professor Katsiaficas wrote, "More than 80 percent of all universities and colleges in the United States experienced protests, and about half of the country's eight million students and 350,000 faculty actively participated in the strike."[23]

The 1971 May Day Rally in Washington, DC. The slogan of this rally was "If the government doesn't stop the war, we'll stop the government."

Student movements turned more radical. Arson and bombings occurred more frequently than ever before, and new disruptive strategies including barricading occupied buildings were attempted. Dozens of ROTC buildings were set on fire. The Weather Underground bombed New York City police headquarters in June. Sterling Hall at the University of Wisconsin–Madison, which housed the Army Mathematics Research Center and was known for its role in informing Che Guevara's location to the CIA, was also bombed.

The government's violent response to these students' protests provoked even more violent forms of resistance from college students. Unfortunately, the civil war began to tire both students and citizens. Professor Katsiaficas, who, as an MIT student, had been imprisoned at the time for his participation in the anti-war protests, explains the aftermath of the Kent State shootings: "The shootings had a chilling effect on many activists who dropped out, moved to the countryside, while others became desperate, going underground to work against the government. All of this meant space of popular engagement was shrinking so the movement gradually dissipated as the war wore down."[24]

In the end, the New Left movement that swept the United States did not develop to form a new political alternative but faded with the end of the Vietnam War. SDS, an ideologically loose association from the outset, once boasted five hundred nationwide branches and more than a hundred thousand members. But it was a fractured organization with a wide range of beliefs and fizzled out shortly after the Vietnam War ended. The anti-war movement, however, raised a serious question about a U.S.-centered world order and offered an important opportunity for students to reflect on the role of universities and to demand reform. Additionally, the movement raised issues related to racial and gender discrimination and nuclear energy applications, and helped progressive values to take root across all areas of society. Various new disciplines including women's studies and African American studies were introduced to universities in its aftermath.

Universities saw significant changes. ROTC was weakened or disappeared from campuses. Admission policies became more flexible. Above all, university administrations could no longer support secret research sponsored by intelligence agencies with the pretext of national security.[25] These changes brought an enormous sense of crisis to the ruling elite and made them increasingly resistant. One example of their reaction is the Trilateral Commission's advocacy of less democracy discussed in the previous chapter.

Professor Chomsky argues that the Trilateral Commission viewed schools as institutions for indoctrination, "for imposing obedience, for blocking the possibility of independent thought, and [that] they play an institutional role in a system of control and coercion."[26] Further,

> The activism in the '60s caused great concern among elite circles. It was too democratic. There were policies undertaken to overcome this . . . all kinds of policies. But one very straightforward policy was just raising tuition. If you look back at that time, tuition was sort of within reach, and now if you go to even state college, you come out with a tremendous debt burden. Okay. That's a control system.[27]

As universities turned from sites intent on maintaining the status quo to bases of anti-war resistance, the ruling elite began to claim that universities were not playing their proper roles. They also came up with a very simple solution to their problem: cutting back federal aid to universities. As a result, federal funding for university research, which had been increasing at an astronomical pace, began decreasing starting in 1968. The table below shows it well. The budget steadily decreased and stagnated until 1972, a presidential election year. The following year, the renegotiation of the peace treaty helped it recover to 1967 levels. Clearly, the anti-war movement had a significant influence on federal support for university budgets. The federal cutback was an effective means to pressure universities, particularly since university administrators felt anxious amid enormous threats from the politicians. The *Harvard Crimson* reported in February 1973 that "Cutbacks in Federal housing grants by the Nixon Administration have jeopardized the plans for two Harvard housing programs and indirectly threaten to force the University to discontinue subsides for community housing."[28]

Federal research and development obligations and budget authority for national defense and civilian functions (1955-75)

Fiscal year	Total
1955	2,533
1956	2,988
Omitted	
1965	14,614
1966	15,320
1967	16,529
1968	15,921
1969	15,641
1970	15,339
1971	15,543
1972	16,496
1973	16,800
1974	17,410
1975	19,039

Source: http://www.nsf.gov/statistics/nsf10323/pdf/tab38.pdf

Graduate Student and Teaching Fellow Union Strike

In the spring of 1972, Harvard graduate students and teaching fellows could not help but feel alarmed. Without prior discussion with students, the university called a meeting, where they announced that they would radically slash scholarships due to cutbacks in federal and corporate support. When the dean left, 150 students formed a union on the spot. Within two weeks, membership to this union increased to 1,100. Margaret Gullette, an active participant in the organization of this union, recollects: "Harvard decided— this was their management style—that its least well-paid employees would take a cut in salaries. Now, the way they did this was to cut tuition waivers. It was a thousand dollars and we were only getting paid at most thirty-two hundred dollars."[29]

Student union members demanded a revised policy from university administrators. After negotiations made little progress, the union decided on a one-day strike for March 28. The strike had a major impact on university operations. As Harvard had expanded since the 1950s, the number of students and classes had rapidly increased as well. Graduate students had taken charge of a considerable proportion of classes. The number of classes taught by graduate students was equivalent to that taught by 340 full-time professors. In other words, without graduate students, Harvard should have employed 340 more full-time faculty members. Undergraduates also widely supported the graduate students' demands.

In response, Harvard administrators suggested that six professors and six student representatives form a committee. Gullette, who had been

Harvard graduate students picketing.

recently appointed to this committee, suggested that organizing a committee and having them investigate the issue was the shrewdest way to stop the movement. Student representatives demanded that the university guarantee full scholarship for students for five years. Meanwhile, the faculty proposed a "need-basis aid." Although "need-basis aid" sounded reasonable enough, it presupposed parents or spouses would assume the primary obligation of tuition payment. Graduate students could not accept the offer. Negotiations lasted a year without much progress. Eventually, facing an intransigent administration, graduate students retreated into their own individual work and dissertations, and the union collapsed without any visible achievement.

University Turned Corporation

While Harvard graduate students were organizing unions and negotiating with university administrators, a very important change was taking place in American society. Neoliberalism was beginning to make its presence felt. Neoliberal policies took off when Friedrich Hayek won the Nobel Prize in Economics in 1974, and Milton Friedman, an advocate of the market economy, won in 1976. Universities began exploring the conversion of their management style into more corporate styles.

Dr. Joshua Humphreys at the Tellus Institute points out that during the 1970s there emerged a revolutionary change in the way capital was managed, especially in educational institutions. "Many universities, especially ones with considerable endowments like Harvard, abandoned past practices of safety-oriented investments and chose to manage their capital professionally."[30]

In fact, it was large corporations themselves that encouraged universities to embrace neoliberal policies. For example, the Ford Foundation had a group of influential investors, lawyers, scholars, directors and charitable foundation officials conduct research on a more aggressive university fund management model. They published the Barker Report, based on data collected from thirty universities nationwide. This report, which happened to take its name after Wall Street investor Robert Barker, argued that

American universities had missed huge investment opportunities during the postwar economic boom by managing their funds too conservatively. The Barker Report encouraged universities to manage their funds far more aggressively.

Why had the Ford Foundation conducted this research? According to Joshua Humphreys, the reason lies with the sense of confusion felt by many in the aftermath of the 1960s anti-war movements. As universities became bases for anti-war movements, corporate charitable foundations no longer viewed universities as attractive investment sites.

With its enormous endowment, Harvard was quick to jump on this bandwagon and established the Harvard Management Company in 1974. That same year, Harvard also established the Harvard Institute for International Development, expressing its interest in expanding global networks. As discussed further in Chapter 7, this institute would play a crucial role in Russia's 1990s economic reform after the collapse of the USSR.

It is also noteworthy that Harvard began decentralizing its administrative structure during this period. After violently suppressing student protests, President Pusey had to step down in 1971. His successor, Derek Bok, demonstrated a markedly different crisis management style when he brought coffee and donuts to dissident students as a way to strike up a conversation. Bok, a labor law professor specializing in organized negotiations, emerged overnight as a new hope to rescue Harvard from its crises.

After Bok's inauguration as president, Harvard transformed itself from a national defense-centered management style to a corporate management style. Bok established the Harvard Management Company and handed over Harvard's endowments to Wall Street fund managers.

During Bok's tenure as president, Harvard's endowments grew rapidly. One Harvard official is known to have said, "Before Bok, Harvard wasn't a business."[31] Bok also instituted four new university vice presidents, dividing up and specializing administrative systems and duties. Professor Katsiaficas noted that this "decentralization" enabled university's central administration to distance itself from social responsibilities.

> One of the demands of the student strikes of the 1970s was the university stop doing war research. MIT divested itself of the Instrumentation Laboratories, but they just renamed it the Draper Lab and moved to a brand new corporate building down the street. Harvard in its decentralization program made the central administration appear to have no accountability for its CIA research that Samuel Huntington and others were involved in and other kinds of research. They moved to a neoliberal corporate style management, which in effect led to a lack of accountability on the part of the central administration.[32]

Three Harvard presidents at the 1971 graduation—left to right: Nathan Pusey, James Conant, and Derek Bok.

Bok's university administration decentralization proved its strategic value when Professor Nadav Safran's CIA-funded research was exposed in the mid-1980s. The scandal erupted when it became known that Safran, the director of Harvard's Center for Middle Eastern Studies, had also taken $45,700 from the CIA in a quasi-clandestine manner to fund a major international conference he was hosting at Harvard on "Islam and Politics in the Contemporary Muslim World." It then came out that Professor Safran had also received a $107,430 grant from the CIA for research that led to his 1985 book *Saudi Arabia: The Ceaseless Quest for Security*. Safran's contract with the CIA stipulated that the agency had the right to review and approve the manuscript before publication and that its role in funding the book would not be disclosed.

When this scandal broke out, President Bok's administration issued a letter of public apology but did not follow it up with any practical measures. The university administration emphasized that it had limited prior knowledge of this incident. As the system became decentralized, the central administration did not need to take any responsibility for what happened in one of its independently managed branches.

What was more surprising was Professor Safran's response to this scandal. He insisted that although he had taken funds, he was still an independent scholar. Professor Ngo Vinh Long mentioned that he was surprised at Professor Safran's shameless actions, and Harvard's reluctance to fire him outright. It was only when this scandal was extensively covered in the *Harvard Crimson* and the *Boston Globe* that Safran resigned from his position as the director of the Center for Middle Eastern Studies—but he retained his position as a full-time Harvard professor.

Professor Safran's shamelessness suggests that his study was only one of many secret research projects, and his only fault was getting caught. At this point, we cannot help asking how deeply intelligence agencies like the CIA were involved in U.S. universities.

Secret Plots Exposed

Militant student movements during the 1960s and 1970s had a strong impact on the relationship between universities and intelligence agencies. As the anti-war movement exposed their intimate involvement, people became enraged and extremely critical. In 1966, when relationships between universities and intelligence agencies remained top-secret, media outlets ran coverage on a Michigan State University secret program that trained South Vietnamese police members in exchange for $25 million from the CIA.

After this expose, it became known that the CIA had funded projects at other universities across the country including MIT, Harvard, Columbia, Miami, and California. Among all involved schools, Harvard's relationship with the CIA was the closest. A large number of Harvard men worked as OSS agents during World War II and played important roles in transforming the OSS into the CIA. Sumner Benson and William Langer are prime examples of such federally involved Harvard men who played major roles in establishing political analysis systems at the CIA. Next to Harvard in terms of close working relations with the CIA was Yale University. About a quarter of early CIA high officials were Yale graduates.[33]

As mentioned earlier, the specifics of the relationship between Harvard and the CIA were revealed during the 1969 student occupation of University Hall. Afterwards, Harvard students published a pamphlet titled *How Harvard Rules* based on secret documents found in administrative buildings. The pamphlet shed light on the intimate working relations between Harvard and the CIA in three major ways.

First, it uncovered influential Harvard graduates directly and indirectly involved in the CIA. Robert Amory, Harvard class of 1936, a member of the Harvard Overseers and former CIA deputy director, was one prime example. Before he entered the CIA, Amory was a professor at Harvard Law. At the CIA, he was a National Security Council Planning Board member. Similar examples are, of course, figures already discussed in this chapter such as McGeorge Bundy, Henry Kissinger, Zbigniew Brzezinski, and William Langer, all of whom were directly involved in the CFIA.

Second, the pamphlet examined Harvard professors who had participated in CIA activities as advisors or conducted research under CIA contracts. In this case, there are too many notable examples to include even a

Cover of *How Harvard Rules,* a pamphlet students published in 1969.

fraction of them. A report sent by economist Arthur Smithies on December 7, 1967, to Dean Ford detailed that Smithies had been working with the CIA for ten years. He also said that he had decided to inform the dean according to orders from the CIA. Dean Ford replied with a casual letter of recognition, thankful to have been informed. A report of April 1967 to the faculty contains information that Harvard had been carrying on thirteen projects worth $450,000 commissioned by the CIA from 1960 to 1966. The nature of these programs ran the gamut from the summer international seminars sponsored by Henry Kissinger to projects in the fields of psychology, philosophy, and sociology.[34]

Third, the pamphlet showed how Harvard occasionally directly managed CIA programs. There were programs carried out by both the Trade Union Program and the International Marketing Institute (IMI) at the Harvard Business School. The IMI received funding from the State Department, the U.S. Agency for International Development (USAID), the Ford Foundation, and the CIA for an enhanced understanding of the marketing and circulation for the global market. Its projects included a program that trained Vietnamese women for managerial positions. The IMI operated similar programs in other developing countries with the ultimate goal of training their managerial classes and, by so doing, strengthen American economic control abroad.

The CIA and the State Department was also involved in Harvard's Trade Union Program, at first glance a seemingly progressive program. The apparent objective of this program was to prepare "union activists to meet the challenges of dynamic leadership within their unions and society." Its true mission, however, was to control and manage potential opponents. It was a program in line with the CIA monetary support for conservative trade unions in Europe and South America. This became an international scandal in 1983 when the *New Zealand Times* exposed the CIA's involvement in this program. Kicked out of the Harvard Business School in the mid-1980s because of a new dean hostile to labor unions, the Trade Union Program brought in new leadership that then embarked on a path free from intelligence agency activities and open to labor activists. Freedom from HBS control may have enabled the program to take a more progressive direction.

Of course, it wasn't just Harvard that had a close relationship with intelligence agencies. According to an article published in 1970, at least 100 universities and 350 scholars and governmental officers secretly worked for the CIA. Brown University's president Barnaby Conrad Keeney had been a high official at the CIA and continued to work as a consultant for the CIA during his tenure as the president of Brown in the 1950s and 1960s. In that capacity he set up a covert funding plan for a secret CIA program to test mind control through drugs and other covert means. He also became chairman of the Human Ecology Fund, a CIA front that experimented on behavior control to torture enemy intelligence agents.[35]

The Vietnam War drove a wedge in the intimate relationship between universities and intelligence agencies. When public opinion became unforgivingly critical of this working dynamic between universities and intelligence agencies, President Johnson banned federal intelligence agencies from secretly funding educational institutions or charitable organizations. The 1974 Watergate Incident and Nixon's ensuing resignation drew more attention to illegal activities by governmental intelligence agencies. With the launching of the U.S. Senate Select Committee to Study Governmental Operations with Respect to Intelligence Activities chaired by Senator Frank Church, illegal research activities in universities began to recede dramatically.

With the tide turning on secret and illegal relationships between universities and intelligence agencies, Harvard adjusted to changed circumstances remarkably quickly. President Derek Bok issued a statement banning illegal secret research at Harvard. There was, of course, no self-criticism or admission of faults concerning its own past activities.

But has Harvard really completely severed its ties to the CIA? Dr. Trumpbour points out that only illegal secret research was banned and nothing more. For example, President Bok applauded professors who openly received research funds from the CIA. Professors had only to announce to related departments that they were conducting joint research with the CIA. On top of this, it was difficult to know who was doing what kind of research in Harvard's decentralized system. Also, following the events of 9/11 the situation changed again, returning to its former direction. The events of 9/11 stimulated excessive patriotic sentiment, once again enabling academia's open collaboration with intelligence agencies. The Nadav Safran Scandal illustrates this continuing secretive relationship between Harvard and the CIA.

John F. Kennedy School of Government: Training Facility for the Pentagon

During President Bok's tenure, Harvard underwent a number of important structural changes. First, its endowment grew rapidly and reached $30 billion in the mid-1980s. Second, Harvard became coed, with Radcliffe College agreeing to merge with Harvard. Third, professional schools including the Kennedy School of Government expanded.

Harvard's Kennedy School illustrates well the continuous partnership between Harvard and the U.S. government. The Kennedy School began when Harvard launched the Graduate School of Government in 1936 with a two million dollar donation from Lucius Littauer, a Harvard graduate, politician, and economist. Harvard changed the school's name to the John F. Kennedy School of Government in 1966. This school has cultivated ties with a number of notorious national security specialists, McGeorge Bundy, Henry Kissinger, and Samuel Huntington, to name a few.

What was the reason for the Kennedy School's rapid expansion during President Bok's tenure? Above all, the anti-war movement made it impossible for area studies to carry out their original mission. As mentioned in Chapter 4, Third World countries began to be cautious about American scholars active in their countries. A few conscientious scholars' self-criticism, combined with the whirlwind of anti-war movement, drove area studies into difficulties.

It is significant, then, that the Kennedy School made remarkable growth when area studies were fading. This growth was especially striking during Dean Graham Allison's tenure between 1977 and 1988, when there was a sevenfold surge in the value of the Kennedy School's endowment.[36] It is also noteworthy that a considerable proportion of those funds came from the U.S. Department of State. Together with this increase in funding, the school's population grew as well. Its faculty grew five times larger, from twenty to a hundred, and the student population almost quadrupled, ballooning from two hundred to seven hundred.[37]

The result was not simply surprising but fearsome. Many world political and economic leaders today pass through the Kennedy School. Mexican president Felipe Calderón, Colombian president Juan Manuel Santos, Liberian president and the first female African commander-in-chief

A forum at Harvard Kennedy School of Government, where three former and current White House spokespersons were invited.

Ellen Johnson Sirleaf, UN secretary general Ban Ki-moon, World Bank chief executive Robert Zoellick, Singapore's prime minister Lee Hsien Loong, and chief executive and president of the Executive Council of Hong Kong Donald Tsang Yam-kuen were all Kennedy School alumni. The internet home page of the Kennedy School in 2012 boasts that its more than forty-six thousand alumni are actively working in governmental and non-governmental organizations in more than two hundred countries worldwide. It may not be an overstatement to say that the past U.S. strategy of managing global hot spots through specialists at the area studies institutes is giving way to a present strategy of cultivating connections to political elites through the Kennedy School and more rarefied networking forums such as the World Economic Forum in Davos.

According to a recent South Korean newspaper article, the Kennedy School's influence on the American political scene grew so powerful it became an unspoken rule for presidential candidates to hold a discussion at the Kennedy School before announcing their candidacy.[38] In other words, a presidential candidate somehow perceives he or she has to be first officially anointed by faculty and students at Kennedy School before even running, an acceptance that shows a person has arrived. Recently elected South Korean president Park Geun-hye, who gave a 2007 talk at the Kennedy School, illustrates a globalized version of this.

The same article also reports on South Korean Representative Pak Jin's "moving" testimony of his eyes being opened towards the state of international affairs through his practical learning at the Kennedy School. One wonders what international state of affairs so opened the eyes of the Korean parliamentary representative. Might it not be the state of affairs as seen through the eyes of American professors? In the end, the Kennedy School might be nothing more than a place where the ideology of *Pax Americana* is maintained and spread through education.

The power of the Kennedy School is clear when we look at its guest list of foreign presidents, cabinet heads, as well as numerous former and current high American government officials. Also, a significant proportion of programs at Kennedy School are related to American governmental agendas. For this reason, some even call the Kennedy School a retreat facility for Pentagon and National Security elites: "They sometimes joke about places like the Kennedy School as a drying-out institution for politicians and former Cabinet figures to come here. But people then make their connections there and build their ties. And that's where people then become a part of a very limited circle."[39]

When I went to Kennedy School events, I often encountered military officers in and out of uniform. Harvard offers a wide range of educational programs for current and former military personnel. Especially considering the Yellow Ribbon Program, which was introduced to support education expenses for current soldiers and veterans on August 1, 2009, many Iraq and Afghanistan war veterans head to Harvard. Noticing the crowd of high officials at the Kennedy School, Professor Katsiaficas commented that the Kennedy School was not a place for the education of public elites but a training site for national security specialists. He also noted the chilling boasts of Kennedy School Professor Ashton Carter concerning a call from the White House for assistance in choosing potential North Korean bombing targets when the United States came close to a first strike in 1994.

Reestablishment of Area Studies

Since its rise in the 1950s, what has since happened to area studies, the product of the Cold War? Professor Immanuel Wallerstein, renowned sociologist best known for his world-systems theory, presents an analysis of the important changes brought on by area studies to American society in his article "The Unintended Consequences of Cold War Area Studies." Non-Western region scholars increased, college curriculums changed dramatically, and traditional research topics eroded. For example, while about ninety-five percent of American historians studied Western civilization in 1945, the percentage of scholars studying non-Western civilization increased to about a third of all American historians. Area studies ended up playing a positive role in the general understanding of non-Western parts of the world. It is analogous to how the internet, initially developed for military uses by the American government, ultimately gave birth to social movements through social media.

In conclusion, area studies portfolios have become significantly more diversified since their inception. Professor David McCann, former director of the Korea Institute at Harvard, notes that many area studies programs still continue to operate based on the support of governmental funding, a prime example of this being the National Defense Foreign Language Study Program. The American government continues to support education of language in priority areas in order to aid American interests. However, according to Professor McCann, these days the funding does not come solely from the government. Funding sources for area studies institutes have become more diverse than ever.[40]

What truly matters is that area studies centers at Harvard play a key role in forming global communities around Harvard. Elites from countries around the world also join their own networks at these area studies research institutes. Professor McCann presents the following analysis of the critical role of Harvard area studies institutes:

> Students at Harvard are going to have real impact in the world after they graduate. And if they go out there without understanding the world at large and other people and other cultures, other forms of artistic expression and also other ways of doing business, other ways of running the government—if they don't have some strong understanding of that, then they are not going to be as effective in the world at large once they are out and in it. So I think Area Studies in that sense is very important.[41]

Such "real influence" of Harvard graduates in the world revealed itself very clearly in the 1990s Russian economic reform. Let's take a careful look at this in the next chapter.

CHAPTER 7

HARVARD'S ROLE IN RUSSIAN ECONOMIC "REFORM"

"The United States alleges that Defendants' actions undercut the fundamental purpose of the United States' program in Russia—the creation of trust and confidence in the emerging Russian financial markets and the promotion of openness, transparency, the rule of law, and fair play in the development of the Russian economy and laws."
—U.S. Department of Justice, *United States v. Harvard, Shleifer, Hay, et al.*, September 26, 2000[1]

In January 1998, a U.S.-Russian Investment Symposium was held at Harvard's Kennedy School of Government. At this symposium, Yuri Luzhkov, the Mayor of Moscow, made what might have seemed to its audience an impolite reference to his hosts. After criticizing Russian high officials including Anatoly Chubais and his monetarist policies, Luzhkov singled out Harvard for the harm its affiliated advisers had inflicted on the Russian people by encouraging Chubais's misguided approach to privatization and monetarism.[2]

What had Harvard done to deserve such public condemnation?

In 1997, Russia was in a state of turmoil. Energy was the country's main source of income, but international oil prices had fallen because of the Asian currency crisis. As speculative foreign capital that had been used to solve Russia's chronic deficit problem began to migrate, the Russian ruble struggled. On August 17, 1998, the Russian government devalued the ruble, defaulted on domestic debts, and declared a moratorium on payment to foreign creditors.

Luzhkov castigated Harvard six months *prior* to this moratorium, suggesting that Harvard was deeply involved in the Russian financial crisis. How deep was Harvard's involvement? Is it really possible for a university, even the most renowned university in the world, to influence a major country's economy?

"Doing Russia"

After the Berlin Wall collapsed in 1989 and the USSR was dismantled in 1991, the Cold War came to an end. The United States was triumphant. Almost immediately, the White House took advantage of the opening to convert the former Soviet bloc into market economies. Cold warriors who had helped the U.S. government develop arms and intelligence took charge again, and Harvard scholars were at the forefront.

Western aid agencies that had poured billions of dollars into eastern European countries turned their eyes toward Russia. Professor Janine R. Wedel, University Professor in the School of Public Policy at George Mason University and Senior Research Fellow at the New America Foundation, who had done extensive research on the economic reform process in eastern European countries including Poland and Hungary, visited Russia to observe Russia's economic reform process and noticed something strange. Whichever organization she visited, she found the same small group of people controlling and exerting influence.[3]

This exclusive, enormously influential group was composed of a few Harvard men and several Russian high officials. In the early 1990s, the U.S. Agency for International Development (USAID) had handed over to Harvard the task of converting the Russian economy into a market system. Russian partners of this group included officials surrounding Anatoly Chubais, "father of Russian privatization," and his cohorts—or as they were often called, the "St. Petersburg Gang" or the "Chubais Clan." This Chubais Clan, together with USAID, took charge of the task of converting the Russian economy, using Western funds.

Lawrence Summers, who later served as president of Harvard, stood behind the reform policies carried out by Harvard and the Chubais Clan. In order to understand Harvard's role in the Russian economic reform, let us briefly look at the profiles of the "dream team" of Harvard gurus and Russian high officials.

Key figures from Harvard. Lawrence Summers became a tenured professor at Harvard in 1983 at the age of twenty-eight. He served as chief economist for the World Bank (1991–93), and then in the U.S. Treasury Department from 1993 to 2001, becoming secretary of the treasury in 1999. As an old friend of Harvard professor Andrei Shleifer, Summers was at the center of the connection between Harvard, the U.S. government, and Russia. He was president of Harvard from 2001 to 2006. Jeffrey Sachs, an economics professor at Harvard, was principal author of the "shock therapy" approach, which promoted a market system through the sudden release of price and currency controls. He directed the Harvard Institute for International Development (HIID) from 1995 to 1999. Andrei Shleifer is a Russian-born American economist who was the HIID's project director in Russia, in which capacity he drafted the Russian aid project. He was later sued by the U.S. government under the False Claims Act and, together with his wife and hedge-fund manager Nancy Zimmerman, ended up paying $2 million in damages. Jonathan Hay, a Harvard Law School graduate, was the HIID's general director in Russia from 1992 to 1997, when he was fired for using his position for personal gain. Together with Shleifer, he founded numerous civilian organizations including the Russian Privatization Center (RPC). Hay helped Chubais draft the blueprint for Russian economic reform. As the HIID's project director in Russia, Hay was a key intermediary between the Chubais Clan and foreign aid agencies. Hay was removed from the HIID's Russia project in May 1997 for alleged "activities for personal gain by [HIID] personnel placed in a position of trust in Russia."[4]

Key figures from Russia. Anatoly Chubais was chairman of the board of the Russian Privatization Center (RPC) and first head of the State Property Committee (GKI), an agency in charge of privatizing state-owned corporations. He also was the campaign manager for President Boris Yeltsin's successful reelection campaign in 1996, after which he became chief of staff and first deputy prime minister. Maxim Boycko was a close Chubais associate. He was CEO of the RPC from 1993 to 1997, and later head of the GKI. Yeltsin fired him from this post when it was revealed that he received $90,000 from a corporation that benefited from privatization.[5] Alfred Kokh was another close Chubais associate. He served as deputy chairman of the RPC and was named head of the GKI in 1996 after Boycko was fired. Yeltsin fired him in 1997 when it was revealed that he too had showed favoritism toward a corporation that benefited from privatization.[6]

Shock Therapy: All Shock, No Therapy

Between the late summer and early fall of 1991, only a few months prior to the official dissolution of the USSR, Western economists gathered at a villa on the outskirts of Moscow. Their mission was to set the future course of the Russian economy. With his experience in Poland, Jeffrey Sachs emerged as the key figure to draft the overall plan for Russian economic reform. Among the attendees at this meeting were a number of Western economists, Yegor Gaidar, the first architect of Russian economic reform, and his successor Anatoly Chubais.

As Russian officials met with Western economists, Chubais and Andrei Shleifer became close friends. Born in Russia in 1961, Shleifer immigrated to the United States in 1976. A fluent Russian speaker, he was also a close associate of Lawrence Summers. Chubais and Shleifer's partnership soon

Jeffrey Sachs, advocate of "shock therapy."

became a major driving force behind Russia's state property privatization.

In late 1991, Yegor Gaidar became Russia's secretary of the treasury. He later served as Deputy Prime Minister, and then prime minister from June to December 1992, introducing Sachs's "shock therapy." The shock therapy consisted of sudden price and currency control releases, state subsidy withdrawals, and immediate trade liberalization. Gaidar sincerely believed that this "therapy" would quickly transform a stagnant Russian economy into a capitalist market system.

But the reforms brought the Russian economy "shock" and little therapy. Seemingly unstoppable hyperinflation drove up the price of commodities by 2,500 percent within a year. As prices of staples soared, many people lost a majority of their assets overnight. The biggest victims were ordinary people who had to spend most of their income to buy essentials.[7] Ultimately, many Russian people suffered extreme poverty.

In late spring of 1992 Chubais also engineered a massive giveaway that was supposed to give to each citizen a share of formerly publicly owned companies. But inflation rendered the vouchers (set at a value of 10,000 rubles) virtually worthless within a year or two. Most of the 98 percent of Russians who received the vouchers also had little idea of their value or what to do with them. Many were persuaded to place them in voucher funds that had been hastily created by speculators, which collapsed or turned out to be scams. Marshall I. Goldman comments, "For most Russians . . . the voucher funds were another example of how ordinary Russians can be abused by the state or financial manipulators. This result helps explain why so many Russians (37 million) ignored the voucher funds and sold their vouchers for cash or a bottle of vodka."[8]

In addition, Wesleyan professor Peter Rutland notes that most of Russia's most profitable firms, in the oil, gas and metal sectors, were excluded from the public giveaway. Instead, Chubais offered the shares to Russian banks in exchange for loans to the government. When the government defaulted on the loans, the banks ended up with vast holdings in the most profitable sectors of the economy, such as the Norilsk nickel mine and the Yukos and Sibneft (now called Gazprom Neft) oil companies. The new oligarchs then helped Yeltsin get reelected in 1996.[9]

Russian voucher.

Harvard's connection to the voucher program comes through Andrei Shleifer, who coauthored an article on voucher privatization with Maxim Boycko in the *Journal of Financial Economics*, in which they described the voucher system as "unprecedented in recent history in that it is comprehensive, rapid, and virtually free."[10] The writers praise the free trade in vouchers in that it allows both the emergence of financial markets and the consolidation of ownership with large investors.[11] On the basis of this article, it seems that the consequences to individual citizens were anticipated from the beginning.

In some Eastern European countries including Poland, "shock therapy" had achieved a measure of success despite initial turmoil. Why, then, did it fail in Russia? Former Prime Minister Gaidar discusses the fundamental difference between Poland and Russia in his 2003 work, *State and Evolution: Russia's Search for a Free Market*. According to Gaidar, unlike Soviet citizens, Poles had retained the memory of the pre-Communist market economy and therefore "had the flexibility to deal with the conversion to a market economy."[12] By introducing shock therapy without providing any social foundations and institutional changes, the economic reform ended in failure, resulting in citizen resistance, resentment, and opposition.

Yegor Gaidar, the first architect of Russian economic reform.

The Harvard Institute for International Development and Its Russian Allies

The Harvard Institute for International Development (HIID) originated when Harvard's Center for International Affairs (CFIA) tried to move away from its controversial past as an institution advising U.S. intelligence agencies on matters relating to arms control, foreign aid and foreign development. In 1962, the Development Advisory Service was established for this purpose. Associated with the CFIA but structurally independent, it was renamed the Harvard Institute for International Development in 1974.

From 1974 to 2000, the HIID was Harvard's center for coordinating development assistance, training, and research in Africa, Asia, Central and Eastern Europe, and Latin America. For example, the HIID took charge of tax reform and financial market liberalization in Indonesia, and economic reform involving neoliberal market economy conversion in Kenya, Pakistan, and Zambia. The conversion of the Russian economy to a market economy was the largest project the HIID had undertaken. The HIID received its first $2.1 million grant from the Bush administration in 1992. Over the next five years, it received $40.4 million in grants for its work in Russia. However, in May 1996 USAID canceled funds earmarked for the HIID, "citing evidence that the two managers were engaged in activities for 'private gain.'"[13]

Professor Janine R. Wedel points out that it was extremely exceptional for the HIID to receive such huge grants in such a short period of time. Even more surprising, USAID not only granted a large amount of funds to the HIID but also entrusted its associates with the task of supervising the USAID fund's control and management. In other words, HIID associates were in the unique position where they could supervise and manage their competitors at the same time as they themselves benefited from major USAID funding.[14]

The two central figures in the Russian project were Andrei Shleifer, the project director, and Jonathan Hay, in his thirties and only a few years out of Harvard Law School. They wielded an unimaginable level of influence and power in Russia. Professor Wedel said that she witnessed numerous times firsthand that older, more experienced figures paid considerable respect to Hay when Hay's role was only that of a consultant.

As for Chubais, as the privatization policies he implemented frequently came under fire, he often skipped parliamentary sanction hearings and relied on presidential decrees to implement his dictates. The result was that the policies drafted by Hay and his associates were directly adopted without democratic procedures. [15] Important economic reform laws on which the country's future depended were created by a handful of pro-West powerholders and foreigners without even going through the motions of parliamentary discussions. The intimate partnership between Chubais and Harvard not only pillaged the Russian economy, but it also ignored Russia's emergent democratic institutions and procedures.

The Chubais Clan raked in huge sums of money in exchange for awarding privileges (or bribes) to their patrons. One example that particularly incensed the public was the Chubais Clan receiving inexplicably large payments for books they were writing or co-authoring. In one case, Chubais and four high officials received $90,000 per person for coauthoring an eighteen-page pamphlet entitled the *History of Russian Privatization*. The publisher

Anatoli Chubais, Gaidar's successor and leader of the Chubais Clan.

of this pamphlet belonged to the Oneksimbank Group, the winner of several fierce privatization battles who had made off with crucial shareholdings in telecommunications giant Svyazinvest and in Norilsk Nickel, the world's largest nickel producer. Chubais and his close associates were widely vilified by the public and media. Under heavy public pressure, Yeltsin fired three officials—but not Chubais. Eventually, he even fired Chubais from the post of Secretary of the Treasury. Still, Yeltsin kept him as First Deputy Prime Minister, turning down Chubais's offer to resign completely from governmental office. Yeltsin claimed that his resignation could "destabilize the situation."[16]

It was to be expected that Yeltsin protected Chubais, the biggest contributor to his own reelection in 1996. Chubais led Yeltsin's campaign from March 1996, and it is known that his team spent more than $5 billion, several hundred times more than legally allowed (about $3.2 million) in his election campaign. There is no doubt that illegal funds accumulated during privatization were funneled into the campaign. On June 19, 1996, only three days after the first votes were cast, two associates of Chubais were caught slipping out of the Russian presidential palace with a cardboard box full of cash—about $538,000 total.[17]

It is bitterly ironic that Harvard was an enthusiastic supporter and collaborator of Chubais's corruption-riddled privatization project. The U.S. government also fully supported Yeltsin, turning a blind eye to corruption in his government because Yeltsin had adopted pro-West policies. When the corruption scandal erupted, it is reported that the U.S. secretary of the treasury said: "We thought it was a good thing. We hoped Yeltsin would get

Russian male life expectancy

elected. We didn't care at all about the election corruption. We wanted to pour money into his campaign."[18]

Correlated to the level of anger and stress that privatization caused the Russian people was the plummeting of the average life expectancy. Since the early 1990s, when privatization and economic reform were rapidly underway, life expectancy had begun to drop rapidly, and it ending up falling by about seven years over a ten-year period.[19]

In her testimony before congress, journalist and Russia specialist Anne Williamson eloquently summed up the cost of the failed Russia policies:

> Clearly, building an empire of finance capitalism is an expensive business. But who pays? U.S. taxpayers, who paid directly through contributions to both multilateral and bilateral assistance efforts, and Russian workers, who paid indirectly by having their wages go unpaid and their national estate continually degraded. Secondly, the Russian people paid by being denied a means of exchange since the banking and trade sectors of the economy were quick to socialize amongst themselves what few rubles the IMF's tight money policies allowed the Russian Central Bank to print.[20]

Missing Aid Money

While Russia was pursuing the privatization of state-owned corporations, the HIID and the Chubais Clan began to carry out a plan to establish an independent agency that would handle aid from a number of international organizations. International aid agencies preferred civilian agencies in order

The United States Agency for International Development (USAID) poured an astronomical amount of money into Russian economic development.

to bypass the bureaucracy. This is when the RPC, the Russian Privatization Center, was born.

Established by the presidential decree of November 1992, the RPC was a window through which an astronomical amount of Western aid money entered the country. Chubais, already chairman of the GKI, became head of RPC as well. Harvard men were involved in its founding, operation, and projects. Andrei Shleifer exercised considerable influence on it as a board member. With the Harvard Institute's help, the RPC received some $45 million from USAID and millions of dollars more in grants from the EU, Japan, Germany, the British Know How Fund, and many governmental and non-governmental organizations. The RPC also received $59 million from the World Bank and $43 million from the European Bank for Reconstruction and Development, all of which had to be repaid at some point by the Russian people.[21]

The HIID used this aid money to establish many civilian organizations. One of them was the Federal Securities Commission, the equivalent to the U.S. Securities and Exchange Commission (SEC). This agency was established by presidential decree. Dmitry Vassiliev, the former Deputy Chairman of GKI under Chubais, moved to this organization to become its deputy chairman under Chubais, its predictable chairman.

Another organization the HIID established, funded by USAID and the World Bank, was the Institute for Law-Based Economy (ILBE). Betraying its original purpose of providing legal guidance for the conversion of Russia's economy to a market economy and establishing a regulatory framework, the ILBE became an example of backdoor dealings and deception. One of its early customers was Nancy Zimmerman, the Boston-based hedge fund manager and Andrei Shleifer's wife. Zimmerman and the ILBE were later accused of collaborating in making illegal investments using insider information.

As controversies continued erupting, a Russian accounting agency, equivalent to the U.S. Federal Audit Agency, began investigating the manner in which aid had been used at the RPC. In its May 1988 report it concluded,

"Money was not spent as designated. Donors paid hundreds of thousands of dollars for nothing . . . for something you couldn't determine."[22]

It is difficult to find out exactly where all this aid money went. We can get some idea, though, from a September 2, 1999 BBC news report. According to this article, New York investigators suspected that more than $10 billion in funds from Russia were illegally deposited in the Bank of New York. Some of this may even have come from the $20 billion that the IMF paid to Russia in 1992 to assist it with its economic reform. As expected, Russian officials "reacted with fury and incomprehension."[23]

Professor Wedel emphasized that all major international financial donors essentially sent aid to the RPC, which was managed by Harvard and the Chubais Clan. She also pointed out that what was even more surprising was that the RPC was officially an NGO:

> Basically every major donor in the international financial institutions was involved in funding the Russian Privatization Center and the Harvard-Chubais group ran it. And the remarkable thing about it was that it was formally a non-government organization, it was formally an NGO. And yet it functioned like a government agency, but it did not have the accountability of a government agency. It is what I call a flex organization.[24]

Virtually all international agencies treated the RPC as if it were a governmental agency since its staff, including Chubais, were all central government officials. Professor Wedel noted that when she asked an officer of the World Bank if his organization aided an NGO financially, the officer denied it. But the World Bank, in fact, sent enormous sums to the RPC as did USAID. In other words, both organizations considered the RPC a governmental agency.

Ambiguity concerning the exact nature of the RPC was clearly intentional from the outset. Its structure as an NGO was a kind of safety device, a convenient front behind which relevant parties could hide, concealing their specific roles and responsibilities should their secret activities be discovered. As a combination of two groups of people with different nationalities and cultures, the two groups could also use each other as shields. Russians could blame Harvard, while Harvard could blame Russian officials. It was a way of insuring deniability.[25]

The two groups—Harvard men and the Chubais Clan—also thoroughly blocked the involvement of other agencies in the Russia project. However, as the two groups' abuse of power became better known, the U.S. Congress decided in 1996 that the U.S. General Accounting Office (GAO) should investigate USAID's activities in Russia and Ukraine. The GAO investigation concluded that the HIID practically controlled the USAID program, but handled their responsibilities with extreme negligence.[26]

The United States Sues Harvard

To Shleifer, Hay and their associates, Russia was a financial boondoggle—an attractive new market where billions of dollars could be made. According to the contract signed by the U.S. government, the HIID, and USAID, however, officers of the HIID and their family members were banned from investing in Russia, a clause intended to mitigate conflicts of interest. In response to this, Shleifer and Hay, the two leaders at the helm of the Russian privatization project, chose to become masters of backdoor deals.

Shleifer and wife Nancy Zimmerman began investing in Russia in July 1994 at the height of Russian privatization. Nancy Zimmerman, a former Goldman Sachs hedge fund manager, owned and managed her own investment firm Farallion.[27] The couple recommended that their friends invest in Russia as well, providing them with insider information and letting them freely use facilities and legal services operated with funds from the HIID.

In August 1994, Shleifer began buying oil company stocks, investing some $4 million until November. About 90 percent of these funds flowed through Farallion, and the rest was through direct investments. In order to hide their identity, they used the name of Shleifer's father-in-law, a real estate developer in Chicago. In 1996, the couple became increasingly bold in their activities and expanded their investments. Zimmerman established a firm in Russia and began buying short-term Russian government bonds with loans. According to U.S. allegations, they transferred profits from these bonds to American banks as if they were repaying bank loans and then retransferred this money to Farallion. Hay, who offered legal advice to the couple, also bought short-term government bonds with his $50,000 and his father's $150,000. Russian short-term government bonds depended on the IMF at that time, and it was Lawrence Summers who approved this IMF loan to the Russian government. Shleifer, Hay, and the Chubais Clan invested and profited from these short-term Russian bonds, as did George Soros, who made significant financial gains through this most profitable paper transaction.

According to an article in the Korean weekly *Hangyoreh 21* (September 3, 1998), investments in these short-term bonds were the reason why the Russian *ruble* was devalued and the Russian government ended up declaring a moratorium on repayment of debts. As part of its economic reform programs, the IMF and the United States recommended that the Russian government issue bonds in order to control inflation and nurture a capitalist market. During the seven years of the Yeltsin presidency, the value of all short-term government bonds issued was some $700 billion, $200 billion of which was owned by foreign investors. When the 1997 Asian Currency Crisis occurred, almost all foreign investors withdrew their funds simultaneously, dropping the value of the *ruble* and leaving the Russian government with no choice but to declare a moratorium.[28]

June 1, 1998, cover of *The Nation*, in which the Harvard-Russia Project scandal was exposed

In August 1996, Hay's friend Elizabeth Herbert won approval for her firm, Pallada Asset Management, as the first mutual fund company in Russia. Together with this approval, Pallada acquired an exclusive right to manage several million dollars of government funds set aside to help investors with their losses. Harvard itself was the greatest beneficiary of these clandestine dealings. As mentioned earlier, the Harvard Management Company raked in enormous profits by participating in insider auctions.

Despite the U.S. GAO report that pointed out problems in the Harvard Russia project, USAID did not take any follow-up measures for a considerable length of time. The tide turned only when the favoritism behind the approval of the mutual fund firm run by Hay's romantic partner Elizabeth Herbert was exposed in February 1997. In May 1997, the Harvard Russia project was terminated, and Hay was fired from the HIID. Shleifer also resigned from his position of director of the Russia project. The contract between USAID and the HIID was terminated. The total of funds transferred from the U.S. government to the HIID came to more than $4 billion, all initially supplied through taxes.

In September 2000, the U.S. government sued Harvard, Andrei Shleifer, Jonathan Hay, Nancy Zimmerman, and Elizabeth Herbert for $1.2 billion. There were eleven charges against them including fraud, contract violation, and making false claims. The main issues were twofold. The first was whether Harvard investors had used resources offered by USAID for their own or their friends' personal business and investment. The second issue was whether they had abused their positions by profiting from insider information. Shleifer argued that the conflict of interest policies did not apply to him as a Russian consultant. Therefore, whether or not Shleifer and Hay violated regulations for government officers became the key issue.

In 2004, U.S. District Judge Douglas Woodlock found Shleifer and Hay liable under the False Claims Act, stating, "I find that the Cooperative Agreements were valid contracts between Harvard and USAID, that they created an obligation to remain free of conflicts of interest."[29] In August 2005, Harvard, Shleifer, and the Justice department reached an agreement under which the university paid $26.5 million to settle the five-year-old lawsuit. Shleifer was also responsible for paying $2 million worth of

President Yeltsin resigned due to administrative incompetence and corruption (left); president Putin, who purged the oligarchy and renationalized basic industries.

damages, and Hay $2 to $4 million depending on his future income. Nancy Zimmerman's firm paid $1.5 million in an out-of-court settlement. The total settlement was $31 million, the largest suit in Harvard University's history.

After the proceedings, an unidentified banker who often visited Russia said, "The Harvard crowd hurt themselves, they hurt Harvard, and they hurt the U.S. government."[30] This judgment may only be half true. The greatest victim of this Harvard-instigated debacle was not Shleifer, Hay, Harvard, or even the U.S. government. It was the Russian people.

What Did the United States Really Want?

In August 1998, while the HIID investigation was in progress, Russia fell into a state of extreme emergency, declaring a debt repayment moratorium after the crash of the ruble. Of course, the Russian economic crisis was not entirely due to Harvard participants. However, Harvard's management of Russian economic reform left nightmarish memories and the stench of corruption in the minds of many Russians. Like most inconvenient incidents related to Harvard discussed in this book, American mainstream media provided little coverage of the Russia scandal. As the five-year-long legal process dragged out, this scandal eventually faded in the minds of many. Most Americans these days do not remember or know the relationship between Harvard and the freshly formed Russian oligarchy, or that Harvard had any involvement in Russian economic reform.

President Yeltsin resigned in December 1999, his approval ratings hitting rock bottom due to his administrative incompetence, corruption, and the economic crisis. His successor Vladimir Putin, elected by an over-whelming majority in 2000, purged the oligarchy that had accumulated wealth under Yeltsin's protection and re-nationalized oil companies and a third of the energy companies. He intensified state authoritarianism as well. Embittered after the failed capitalist economic reform, people were receptive to these changes.

A most interesting question is whether or not the U.S. government knew what was going on during Russia's privatization debacle. In November 1998, the New York Times ran an article exposing vice president Al Gore's intentional dismissal of a CIA report on Russian prime minister Viktor Chernomyrdin's (1992–98) corruption. The CIA was ordered not to report on the matter afterwards. The article also pointed out that the U.S. govern-ment did not pay any attention to numerous corruption scandals then in progress, citing the aforementioned Russian officials' pamphlet deal as one example of such inattention.[31]

The CIA, however, was actually paying close attention to the situation in Russia. The U.S. government was not as oblivious as they claimed. One can deduce that the government either did not care if the Russian economy was destroyed, or that they may have actually desired it. What the United States wanted from Russia after the collapse of its Communist system must have been the reorganization of its political and economic system to suit American needs—or at the very least, for Russia to never become powerful enough to confront the United States again.

It's interesting to note how the media constructed the narrative of Russia's "progress" to a market economy and privatization. Soviet expert Stephen F. Cohen writes that Russia was designated as the "best-performing emerging market" in the 1990s, even though it was the worst-performing modern economy at the time. Similarly, the impoverishment of some 75 percent of the nation, the transformation of a superpower into a beggar state and Russia's experience of the worst peacetime industrial depression of the twentieth century were called "reform, remarkable progress," and a "success story."[32]

Update on the Dream Team

How are the protagonists of the Russian scandal doing these days? According to Professor Wedel, the Chubais Clan still maintains technocratic govern-ment posts. Chubais was head of the state-owned electrical power company from 1998 to 2008 and is currently director of the Russian Nanotechnology Corporation. A 2004 survey by Pricewaterhouse Coopers and the Financial Times named him the world's 54th most respected business leader. He has also been a member of the Advisory Council for JPMorgan Chase since September 2008. He survived an assassination attempt in 2005.

How about Harvard's Financial Geniuses?

The *New York Times* suggested in 2006 that David McLintick's exposé of Harvard's role in the disastrous Russian privatization played a role in the dismissal of Lawrence Summers from the Harvard presidency.[33] Despite this, after a prosperous career as a consultant following his resignation, Summers was tapped by President Obama to be director of the White House National Economic Council. Following his appointment, he played a key role in rescuing Wall Street from the finan-

Lawrence Summers was inaugurated as Harvard's president in the aftermath of Harvard-Russia scandal.

cial recession they had largely created. Since his resignation in 2010, when the Obama economic team shifted gears, Summers has taught at Harvard's Kennedy School.

Shleifer, who remains on the Harvard faculty, was awarded the John Bates Clark Medal in 1999, one of the two most prestigious honors in the field of economics. Milton Friedman, Nobel laureate and neoliberal evangelist, had received that same medal in 1951, with Summers following in 1993.

Jonathan Hay worked as an international lawyer at a New York-based law firm and is currently employed by a real estate development company in Ukraine. After the termination of the Russia project, he married Elizabeth Hebert; Herbert sold her mutual fund firm in 1998.

Jeffrey Sachs resigned from the directorship of the HIID in 1999, and became director of the Center for International Development (CID) at the Kennedy School. This center focused on research in developing countries rather than foreign consulting. After the dismantlement of the HIID, its $1.3 million fund was transferred to the CID. In 2002, Sachs left Harvard to become director of the Earth Institute at Columbia University.

The protagonists of the Harvard Russian project have thus remained largely unaffected by their scandals and disastrous decisions. The Harvard connection remains so powerful that poor decisions seem to have little influence on one's personal trajectory. Professor Wedel argues that this is partly due to the blame for the Harvard Russian scandal falling upon only a few individuals rather than an entire organization. Investigators missed an opportunity to look deeply into the U.S. government, Harvard individuals, and the Harvard Corporation as a whole. Through observing Harvard and the Chubais Clan, Wedel told me that she came to the realization that a new group had emerged, one that exercised its powers and influence in a completely different way than in the past.

The profile of today's top powerbrokers is that of someone who performs multiple and overlapping roles as a government consultant, as a business consultant, perhaps affiliated with a think-tank, and working with the media promoting his views. And all the while he's saying that he's working in the public interest but in fact he's serving his own agenda. The new powerbroker is also much less visible than in the past. He's much more peripatetic. I think we are really in a very dangerous era, one in which there is not the same accountability that was tied to the state and to organizations; today's top players are connecting dots that are global in reach.[34]

The Harvard Russia scandal reminds us that we need to maintain a watchful eye on small, elite minorities that exercise vast power but remain completely free of social responsibility.

CHAPTER 8

HARVARD'S LABOR POLICY AND THE 2001 OCCUPATION

"Harvard has prestige. That is probably the single thing which brings back to mind the campaign of Harvard clerical workers when they tried to organize against poor working conditions. Their slogan was 'you can't eat prestige.'"
—Victor Wallis[1]

"Did you know that you might not get any better—in fact might get less—salary and benefits through collective bargaining? Did you know that no union can guarantee job security?"
—Letter from the Personnel Office to the Medical Area staff dated June 1, 1977, to encourage them to vote "no" on the district 65 representation election[2]

Close your eyes and imagine Harvard. What do you see? Scholars sitting next to sunny windows perusing old library books? Athletes dashing across the Harvard Stadium field as the audience roars their approval? Elderly professors engaging in deep discussions with students? There is a unique aura that surrounds Harvard University, an aura that comes from the bright, talented student body and the school's many brilliant scholars.

There is another side of Harvard, however, that we shouldn't ignore. There is Harvard the educational institution, and then there is Harvard the mega-corporation, employer to thousands in the greater Boston area. With some eighteen thousand employees including professors, research fellows, teaching fellows, interns, and staff members, Harvard is actually the second largest corporation in the greater Boston area. In addition, Harvard hires employees such as security guards and service workers through subcontracted companies. Harvard's labor policies and decisions have an immediate impact on neighboring communities.

So, what are the labor policies at Harvard University, one of the most prestigious and well-funded universities in the world? In 1987, Vladimir Escalante, who was involved in Harvard's labor union activities while writing his doctoral dissertation, wrote a report on Harvard's anti-worker labor policies and its workers' ceaseless efforts to improve their working conditions. According to his observations, Harvard has one of the most sophisticated and refined union-busting strategies. Wayne Langley, director of the Higher Education Division of the Service Employees International Union (SEIU), testifies to Harvard's labor policy as "never give anybody anything without a fight."

Interestingly, it was the students of Harvard who demanded improved labor treatment, fighting against Harvard's anti-worker policy. In 2001, students occupied Massachusetts Hall, site of the Harvard president's office, during their fight for a living wage. In May 2007, in the middle of a hunger strike for a wage increase for Harvard security guards, nine students were taken to the hospital. It was only after this that the Harvard administration changed its position and accepted students' demands. In this chapter I will briefly examine Harvard University's treatment of its workers. What kind of corporate employer has the renowned educational institution Harvard University been to its workers?

The Labor Policy of a Wealthy University

That Harvard was originally a college for affluent, fairly well-known families in the greater Boston area can tell us a lot about Harvard's labor policy. In the late nineteenth and early twentieth centuries, the number of industrial laborers rapidly increased in the United States along with an accompanying struggle to improve their working and living conditions. It might have been inevitable for Harvard University to be on the side of industrialists, who were, after all, Harvard members and backers. For example, Harvard patron Henry Lee Higginson once said in an anti-union fundraising letter of 1886: "Educate, and save ourselves and our families from mobs."[3]

When Lawrence textile workers went on strike during the Bread and Roses uprising of 1912, Harvard immediately sided with the factory owners and offered academic credits to students who joined the ranks of strikebreakers. Harvard supported its stance with the motto "Defend Your Class!" When the Boston Police went on strike in 1919, Harvard appealed for an immediate action from its members, enlisting some two hundred enthusiastic volunteers to join the strikebreakers.

When basic worker rights began to be legislated, Harvard found a way to bypass the law rather than improve working conditions. For example, Harvard fired nineteen scrubwomen without advance notice in 1929 and employed men instead. A handwritten note explained President Abbott Lawrence Lowell's reasoning: "the minimum wage board has been complaining of our employing women for less than 37 cents an hour, and, hence, the University has felt constrained to replace them with men. Their

Harvard students carried out a concerted campaign to end the school's investment in South Africa.

replacement by men was prompted by the fact that the law that prescribed minimum wages for 'scrubwomen' did not protect men."[4]

In order to bypass laws that prescribed a minimum wage for scrubwomen, Harvard changed their title from scrubwomen to chambermaids. These "chambermaids" swept and cleaned the Widener Library building from six in the morning till eleven at night on a thirty-two-cents-per-hour wage, a much lower rate than the legally prescribed minimum wage for scrubwomen. Considered substitute income-earners, women workers were often paid considerably lower wages than male workers performing the same jobs. By and large, Harvard has maintained a feudalistic relationship with its laborers for years, and as a result university administrators and workers continue to have friction to this day.

Workers' demands were also not only limited to the issues of wages and working conditions. In the midst of the social upheaval of the 1960s and 1970s, workers' interests also expanded to social and political issues. Harvard students fought together with workers, despite the university administration's persistent attempts to drive a wedge between them, claiming, for example, that the school would have to raise student tuition and cut scholarships in order to raise workers' wages. Nevertheless, events like the anti-war movement offered a great opportunity for Harvard students and workers to fight alongside each other. After Nixon announced that the United States had invaded Cambodia on April 30, 1970, the anti-war movement spread to every corner of the country and students began to strike on university campuses all over the country. At Harvard, 2,700 students, professors, and staff members assembled and began a general strike.

In 1986, when Harvard students carried out a movement to demand the school administration withdraw its investments in South Africa, union activists actively participated as well. In May 1986, activists briefly occupied the Holyoke Center office used to plan Harvard's 350th anniversary celebration. Several months later, on September 4, union activists joined students in demanding divestment from companies doing business in South Africa by interrupting a party to honor Harvard's most affluent alumni. President Bok cancelled the party, worried about the public response and potential media coverage of the event.[5]

Labor Unions Are Necessities, Except at Harvard

It is not easy to uncover the history of Harvard's treatment of its workers. Although Harvard scholars and research institutes teach extensively on the subject of labor policy, the college hasn't really studied its own labor policies. Additionally, Harvard's employment structure is extremely complicated. There are many categories of workers from managerial staff to faculty, office clerks, undergraduate and graduate students working part-time, and service workers. Faculty members are also divided into various classes from tenured professors to contract-based adjunct professors. Since Harvard professors cannot form a union according to the Supreme Court's 1980 *National Labor Relations Board v. Yeshiva University* decision, let's take a look at the cases of office staff and service workers. According to labor data published by Harvard in 2011, about 5,800 Harvard employees belong to seven different labor unions.

The oldest among them is the food service union, dating back to 1937. Clerical and technical worker unions, as well as security unions, were organized relatively recently. The Harvard Union of Clerical and Technical Workers (HUCTW) was the largest of its kind when it was established in 1989, but until Harvard recognized it more than a decade later, the HUCTW had to go through a fifteen-year-long war with Harvard, enduring numerous trials and testifying to Harvard's brutal labor policy history.

Clerical and technical workers at Harvard began their unionization efforts in the early 1970s. The core members of this initial movement were Harvard medical school employees. At that time, most of these workers were women working short-term until they finished their graduate work. Harvard took advantage of this situation and used high quality labor at a very low wage. These female lower-rung managerial staff members not only suffered from low wages and lack of job security, but it was also almost impossible for them to move up the career ladder. In short, they were almost invisible members of the campus.

Harvard University Campus Unions

Area Trade Council (ATC): represents about 240 operating engineers, electrical workers, plumbers and gasfitters, and carpenters.

Harvard Union of Clerical and Technical Workers (HUCTW): represents about 4,800 members.

Harvard University Police Association (HUPA): represents about 60 members.

Harvard University Security, Parking & Museum Guards Union (HUSPMGU): represents about 55 members.

Service Employees' International Union (SEIU), Local 615: represents about 355 custodial employees.

Hotel Employees and Restaurant Employees International Union, Local 26: represents about 440 food service employees.

Project labor Agreement (PLA): a collective bargaining agreement between Harvard University and multiple local constructions trade unions to cover employment terms and conditions at selected renovation and construction projects across the university.

Source: http://laborrelations.harvard.edu

The Harvard University clerical and technical employees tried voting twice—in 1977 and 1981—in order to establish a union. But university administrators campaigned to block them. In 1977, just before the vote, Harvard administrators sent out letters to employees presenting ominous "facts" like the following:

> Did you know that as a union member you have to pay union dues, averaging more than $120 each year? Did you know that as a union member you would have to attend union meetings, or pay a fine unless your absence was excused by your shop steward? . . . Did you know that you might not get any better—in fact might get less—salary and benefits through collective-bargaining? Did you know that no union can guarantee job security?[6]

Harvard's anti-union campaign was successful. Many employees were too afraid to commit, causing the 1977 vote to fail to form a union.

The workers made another attempt in 1981, and the Harvard administration again launched a full-scale anti-union campaign. Harvard distributed a booklet titled "Union Representation Election Briefing Book for Administrators and Supervisors" a few days before the general election. The information in this booklet, to be delivered to the employees under supervision, included:

> It is very difficult to get a union out once it gets in. Legally, a union can be decertified by a majority vote of individual employees. . . . As

a result of collective bargaining, pay and benefits can be essentially
the same, better than or worse than prior to agreement. . . . The university would continue all normal activities to the best of its ability
during a strike. . . . The law allows an employer to replace economic
strikers permanently. . . . University supporting staff members not
represented by the union receive salary increases and benefits equal
to or better then the service department employees.[7]

The heart of the message Harvard sent to its employees can be summarized as: "We're Harvard, we're big, we know what you're doing, and we'll
get you. If you think you have a prayer against us, you're wrong."[8] Eventually,
the 1981 attempt to form a union again was also defeated by only the slim-
mest margin, 380 for "no" and 328 for "yes." Activists appealed to the
National Labor Relations Board, charging that Harvard had acted unfairly.
The board, which usually loyally complied with the anti-union policies of
the Reagan administration, ruled in favor of the Harvard administration.

However, despite the anti-union campaigns of the Harvard administration, the Harvard Union of Clerical and Technical Workers, based in all
Harvard workplaces, successfully formed in 1988. It is noteworthy that 83
percent of its members were women. In October of the same year, Harvard
petitioned the National Labor Relations Board, claiming unfairness on the
part of the labor union, but this time the board sided with the union. It was
a victory achieved after fifteen years of hard work.

Elaine Bernard, executive director of the Labor and Worklife Program
at Harvard Law School, points out President Bok's hypocrisy in opposing the
clerical workers' union. As a labor law specialist, Bok knew very well about
the workers' rights to unionize. He was also known to have supported the
need for unions. The problem was his contradictory attitude of believing
unions were a necessity, except at Harvard.

According to Dr. Bernard, corporations often oppose unions because
they mistakenly believe that a union's purpose is to punish bad employers.
Of course, in comparison to the Coca-Cola company that has used "death
squads" to assassinate union leaders in Colombia, or the Samsung conglomerate that boasts of its "no labor union" myth, Harvard's anti-union
activities were fairly moderate. No workers were ever fired for their union
activities. Harvard, however, adopted a much cleverer strategy, advancing
union leaders to managerial positions and automatically depriving them of
union membership.

Given that Harvard Corporation fellows are mostly managers of large
corporations, Harvard's anti-union campaigns should not be surprising.
Recently, Harvard has outsourced many of its service jobs. This is partially
why it is hard for us to know the exact number of Harvard employees or the

nature of their working conditions. According to an official 2011 Harvard report, the number of custodial staff and security, parking and museum guards directly employed by Harvard is around nine hundred, and the other eight hundred and forty staff members are employed through sixteen outside companies.[9]

Harvard's service staff outsourcing dates back to the 1980s when neo-liberalism was beginning to expand its influence. For example, the *Harvard Crimson* reported in 1984 that local union activists and on-campus workers expressed growing dissatisfaction with Harvard's increasing its "contracting out" strategy.[10] Apparently Harvard first became interested in "contracting out" as an "attractive alternative to in-house labor that may increase efficiency and lower costs." As a result, Harvard gradually contracted out food service staff and maintenance crew such as plumbers, carpenters, and electricians. According to a local union activist, as of 1984 about 50 percent of Harvard's graduate school food service staff and about 10-20 percent of undergraduate food service staff were outsourced. Local union activists and Harvard staff members criticized this policy as a tactic to pressure Harvard staff members to end their labor union activities. They argued that cost efficiency could not be Harvard's only priority; Harvard was an educational institution, after all.

These concerns of local union activists reflected a larger issue of the influence of Harvard's managerial policies on other institutions in the area. As expected, outsourcing spread rapidly from the manufacturing sector to all areas of U.S. industry in the 1980s—and subsequently all over the world.

Thanks to outsourcing, Harvard can now more easily manage its staff. While Harvard's fund managers were making millions of dollars in bonuses every year, its service workers had to accept wages less than minimum living costs. In the end, Harvard's union-busting policies and low wages invited the 2001 student occupation of Massachusetts Hall.

Spend Freely and Throw Away

On April 18, 2001, some fifty Harvard students entered and occupied Massachusetts Hall, the building with the office of Harvard's president. Surprisingly, they demanded a "living wage" for Harvard's service workers, a demand that didn't appear to have any direct relationship to students.

At that time, Harvard's endowments were growing rapidly, breaking new records every year and surpassing $20 billion in 2001. Throughout the 1990s, however, Harvard service workers' wages gradually decreased. According to the leaflet protesters were distributing, Harvard guards were earning less than $10 per hour compared to the $14 per hour they were earning in 1994. This wage reduction remained in effect at the same time when Boston area real estate prices nearly doubled. The leaflet also noted

Logo of the Harvard living wage struggle.

that, since it was impossible for workers to make ends meet with their jobs at Harvard, many service workers were juggling two jobs, working from dawn to midnight.

The history of Harvard's wage campaign began in the late 1990s when a group of Harvard students started a movement against the sweatshop practices of companies producing Harvard merchandise. Many universities—including Harvard—sold clothing companies the rights to use their names in products. As a result, university-related clothing companies were making $30 billion a year manufacturing T-shirts in overseas sweatshops. Anti-sweatshop campaigns spread across campuses all over the country.

As this campaign progressed, Harvard students eventually formed the Progressive Students Labor Movement (PSLM) and turned their gaze inward at their own school's labor practices. While interviewing Harvard's service workers and union members, students learned that these workers' situations were not so different from those working in Third World countries. Upon discovering the workers' plight, students began to demand improved working conditions and living wages, calculated using the minimum living expenses in Cambridge.

The Harvard administration consistently ignored repeated appeals from students and residents. PSLM's every attempt to meet Harvard's president and Harvard Corporation officials met with frustration. In February 2001, Harvard declared that it would allow its workers to take certain courses free of charge, declaring an end to any further discussion on the matter. Justification for this concession was that workers could acquire higher paying jobs if better educated, still ultimately ignoring the reality of workers who had to work two grueling job workdays.

Students understood that no further dialogue was possible with school administrators. For two months, they prepared intensively for a civil disobedience struggle. Eventually, they came up with the plan to occupy Massachusetts Hall and organized two teams—the occupation team and the support team. They prepared very carefully because of their worries about the negative images of an occupation struggle. Throughout all of their planning, no one expected that they would occupy Massachusetts Hall for three long weeks. According to Maple Razsa, one of the campaign's leaders: "When we initially started to plan the sit-in, we thought maybe

Maple Razsa, one of the leaders of the Massachusetts Hall occupation.

we'd be inside the building for a few hours and then we'd be arrested, and it would all be very quick, but at least we'd draw attention to this problem. But given the history of student protest at Harvard, the university decided to just ignore us and say, 'It's just free speech, no problem,' and then just wait until we gave up."[11] On April 18, nearly fifty students gathered in a dormitory near Massachusetts Hall with their toiletries and basic necessities. At one in the afternoon, they made their way toward Massachusetts Hall, only about thirty meters away, and successfully occupied the building.

Neil Rudenstine was president of Harvard at the time, but he was planning to step down, having completed a grueling six-year fundraising campaign raising $2.6 billion. After a nine-month process, Lawrence Summers had already been selected as the next president. Dr. Elaine Bernard said that the students might have felt the urgent need to raise this issue before Summers was inaugurated. Rudenstine, a humanist and supporter of the African American studies program, would make a more receptive opponent than Summers, known for his stubbornness and arrogance. One Harvard official said that Rudenstine and Summers were similar in that they could bring in large sums of donations during their term. Rudenstine attracted sizeable donations during his ten-year presidency (1991–2001), while Summers generated enormous profits by managing Harvard's endowment like a hedge fund during his five-year tenure. But their similarities ended there. Their characters were actually almost polar opposites of each other. While Summers arrogantly demanded donations from potential benefactors, Rudenstine was considerate and polite, sending handwritten thank-you

Massachusetts Hall.

notes to individual donors. Who wouldn't feel moved after receiving a handwritten thank-you letter from the president of Harvard? Thanks to Rudenstine's gentle manners, donations grew rapidly. Some people even joked that Rudenstine hurt his health writing so many thank-you letters.

Surprised at the news of occupation, Rudenstine quickly left the building through the back door. Provost Harvey Fineberg, occupying the office next to President Rudenstine's, also left, refusing to respond to students' proposal to engage in a dialogue. Students remained in the building, saying that they wouldn't budge an inch until the school responded to their demand to have a conversation. As Harvard had already had the precedent of a general strike as a result of violent police arrests, Harvard administrators felt that their hands were tied. University administrations decided to shut the building down and wait the students out. The result was a three-week-long occupation. As Maple Razsa recalled,

> What changed once we were there were two things. One, the energy, the excitement, and power of working together as a group and being involved in this civil disobedience really allowed us to bond together. And there was the great sense of group purpose. But also, every night we stayed there, the police surrounded the building. But at night, when it was quieter, the workers would come and talk to us. And they would tell us about the kinds of things happening to them, day-to-day life, how much it meant to them. . . . [They] also said, for the first time, people they worked with asked them about the conditions

they faced, what was life like [for them], and suddenly they weren't invisible anymore in campus. So hearing from the workers, [our fight] already changed the atmosphere on campus. It was a really amazing experience.[12]

Student protesters were isolated in Massachusetts Hall but they were not alone. Outside, rallies supporting their action occurred everyday, with more supporters from the Harvard community gradually joining their movement. Food service workers would bring pizzas late at night after their day's work. Workers who had remained silent for fear of being fired organized large-scale rallies and began voicing their opinions. More than three hundred professors issued a statement supporting the protesters, and Harvard alumni and local residents also joined in. Every night, candlelight vigils encouraged the students isolated within Massachusetts Hall, and dozens of tents were set up in Harvard Yard. The number of various-sized colored tents grew from about ten the first night to some eighty on the seventeenth night. Students and nearby area residents debated, marched, and chanted slogans all day and night.

As the sit-in dragged on, the media began to pay attention. In the beginning, only local newspapers and television stations paid attention, but eventually the national media covered Harvard students' living wage struggle. Following national coverage, the situation changed dramatically. Harvard University issued a statement of apology for not having paid living wages to its workers. Harvard wanted to leave this incident behind as soon as possible. According to Maple Razsa:

> What they [Harvard administrators] were much more scared of was [that] this would be an example of proof when popular pressure forced Harvard to make a different decision, one they didn't want, and they were very scared of that kind of democratization of the university. They were more scared of appearing to give in than about the money. So really what was at stake, then, was how [Harvard administrators] can appear still to be in control of things. So secretly, they agreed to everything we asked for and more, but they didn't want it to be admitted publicly.[13]

Students demanded that Harvard raise service workers' hourly rate to $10.25, the living wage for Cambridge residents. According to students' calculation, this raise would require about $10 million a year, which just 0.5 percent of Harvard endowment's annual profit could easily cover. Harvard promised that they would pay a $10.83 hourly rate, more than the rate students demanded. This promise would apply to outsourced workers as well. Workers would also get health insurance coverage, vacation time, and

The living wage struggle.

sick leave. This was an incredible victory after weeks of collaboration among students, workers, and local communities.

On May 8, after their agreement with the university administration was made public on the school homepage, students walked out of Massachusetts Hall amid cheers and applause. In the end, their struggle wasn't only about wage increases and improved benefits for service workers. The biggest accomplishment of this struggle was attracting public attention to the world's richest university's ruthless exploitation of its workers.

With more than $20 billion in endowment, Harvard did not choose a low-wage policy because of financial difficulties. They simply adopted their market economy-based policy based on neoliberal beliefs and philosophies. It was easy for a powerful university like Harvard to employ people at minimal costs.

Of course, Harvard's labor policy was not far worse than other universities' policies. Many U.S. universities have mistreated their workers, producing a wide range of workers' strikes and struggles. Some might argue that

Harvard members picketing against layoffs, 2012.

universities are corporations as well, and so it is only natural for them to try to create the most profit by squeezing workers and busting unions. But are universities really nothing more than corporations?

Universities do not produce products for the market, but knowledge for the public good. It is because of our society's expectation that this knowledge will create important social values and improve the quality of people's lives that universities are given tax-exemption status and taxpayer funded support. In other words, there is an underlying consensus in our society that universities produce knowledge that will benefit the lives of the majority rather than the interests of a super-rich small minority. There is no reason why a university should get tax benefits, if they are like any factory producing jeans or toys.

Another significant aspect of the 2001 living wage struggle was that students understood their struggle was part of a kind of anti-globalization movement. Students found an essential connection between the sweatshops in the Third World countries squeezing workers for the highest profit and Harvard's labor policy denying collective bargaining rights from its employees. In this sense, the 2001 Harvard occupation struggle was an incident that boldly challenged Harvard's overall neoliberal policies.

However, this student occupation struggle could not put a complete stop to Harvard's neoliberal policies. Harvard has been actively welcoming neoliberal ideas since the mid-1970s when Western capitalism began the transition to neoliberalism, and the university increased its profits by managing its endowments like a hedge fund. After the 2008 financial crisis,

Harvard lost a significant portion of its endowment, after which it laid off almost a thousand workers. Additionally, Harvard planned a mass layoff of its library staff in 2012. For now, Harvard has put a stop to this plan due to public pressure, opting mostly for early retirement of some sixty library staff members instead.

Does Harvard plan to make cuts to its essential educational services? In the next chapter, let's examine how Harvard has been managing its endowment.

CHAPTER 9

A HEDGE FUND WITH LIBRARIES: THE FINANCIAL CRISIS OF 2008

"Others have said that Harvard is a giant financial, stock market, and real estate investment firm that happens to have classes on the side so that it can keep its tax-exempt status."
—John Trumpbour[1]

"People have called Harvard a hedge fund with libraries, all right, and it is more true than not."
—Wayne Langley[2]

One of the biggest events of 2011 was the Occupy Wall Street movement. This movement with its "We are the 99 percent" banner proves that we now live in an age when simultaneous worldwide uprisings are possible thanks to social networks and the internet. The yearning for a fairer and more just society seen with Occupy Wall Street has also affected tranquil college campuses. On November 2, 2011, a group of Harvard students left class in solidarity with the Occupy Wall Street movement. The class they left was Economics 10, taught by Professor Greg Mankiw.

A conservative economist, Professor Mankiw was chairman of the Council of Economic Advisers under President Bush from 2003 to 2005. In 2006, he became an economic advisor to Mitt Romney and continued in this capacity during Romney's failed 2012 presidential bid. His book *Principles of Economics*, which systematically summarizes economic principles, is a best-selling textbook that has been translated into seventeen languages and has sold more than one million copies. His Economics 10 course is also widely popular among Harvard undergraduates, regularly registering more than seven hundred students every semester.

So what prompted students to walk out of this incredibly popular, near-legendary class? In an open letter, the students recognized that his kind of conservative curriculum contributed to the current worldwide economic crisis:

> We found a course that espouses a specific—and limited—view of economics that we believe perpetuates problematic and inefficient systems of economic inequality in our society today. . . . Harvard graduates play major roles in the financial institutions and in shaping public policy around the world. If Harvard fails to equip its students with a broad and critical understanding of economics, their actions are likely to harm the global financial system. The last five years of economic turmoil have been proof enough of this.[3]

As students left the classroom they headed immediately to Dewey Square, Boston's local Occupy site. Although only about seventy students—roughly 10 percent of students taking his course—participated in the walkout, their actions indicated that students pointed to academic intellectuals as one of the most important culprits who brought about today's economic inequality.

In fact, Harvard University has actively espoused neoliberalism as its key management principle since the 1970s, greatly influencing other universities' philosophies as well. This chapter will examine the changes that have occurred in universities during our present neoliberal age, focusing on the way universities manage their endowments.

Neoliberalism and Endowment Management

Neoliberalism emerged as a new ideology that would restructure the relationship between market and state when the Oil Shock and other critical events in the 1970s challenged the postwar Western economic boom. Neoliberal economists argued that it was time to depart from Keynesian economic theory, which advocated active governmental intervention in the market. It was time to accept a market liberalism that advocated minimal governmental intervention, leaving everything to the market. Neoliberalism began to be incorporated into mainstream ideas when Friedrich Hayek, the father of neoliberalism, and Milton Friedman received Nobel Prizes in economics in 1974 and 1976, respectively. Especially leading the charge was the Chicago School of Economics, headed by Milton Friedman, which for thirty years has supplied the theoretical foundation for neoliberal policies.

Ironically, while neoliberalism advocated minimal state intervention, policies were implemented through strong state intervention. Britain and the U.S. government were among the first countries to adopt neoliberal policies. Margaret Thatcher, who rose to Conservative Party leadership in 1975, was known to have carried Hayek's book in her briefcase. When she became prime minster of the United Kingdom in 1979, she briskly implemented neoliberal policies emphasizing deregulation, policies that have since come to be known as Thatcherism. From the outset, she reduced expenditures on social services, oppressed labor unions, and privatized state-owned industries.

In the same period, the Reagan administration (1981–89) also energetically pursued neoliberal policies, known as "Reaganomics," which also emphasized deregulation, tax cuts, and a hardline policy towards

Milton Friedman

labor unions. The Reagan administration drastically slashed social service budgets and greatly reduced tax rates for the wealthiest, further widening America's wealth gap. His administration also allowed large corporations to outsource product lines for the sake of reducing production costs, ultimately causing mass unemployment in the domestic manufacturing sector and a continuous fall in workers' real wages. The only economic figures that increased during Reagan's administration were public subsidies for the wealthy and the military budget. Additionally, Reagan adopted an aggressive anti-union policy, as illustrated by his actions during the 1981 Professional Air Traffic Controllers Organization strike. Declaring the situation an emergency, Reagan fired 11,345 striking air traffic controllers who did "not report for work within forty-eight hours." Having firmly taken root during the Reagan administration, neoliberal policies bloomed during the Clinton administration together with increasing deregulation.

Neoliberalism was, by then, spreading all over the world. Chile, where neoliberalism was introduced in 1975, was often showcased as the success story of neoliberal reform. Socialist candidate Salvador Allende was elected as Chile's president in a democratic election in April 1970. When Allende's government adopted policies of nationalization of industries and collectivization, army general Augusto Pinochet ousted Allende and took power through a military coup d'état under the auspices of the United States in 1973. The "bloody dictator" Pinochet murdered more than three thousand people during his seventeen-year reign. There were also tens of thousands of torture victims and missing persons reported under Pinochet's rule. Freedom of the press and civil rights were heavily suppressed. In 1975, Milton Friedman went to Chile to advocate neoliberal economic policies, and Pinochet hired a group of economists—"The Chicago Boys"—and had them carry out grand-scale neoliberal economic reform in Chile. As a result, Chile emerged as a rising star among developing countries, drawing world-wide attention and eventually was honored by being admitted to the OECD. At the same time, however, Chile acquired the label of having the highest level of economic inequality among OECD countries.

Professor Emeritus James Petras at Binghamton University, a progressive scholar and specialist in Latin America, argues that the first wave of neoliberalism came to Latin America during periods of military dictatorship. This includes Chile's Pinochet rule (1973–89), Argentina (1976–84), Uruguay (1972–85), Bolivia (1971–84), and Peru (1991–2001). The same is true of Turkey after a military coup d'état in 1980. In all these countries, military *juntas* pursued neoliberal policies through violent means, establishing bridgeheads for large-scale privatization by oppressing labor unions, political parties, and grassroots movements.

All these countries, however, ended up having to face financial crises together with extreme abuses of power, which then functioned as excuses for the second wave of neoliberal policy implementations. During these second waves, the economies of these countries became subject to the IMF and the World Bank and their state-owned industries were privatized en masse. In the end, thanks to these neoliberal policies, socioeconomic inequality intensified and class conflict deepened. A third wave of neoliberalism came with the new millennium. Neoliberals who had come to power combined deepening subordination of national industries to foreign capital with an introduction of "poverty programs" intended to neutralize popular resistance, offering incentives that would supposedly stimulate the growth of "national bourgeoisie."[4]

Recently, an argument was raised that South Korea switched to a neoliberal approach about the same time as Latin America and Turkey. Professor George Katsiaficas, a progressive scholar who conducted in-depth research on Asian social movements, argues that the most critical reason why the U.S. State Department approved the brutal suppression of the Gwangju Uprising of May 1980 was to carry out neoliberal economic policies in South Korea. He came to this conclusion after doing research on thousands of messages exchanged within the State Department during the uprising. This theory also supports the recent analysis that the "Comprehensive Program for Economic Stabilization" announced in April 1979 by President Park Chung-hee was the first step towards introducing neoliberal policies in Korea. At the time, Western capitalist forces were eager to open the Korean market and the Gwangju Uprising of May 18 was an excellent opportunity for the West to force it open. On May 22, White House elites approved Chun Doo-hwan's request to send troops to suppress the Gwangju Uprising. On May 30, only three days after the uprising's bloody suppression, Ambassador to Korea William H. Gleysteen contributed an article to *Nation's Business*, the magazine of the U.S. Chamber of Commerce, in which he said the following:

> Economically, the country is going through a massive shifting of gears, from the almost frenetic growth of the past two decades to more moderate, stable, and market-oriented growth better suited to the economy's present stage of development. . . . The next crucial step in the country's economy development—liberalization of the economy from this tight central control to a greater reliance on market forces— is one which has been accepted in principle and is being pursued as conditions permit.[5]

What Gleysteen meant by "liberalization of the economy from this tight central control to a greater reliance on market forces" was clearly neoliberal economic reform. Pointing out that "foreign loans" are an instrument for neoliberalism to trap countries, Professor Katsiaficas argues, "In the first four years of his [Chun Doo-hwan's] government, the country's foreign debt more than doubled, giving South Korea the dubious distinction of fourth place among the world's debtor nations behind Argentina, Brazil and Mexico."[6] He also points out that by revising the Foreign Capital Inducement Law, Chun's regime removed nearly all restrictions on profit-taking and capital flow out of the country, thereby enabling foreign investors to gain enormous profits.

As these examples show, Western capitalism spearheaded by the United States intervened in the politics of developing countries in order to force their economies to switch to neoliberal systems. The easy transition to neoliberal system in strongly autocratic countries where military *juntas* took power through violent coup d'état evinces the duplicity inherent in neoliberalism. Although advocates for neoliberal economy argue for free markets and minimal governmental intervention, all countries adopting neoliberal policies did not hesitate to resort to active state intervention to bust labor unions or to pressure other countries to open their markets.

What changes have neoliberal economic policies brought to our lives? Corporations pay fewer taxes and basic national industries and public corporations have been privatized. Regular employment has been reduced as temporary jobs replace regular positions under the pretext of "flexible employment." As the influx of foreign capital increases, national debts snowball. The wealth gap increases, social polarization deepens, and the poorest population expands daily. In short, neoliberal policies make the rich richer and the poor poorer. A 1996 report shows that the assets owned by the 358 richest men in the world are equivalent to the income earned by 45 percent of the world population, the poorest 2.3 billion people, a clear summary of the essence of neoliberalism. According to another report, the net worth of the world's two hundred richest people increased from $440 billion to over $1 trillion within only four years from 1994 to 1998.[7] Although the American economy enjoyed a record boom during the 1990s thanks to the introduction of neoliberal policies, workers' real wages dropped drastically as illustrated in the above-mentioned case of Harvard service workers. These are the circumstances behind the Occupy Wall Street movement.

In fact, one of the most harmful effect of neoliberalism was revealed within universities. As universities changed their fund management style, they practically became hedge fund firms with educational institutions as their fronts. As we have examined in Chapter 6, the 1960s anti-war movement had a strong influence on the way university fund management style changed. Foundations based on large corporations became more reluctant to support universities, which had become bases for anti-war movements. Universities had to come up with different ways to manage their endowments.

The word, "endowment," means a gift, quite different from the concept of "fund." Endowments have been given to universities to help them carry out their original educational mission. The table below, based on a 2015 source, shows the status of endowments in U.S. universities. When neoliberal management systems were introduced, the purpose of these endowments changed entirely. They were no longer safety funds that would support university finances but speculative tools to increase university's assets. At the same time, they became an important index to rank universities. This is why U.S. universities rush to publish the size of their endowments every year. Neoliberalism, for which financial capital is everything, has distorted the original purpose of university endowments.

Ten Largest U.S. University Endowments (2014)

University	Endowment
1. Harvard University	$35,883,691,000
2. University of Texas System	$25,452,922,000
3. Yale University	$23,900,000,000
4. Stanford University	$21,446,006,000
5. Princeton University	$20,995,518,000
6. Massachusetts Institute of Technology	$12,425,131,000
7. Texas A&M University System & Foundations	$11,103,880,000
8. Northwestern University	$9,778,112,000
9. University of Michigan	$9,731,460,000
10. University of Pennsylvania	$9,582,335,000

Source: National Association of College and University Business Officers (NACUBO)

Palace of Usury

David Swensen, the Chief Investment Officer at Yale University, invented what has become known as "The Yale Model," an application of modern portfolio theory. An economics PhD from Yale, Swensen spent six years on Wall Street at such powerful firms as Lehman Brothers and the Salomon Brothers. Utilizing his Wall Street experience, Swensen radically changed the way Yale University managed its endowment. Before his arrival, the endowment was managed conservatively with 65 percent stocks and 25 percent bonds. By applying a modern portfolio theory, Swenson divided the portfolio into five or six roughly equal parts and invested each in a different asset class. Central to his model was broad diversification and an equity orientation, avoiding asset classes with low expected returns such as fixed income and commodities. Particularly revolutionary at the time was his recognition that liquidity was a poor investment, one to be avoided rather than sought out, bringing with it a heavy price in the form of lower returns. In particular, he bought forested land not for research but for profit.[8]

Many larger endowments and foundations including Harvard University followed this investment model, diversifying their portfolios and investing in complicated financial derivatives. The Harvard portfolio then included such non-traditional assets as hedge funds, venture capital, and private equity funds, as well as investments in real estate, raw materials, and forested land. While other universities including Yale hired outside investment firms for their fund investments, Harvard established its own management company, the Harvard Management Company, Inc. (HMC) during Derek Bok's presidency. They did this at the same time as Bok actively introduced a neoliberal management system centered on the decentralization of the university administration. The HMC office was located not on campus but at the Federal Bank building at the heart of the Boston financial district, near Dewey Square, the site of the Occupy Boston movement.

During Pusey's presidency, it is said that the Harvard Corporation fellow in charge of the treasury orally reported the result of the previous year's investment to other fellows. Their investment method was, then, quite simple. The situation changed radically, however, with the establishment of the Harvard Management Company. After Jack Meyer, who became the company's CEO in 1990, introduced the performance-based pay system, HMC's investment style became even more aggressive. As the Clinton and Bush administrations accelerated the deregulation that had begun during the Reagan administration, the HMC had no impediments to its goals. The graph below shows the changes in Harvard endowment from 1990 to 2009. Harvard's endowment continued to grow throughout the 1990s and their growth was curving steeply upwards before the 2008 financial crisis. In

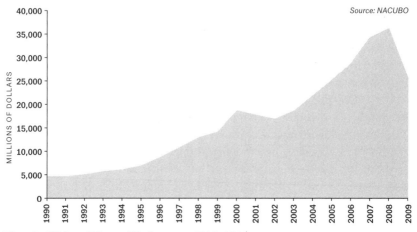

Historical Value of Harvard Endowment 1990–2009

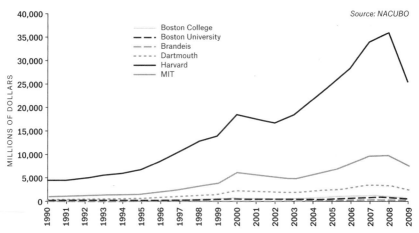

Historical Value of Endowments in Six New England Universities including Harvard 1990–2009

comparison to the other five New England colleges, Harvard endowment performed much better in overall size and growth.

In 2010, the Tellus Institute, a nonprofit research and Boston-based policy organization intent on advancing the transition to a sustainable, equitable, and humane global civilization, published a report entitled "Educational Endowments and the Financial Crisis: Social Costs and Systemic Risks in the Shadow Banking System." This report, which studied the influence of the endowment management methods of six New England universities, drew the public's attention to the way in which these universities' speculative investment played a significant role in the 2008 financial crisis. Dr. Joshua Humphreys, principal investigator and lead author, pointed out how the investment model adopted by Harvard and Yale stimulated other educational institutions into adopting much riskier means of managing their endowments than traditional ones based on security-focused models.

When the dot-com boom busted and that bubble popped in the beginning of this last decade, endowments like Harvard and Yale—precisely because they had diversified away from the U.S. capital markets—did very well during the tech-bubble when it burst, and seemed to have developed some kind of magical strategy for avoiding what seemed to be the really radical volatility of the capital markets. . . . But precisely because they succeeded so well during that period of volatility, everyone suddenly wanted to imitate Harvard and Yale. . . . Suddenly you had all kinds of smaller institutions crowding into timberland, crowding into property, crowding into commodities, gas and oil, using hedging strategy, using private equity, trying to make venture capital investments. And the crowding effects in these corners of the capital markets that had not traditionally seen so much capital actually created all kinds of new forms of systemic risk.[9]

While individuals and corporations had to pay tax on their profits, universities enjoyed the privilege of tax exemption based on the assumption that they were nonprofit educational organizations. Universities could invest as they pleased without worrying about taxes. It is said that David Swensen encouraged investment bankers to adjust Yale investments in real time everyday. Tax exemption status had the effect of encouraging universities to manage their endowments more aggressively.

The HMC went a step further and even borrowed funds to reinvest, raking in tax-free profits. At one point, the HMC's debt vs. capital ratio reached 15:1. Humphreys maintains that this was the background against which the HMC could make aggressive investments: "They [Harvard] have received tax-exempt debt and, to some extent, taxable debt as well, often at very low concessionary interest rate, and this is providing them with infusions of cash, basically going into debt, and that is how they'd be able to get infusions of cash to meet their capital calls and to unwind whole series of other kinds of investment strategy that proved to be absolutely disastrous during the financial crisis."[10]

This strategy of maximizing profitability by way of debt leverage was, of course, much riskier than more traditional investment methods. For example, Sowood Capital, established by Jeffrey Larson, collapsed in the summer of 2007. Jeffrey Larson, a star investor of the HMC, established his private firm with $7 billion he borrowed from the HMC as seed money in 2004. He invested in a variety of derivatives using leverage, his debt vs. capital ratio reaching 12:1 at one point. But when the situation went sour, Larson lost more than half of the $30 billion he was managing for foundations, universities, and pension funds. Harvard also lost $3.5 billion, more than 10

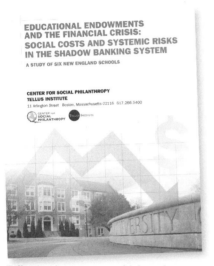

EDUCATIONAL ENDOWMENTS AND THE FINANCIAL CRISIS: SOCIAL COSTS AND SYSTEMIC RISKS IN THE SHADOW BANKING SYSTEM
A STUDY OF SIX NEW ENGLAND SCHOOLS

CENTER FOR SOCIAL PHILANTHROPY
TELLUS INSTITUTE
11 Arlington Street Boston, Massachusetts 02116 617.266.5400

Tellus Institute report, which analyzes the effects of risky investment strategies adopted by universities.

percent of its entire fund. Failing to secure cash, Sowood Capital ended up being sold to Citadel LLC, an investment firm based in Chicago. This was a predictable result of an excessively speculative investment.

According to the report by the Tellus Institute, another problem was that many of the university board directors were directly related to investment firms that managed university endowments. For example, at Dartmouth College, more than half of its board directors were connected to the investment firms that managed the college's more than one billion dollar endowment. In this situation, it is hard to expect the directors could objectively evaluate the endowment's management. It is also clearly in violation of the conflict of interest principle.

Annual Salary: Janitors vs. Fund Managers

During the fifteen years Jack Meyer was leading HMC, Harvard's endowment more than quintupled, skyrocketing from $5 billion to $26 billion—and awarding its fund managers with astronomical salaries. The table below shows Harvard's highest salaries and their recipients since 2000. Those who earned the highest salaries were all fund managers at HMC. Maurice Samuels earned more than $35 million in 2003. If we add up the five highest salaries in 2003, it becomes more than $107 million, and if we add up all the salaries Harvard fund managers took, the total could educate more than four thousand students for a year at Harvard. Even Yale's David Swensen criticized Harvard's excessive bonus system and warned against its risks. In comparison, a fund manager at the University of Texas with the second largest endowment the same year earned about $740,000, and Yale's Swensen earned a little over $1 million.[11]

If we compare the highest annual salary at Harvard in 2003 with the $18,000 annual janitor salary during the 2001 living wage struggle, the difference in salaries in the same university community was two thousand times greater. Of course, one might argue that it is unfair to compare the salary of a fund manager to that of a janitor. In that case, we can try a different comparison. The average salary of a Harvard professor in 2003 was about $150,000. In other words, the fund manager who earned the highest salary in 2003 made two hundred times more than a Harvard professor, the school's actual educator. As it was, we can presume how dissatisfied even Harvard insiders would have been about these excessive salary differences.

Highest Salary Ranking at Harvard since 2000

Name	Division	Salary	Financial Year
Maurice Samuels	HMC	$35,099,300	2003
David R. Mittelman	HMC	$33,979,230	2003
David R. Mittelman	HMC	$17,395,300	2002
Jeffrey Larson	HMC	$17,360,300	2002
Jeffrey Larson	HMC	$17,256,161	2003
Maurice Samuels	HMC	$15,867,650	2002
Jack Meyer	HMC (president)	$7,195,680	2004
Mohamed El-Erian	HMC (president)	$6,500,000	2007
Stephen Blyth	HMC	$6,373,750	2008
Marc Seidner	HMC	$6,288,750	2008

Source: "Educational Endowments and the Financial Crisis: Social Costs and Systemic Risks in the Shadow Banking System"

Controversy surrounding the astronomical salaries of Harvard fund managers drew even mainstream media attention. Of course, Harvard fund managers were also dissatisfied with the controversy. Their attitude, however, was "We can get even more than this on Wall Street." In fact, after the controversy broke out, a few star fund managers left Harvard and established their own private firms. The HMC fully supported their ventures, lending them a portion of Harvard funds for seed money. They did not always get good results, however. Jeffrey Larson is a good example of this. Also, Jack Meyer, who had led HMC for fifteen years, left Harvard most likely because of the fund manager salary controversy. Meyer took with him thirty fund managers of the HMC as well as $5 billion in Harvard funds. However, it is generally known that his early investment record was less than impressive.

The excessive difference in salaries within the Harvard community is a mirror reflecting the polarization of an American society within a neoliberal system. While real wages of workers have been declining, fund managers on Wall Street have been raking in tens of millions of dollars every year, throwing bonus parties in their own honor. As soon as Wall Street, chief instigators of the 2008 financial crisis, barely managed to survive thanks to bailouts using public funds, Wall Street fund managers again got paid astronomical bonuses, bringing more public ire upon themselves. The CEO of JPMorgan Chase, Jamie Dimon, made more than $20 million in 2009, and his direct employees were paid close to $500,000 each. One of the direct causes that touched off the 2011 Occupy Wall Street movement was the bonus party at

Harvard's logo changed to satirize its pursuit of money.

the Bank of America. In the midst of large scale restructuring, the Bank of America decided to pay astronomical sums to a few of its managerial staff. As this information was revealed, citizens were extremely angry at the greed and corruption of the 1 percent symbolized by Wall Street.[12]

When we understand how Harvard has managed its funds, we can understand why some people call Harvard a "hedge fund with libraries." It is certainly unclear why these educational institutions madly dashing for profits should get tax-exemption privileges. I changed the title *Veritas* to *Verita$* in my Harvard documentary film for good reason.

In fact, most people don't care about the way universities manage their endowments. Even if they wanted to discover the truth, they have few ways to find out since most endowments are not managed transparently and universities have no obligations to make this information available to the public. Civil society began paying attention to it only a few years ago, during the historic 2008 financial crisis.

The 2008 Financial Crisis and Harvard

The financial crisis that had begun with the 2007 subprime mortgage crisis, reached its height when U.S. investment firm Lehman Brothers filed for bankruptcy in September 2008. The world economy entered the worst recession since the 1929 Great Depression. Prices of almost all goods plummeted and universities also had to witness the value of their assets quickly dropping.

During severe market downturns, corporations sell their assets in order to reduce their debts and secure cash. This is called deleveraging. The biggest problem during the 2008 financial crisis that Harvard had to confront was that a considerable proportion of their endowment was invested in non-current assets. Even Harvard's "exquisite" investment model fell apart in the midst of the financial crisis and ensuing credit crunch. They needed cash to pay for capital calls. Also, they had to come up with university operating costs as they had already used that money to invest. Since Harvard procured about 35 percent of its operating costs from endowment earnings, it was facing a crisis that could paralyze its day-to-day functions. In the fall of 2008, Harvard decided to sell its $15 billion in private equity funds on the secondary market. According to the Tellus Institute's report, this decision by Harvard played a decisive role in causing the stock market crash. As Joshua Humphreys explained,

> Everything was going down after the collapse of Lehman Brothers, and suddenly they [university fund managers] saw their values, the value of their endowments, declining rapidly. They looked around and they tried to sell whatever they could. Word on the street was that Harvard was selling its private equity interests in the secondary market, and suddenly you see a rush of institutional investors and other endowments. Stanford, Duke, Columbia, large institutional investors like pension funds, all crowding into this relatively small secondary market trying to sell their private equity interests. And when you've got so much sudden supply coming to the market and very little demand, the floor just went out on this market.[13]

According to Humphreys, the worth of the entire U.S. circulation market was $35-40 billion. The value of Harvard's endowments evaluated in 2008 was $36.9 billion, about the same as the worth of the entire U.S. circulation market. This tells us how great an impact Harvard's action can have on the market.

When the stock market crashed, many universities lost a significant chunk of their endowments. As a university with the largest endowment in the world and the most aggressive fund management model, Harvard could not help losing more of its endowment than any other university. The following table shows Harvard's loss at 30 percent within a single year alone, far more than any other university.

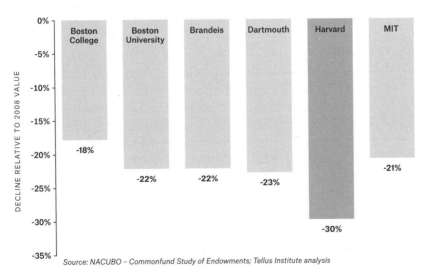

Source: NACUBO – Commonfund Study of Endowments; Tellus Institute analysis

Decline in Endowment Value during the Financial Crisis of 2008–2009.

Harvard dumped the consequences of its flawed policy onto uninvolved workers.

According to a 2009 announcement, Harvard lost about $11 billion of its endowment within one year. Harvard's loss in property funds was also enormous. The *Wall Street Journal* reported in August 2010 that Harvard sustained more than a 50 percent loss in property funds in the 2009 fiscal year.[14] The same report also included the uncomfortable news that China Investment Corporation (CIC), the country's sovereign wealth fund, was in talks with Harvard endowment to buy its property fund stakes worth about $500 million. For a while, it actually did not look very good for a mammoth institutional investor like Harvard to try to pare down its $5.4 billion real estate portfolio to reduce its exposure to illiquid assets in comparison to China's attempt to tap properties in the distressed U.S. commercial real estate sector.

HMC fund managers who had regularly raked in tens of millions of dollars of bonuses were at a loss in the face of the financial crisis. The sparks fell, though, onto other members of Harvard who had never received enormous bonuses. In June 2009, Harvard University announced its decision to lay off 275 of its employees. Harvard had already made the decision to withhold raises for about 9,000 faculty and non-union staff members for the next year. It had also offered a voluntary early retirement program to about 1,600 staff members that ultimately shed more than 500 employees.[15] In short, Harvard dumped the consequences of its flawed policy onto uninvolved service and academic employees.

According to Wayne Langley, director of higher education at Service Employees International Union Local 615, Harvard laid off about a thousand workers at that time. President Drew Faust received a 6 percent raise on her salary as a reward for her services. A considerable proportion of laid-off employees had worked at Harvard for twenty-five to thirty years. Harvard, an educational institution that always seemed proud of its educational mission, changed its face to that of an entirely business-minded entrepreneur in the face of the financial crisis. Other universities took similar measures. Some universities laid off women employees first.

Harvard's labor policies had a far-reaching impact on local communities considering it was the second largest employer in the area. Workers who lost their jobs overnight and neighboring communities where Harvard stopped its projects were all victims of Harvard's flawed investment and labor policies. In particular, Allston, site of a large Harvard development project, suffered the most.

Allston in Ruins

Allston suffered, and continues to suffer from massive collateral damage caused by Harvard's neoliberal policies. Allston is a small town across the Charles River from Cambridge that houses Harvard's main campus. Harvard Business School is located in Allston, although its residents are mostly blue-collar workers.

The history of the Harvard Allston Expansion Project goes back to Derek Bok's presidency (1971–91). Harvard's Cambridge campus was already used to full capacity at that time. Planning to expand its campus to Allston just across the Charles River, the Harvard Corporation began secretly buying land through a front company. Allston residents sold their homes and properties without knowing the buyer was Harvard University, which ended up securing a considerable bulk of the land and buildings in Allston.

Only in 1997 when Harvard University announced that it had secured about 52.6 acres of land did it become known that the real buyer was Harvard. Currently, Harvard University owns 359 acres of land in Allston, twice the size of its property in Cambridge. When you walk around the streets of Allston and neighboring Brighton, you can easily find a sign that reads, "Harvard Real Estate owns and manages this property." Although some people harshly criticized Harvard's secretive real estate purchase strategy, calling it "land pillaging," many Allston residents welcomed Harvard's expansion project. Wouldn't it be nice to have the Harvard campus in your own backyard—especially with its world's largest endowment and its name as one of the most prestigious educational institutions! Problematically, Harvard bought land without specific plans and the expansion plan for such a large institution could take more than a few decades or even a century.

Without any specific plan, Harvard drove out many small and large businesses from Allston and Brighton. Many businesses, including Volkswagen,

A flyer on an electric pole in Allston (above); enormous wall surrounding the Harvard construction site in central Allston (below).

offered workplaces to Allston residents and soon disappeared one after another, leaving mass unemployment. Harvard promised that it would offer better workplace environments, but progress was slow. As buildings were being abandoned, the remaining Allston residents' complaints became louder and more attentive to Harvard's actions.

It was President Lawrence Summers who aggressively pushed through the Allston development project. Intensely interested in stem cell research, Summers wanted to build a grand science complex. Many thought that this interest of Summers's had to do with his experience of surviving Hodgkin's lymphoma. He was known to have been shocked after discovering that his treatment had been discovered only fifteen years before.

Although it was Summers's ambition to build a large science complex housing a biotechnology center and to grow Harvard into a center of science-based industry, the project was launched only after he left. In 2007, Harvard University launched an ambitious $1 billion construction project, and Allston residents were in full support. However, before the builders could even finish the construction of the site's foundation, the financial crisis struck. Harvard announced that it would temporarily halt construction as soon as the foundation was completed. There was no mention of a future start date. About ten acres of land was dug up at the heart of Allston, and only swarms of mice frequent there to the surprise of neighbors. Abandoned buildings and unfinished construction populate Allston's desolate landscape. The sight of it alone is a blight upon the city, not to mention the deserted area welcoming petty crime and theft. It is no wonder residents who have to look at the wall surrounding the gigantic abandoned site everyday feel frustrated and furious.

According to SEIU's Wayne Langley, the financial loss to the Allston-Brighton community due to Harvard's halted construction amounts to $27 million in wages over the past three years and $86 million in other lost economic opportunities. The overall losses to the Allston community totals over $100 million. Langley stated that Harvard should have been more thoughtful with their project and argued that a university hurting local communities does not deserve tax exemption.[16]

On a cold winter evening in December of 2010, I attended the Harvard Allston Task Force meeting for my documentary film on Harvard. As Harvard announced that it was planning to resume the construction a few days previously, many residents came to attend the meeting in excited anticipation. They appeared to be very attentive to the meeting agenda, concerned with the future of their own community. The major agenda items were the proposed Harvard Innovative Lab (HIL) and Tata Hall, future home to the expanded Harvard Business School Executive Education program. When the residents found out that the agenda did not include the construction of the Allston Science Complex, many openly expressed their frustrations.

> How long is this task force supposed to go on? We already knew about what you presented today. There was no new information. I have never attended community meetings that dragged on and on in this way.
>
> What is the City doing to find financing for Harvard and also how can the City issue Harvard a building permit for 125 Western when Harvard hasn't finished the science complex project?

Complaints went on and on. One of the residents in attendance claimed the main culprits of the current financial crisis were graduates of the Harvard Business School in Allston and wondered aloud what on earth Harvard was teaching its students, eliciting laughs from the entire audience. A member of the Harvard Work Team responded that they were focusing on academic priorities and that they needed to decide what was possible in the current market. In the end, the meeting ended without any visible achievements. The Harvard Allston Task Force is currently still operating, and it is unclear how many more meetings they will need before they see clear results.

When criticized for its layoffs and the results of their aborted Allston Project, Harvard, of course, claimed that it is also a victim, saying that no one knew that Harvard would face the kind of financial difficulty in which it was mired. New information, however, continues to reveal that this is not entirely the case. Evidence shows that Harvard had been ignoring warning signs far before the 2008 financial crisis. The person who ignored it? None other than President Summers.

Summers Ignoring the Red Light

The name Lawrence Summers always comes up whenever people discuss Harvard's colossal financial losses. Summers was born into a renowned scholarly family, studied mathematics at MIT, received a PhD in economics at Harvard and became a tenured professor at the young age of twenty-eight. Having served as the U.S. secretary of the treasury at an early age, he was often praised as the most successful scholar in the political world. Some even called him the first Harvard president for whom becoming the president of Harvard would feel like climbing down the career ladder.

Scanning Summers's career, we realize that he was a neoliberal economist through and through. While chief economist of the World Bank, Summers was widely criticized for a confidential memo he signed in December 1991 after the memo was leaked and published in the *Economist*. This memo presented the corporation's justification for dumping toxic waste in Third World countries for perceived economic benefits: "I think the economic logic behind dumping a load of toxic waste in the lowest wage country is impeccable and we should face up to that. . . . The concern over an agent that causes a one in a million change in the odds of prostate cancer is obviously going to be much higher in a country where people survive to get prostate cancer than in a country where under 5 mortality is 200 per thousand."

Predictably, this memo incensed the general public and environmentalists alike. Summers became the target of fierce criticism and political furor. It was later discovered that the actual writer of the memo was Lant Pritchett, Summers's assistant at the World Bank. Pritchett had wanted to clarify this fact at the beginning of the controversy, but other staff members of the World Bank dissuaded him from doing so. Although Summers was subject to public furor, it is said that he was praised for taking the bullet for his assistant. Lant Pritchett, who wrote the memo, is now a professor at the Harvard Kennedy School of Government.

Summers's power is visible on the cover of the February 1999 issue of *Time* magazine, where Secretary of the Treasury Robert Rubin, Federal Reserve Bank Chairman Alan Greenspan, and then Deputy Secretary of the Treasury Lawrence Summers were featured under the title "The Committee to Save the World." Summers succeeded Robert Rubin to become Secretary of the Treasury the same year near the end of the Clinton administration. He became stranded, though, with the election of George W. Bush. It was then that Harvard came to his rescue by appointing him as its president. Throughout the 1990s, Harvard's endowment had rapidly grown to about $20 billion. When Harvard wanted a powerful leader to lead Harvard to continue their financial growth, Summers appeared to be the right man for the job.

During his short five-year presidency, Summers was repeatedly at the center of negative controversies. As soon as he was inaugurated, he caused friction with many professors for his arrogant management style, which he must have learned in Washington political settings. A few professors, including Cornel West, star of African American Studies, left Harvard along with a number of tenured women professors. Of course, Summers was praised for his reform of the traditional curriculum and for the introduction of unprecedented financial aid policies that waived the entire tuition bill for low-income students.

But Summers often caused controversy because of his blunt remarks. At the 2004 Harvard Summer School Welcome Party he was reported to have claimed that in Seoul "there were a million child prostitutes a generation ago and today there are almost none."[17] We can certainly interpret his remark to mean that there were once far more child prostitutes in Seoul. But as an economist, he should have known how careful one must be in quoting statistics. Seoul's population in June 1970 had just surpassed 5 million. That would mean even if 2.5 million, half of its population, were women, girls in their teens could not have surpassed a million. In other words, Summers was inadvertently claiming all underage girls in Seoul at that time were prostitutes.

In January 2005, at a National Bureau of Economic Research sponsored conference on the diversification of the science and engineering workforce, Summers sparked worldwide controversy with his discussion on why women may have been underrepresented in tenured science and engineering positions at top universities and research institutions. His argument was that women were underrepresented because "there are issues of intrinsic aptitude, and particularly of the variability of aptitude." In the end, Summers voluntarily resigned after members of the Harvard Faculty of Arts and Sciences passed a motion of "lack of confidence" and the Harvard Corporation repeatedly pressured him into resigning.

After leaving Harvard, Summers reaped high dividends as a consultant to various corporations, earning, for example, $135,000 for a single lecture at Goldman Sachs. During eight years from 2001 and 2009 and until he joined the Obama administration, Summers earned more than $20 million from financial service sector industries.[18] As director of the White House U.S. National Economic Council for President Obama, Summers repaid their favor by spearheading the Wall Street bailout.

As Harvard president, Summers encouraged the university's aggressive endowment management. Despite warnings from Jack Meyer who had been directing Harvard Management Company, Summers ordered the company to invest 100 percent of Harvard's cash, including its administrative budget. Of course, Summers was not the only one responsible for these kinds of practices; Harvard had already been doing this for some time. During Rudenstine's presidency, Harvard made $2 billion by investing its $290 million administrative budget. Still, economist Summers must have known about investing better than any of Harvard's previous presidents and greatly influenced the endowment investments. When Harvard's treasurer regretted not setting aside cash reserves in the face of the 2008 financial crisis, Summers was no longer at Harvard to take responsibility.

Back in 2002, a new employee of the Harvard Management Company named Iris Mack wrote a letter to Summers in which she warned him of the HMC's risky moves. A Harvard graduate and a derivatives specialist, Mack realized that the endowment was taking on too much risk in derivatives investment. When she approached Summers about this, she asked him to keep her communications confidential or risk making her life "a living hell." But soon afterwards, she was called into a meeting by her boss, Jack Meyer, who was holding copies of her communication with Summers. She was fired the next day.[19]

Summers continued to arrogantly ignore the warning signs. In 2005, at an annual conference of the world's leading central bankers, the chief economist of the IMF presented a paper that warned of the coming crisis. This economist warned the current bonus culture on the financial sector that rewarded bankers for actions that could destroy their own institutions, or even the entire system, could soon generate a "full-blown financial crisis" and a "catastrophic meltdown." After this presentation, Summers attacked the economist, calling him a "Luddite," and "warning that increased regulation would reduce the productivity of the financial sector."[20]

Summers proved his remarkable ability to shut down opposing opinions through personal attacks and humiliation. There is no doubt that Summers repeatedly ignored the warnings signs before America's catastrophic economic meltdown. To appoint him to the position of director of the National Economic Council was like asking the perpetrator of a crime to investigate its damage and to find a way to compensate.

Harvard Is Still Speculating

The financial crisis that began on Wall Street in 2008 drove not only the American economy but also the world economy into panic mode. Real estate prices plummeted, the domestic market shrank, companies large and small shut down, and unemployment rapidly increased. In order to save

Wall Street, the government poured more than $1 trillion in bailout money, including the initial $700 billion, onto Wall Street companies. The crisis caused by the greed of financial companies was handled with people's tax money. Nevertheless, the economy did not show any signs of recovery and ordinary people's lives were getting harder and harder. In the midst of all this, Wall Street was still on a roll. Statistics show that Wall Street traders profited more under Obama than in eight years under Bush.[21]

The same is true of Harvard. The brunt of Harvard's endowment losses was borne by Harvard educators and service employees through salary freezes, budget cuts, layoffs, and early retirement packages. Dealt with the hard blow of major project suspension, Allston turned into a ghost town. The Harvard Management Company learned a hard lesson from the 2008 financial meltdown and increased its cash reserves. According to a 2004 report, the Harvard Management Company's cash reserve rate was 2 percent of the entire fund, not a small sum, considering the size of the $27 billion endowment.

However, Harvard still holds on to an aggressive investment model and exercises global influence. In 2010, Harvard drew public scorn for purchasing, unrelated to any educational purpose, a large dairy farm worth $2.8 million in New Zealand.

In August 2011, the Oakland Institute published a shocking report, titled "Understanding Land Investment Deals in Africa," which reported that Harvard and other major American universities work through British hedge funds and European financial speculators to buy or lease vast areas of African farmland. Western media outlets had been criticizing China, India, and Middle Eastern countries for buying developing countries' lands at bargain prices. The Oakland Institute report revealed that the parties behind these veiled purchases were, in fact, American and European capital, shocking the entire world. This report and research by the World Bank suggests that foreign companies had bought or leased nearly sixty million hectares—an area the size of France—in Africa over the past three years. About 70 percent of these deals happened in Africa, and it was here to which funds flowed from American universities like Harvard, Vanderbilt, Spellman, and Iowa Universities.

According to Anuradha Mittal, the executive director of the Oakland Institute, Harvard University was the cornerstone investor of Emergent Asset Management, the UK-based hedge fund firm involved in these deals.[22] Although a Harvard University spokesperson declined to comment, Mittal claimed that the Emergent Asset Management had told the institute that they were contractually obligated to not talk about Harvard's role as an investor. Mittal pointed out that this disclaimer itself was proof of Harvard's hand in the whole affair.

Some may argue that an infusion of Western capital into Africa could lead to quicker development and improved quality of life. This, however, could not end up being further from the truth. In Ethiopia, 700,000 natives were about to be kicked out of their ancestral land. In Samana Dugu in 2010, bulldozers moved in to clear great swathes of land. Men, women, and children from the community protested but were met by police who savagely beat and arrested them. In Tanzania, 162,000 Burundi refugees who had been farming the land for almost forty years are now facing forced eviction.

The report also points out that the argument by investors that foreign capital investment in agriculture would spur economic development and job creation has not resulted in those promised benefits. For example, investors claimed that they could create several thousand jobs by developing a 100,000 hectares farm in Africa. But how many jobs could this area of land support? According to a UN report only two hectares are enough for an African farmer to feed his or her family. So what is actually happening is that a large farm capable of employing only a few thousand jobs is replacing land that could employ and sustain at least 50,000 families. As a result, the remaining 45,000 families would be left to find their own land or alternative employment.[23]

Through this kind of aggressive and daring investment strategy, the Harvard endowment in 2011 rose by 21.4 percent in comparison to 2010 to $32 billion. This is remarkable, considering that the world as well as the U.S. economy was still struggling with a recession. The risk still remains, though. Although the Harvard Management Company increased its cash reserves, there is no guarantee that they will not face another crisis as long as they insist on their risky investment model. In fact, it is very difficult to find out where and how Harvard invests. Social organizations strongly urge that university funds should offer more transparency. Dr. Joshua Humphreys argues that universities like Harvard should carefully consider the influence their investment will have on their society, economy, and environment:

> When you start to deal with large institutional investors like Harvard University, the stewardship geography is basically the entire world because the footprint of the Harvard endowment is global. And the impacts on the environment, on society, [and] on the communities, in which those companies and instruments, in which Harvard invests, really reach across the entire globe. And what's tragic is that rarely do institutions like Harvard actually take the environmental and social impact of their investment seriously into consideration when they make those kinds of trades.[24]

Imagine the positive effect that more thoughtful investments by universities like Harvard could have! If they were to refuse to invest in environment-polluting companies, union-busting corporations, and countries ruled by savage dictators, their impact could be enormous.

As long as universities enjoy tax exemption privileges as nonprofit organizations, they must manage their funds more safely and transparently. Legal and systemic measures that can monitor their fund management should be introduced and implemented as soon as possible. By exempting universities from taxation, society is taking on considerable burdens for their sake. Also, concentrating power in a very limited minority, especially a minority in control of industries and the general financial climate, is a critical cause of problems that universities face today. Universities should be managed in a different manner than for-profit corporations. It is simply shocking that only seven different individuals have made all university policy decisions, including ones related to an endowment like Harvard's which has more capital than some countries' entire GNPs.

The change in the way universities have managed their endowments is only one aspect of the overall neoliberal university management method. An even more serious consequence of neoliberalism is the deterioration of the universities' mission. If universities subjected themselves to state and governmental intelligence agencies in the past, they have now become subservient to corporations. Universities are now not where knowledge is produced, but where knowledge capable of generating money is produced. Professors take for granted that they are supported by corporations related to their specialty, enjoying the respect and admiration accompanying multi-sponsor support.

The reality of professors getting sponsored by corporations has gone on for some time now. For example, Professor Martin Feldstein, the George F. Baker Professor of Economics at Harvard University, drafted deregulation policies as chairman of the Council of Economic Advisors and chief economic advisor to President Reagan. Since then, he has served as the president of the National Bureau of Economic Research (1977–82; currently, he is its president emeritus) as well as a board member for twenty years. He has made more than $6 million in this capacity.[25] Derivatives of AIG Financial Products, whose board Feldstein was also on, destroyed the company in 2008, and, subsequently, contributed to the 2008 Financial Crisis. The U.S. government had to pour $180 billion in bailout money into AIG to rescue it from its self-inflicted crisis. In the award-winning documentary about the 2008 financial crisis, *Inside Job*, one of the film directors asks Feldstein if he didn't have any regrets serving as a board member for AIG. Feldstein's answer was a proud "Absolutely none!"

As society becomes more aware of the role scholars played in the financial crisis, public consensus is growing concerning the need to apply more strict moral codes to professors. Harvard is no exception. In 2009, a group of Harvard Medical School students raised questions about their professors' work as paid consultants to pharmaceutical companies. Students formed a committee that investigated the connection between Harvard Medical School faculty, drug companies, and other related industries. One professor's disclosure listed no fewer than forty-seven company affiliations.[26] As a result of the committee's investigation, Harvard Medical School has been more strictly applying its conflict of interest policy since 2010. Of course, Harvard is not the only university that has this problem. As I discussed, it has been some time since education became a mere business. But now that the 99 percent have risen up against the 1 percent, exploring alternative systems should start at the universities that were the origin of ideological distortion and deterioration. Could it be that Harvard students walked out on their star economist's class because they recognized this fact? Those students raised the standard of revolt against not only a conservative economist but also against a form of neoliberalism that has thoroughly corrupted contemporary university education. And this was indeed "just the beginning."

CHAPTER 10

HARVARD AT A CROSSROADS

"Universities no longer train students to think critically, to examine and critique systems of power and cultural and political assumptions, to ask the broad questions of meaning and morality once sustained by the humanities. These institutions have transformed themselves into vocational schools. They have become breeding grounds for systems managers trained to serve the corporate state."
—Chris Hedges, journalist[1]

On November 9, 2011, amid the worldwide spread of the Occupy Wall Street movement, hundreds of Harvard students also "occupied" their campus to show their solidarity with the Occupy movement and to protest Harvard's alliance with the top 1 percent. Dozens of tents filled the yard in front of the statue of John Harvard—ordinarily surrounded by tourists—a mere week after students had walked out of Professor Mankiw's class. This walkout would turn out to be more than a one-time event. It would signal the beginning of a lengthy fight.

Among other things, protesting Harvard students primarily found issue with "the corporatization of higher education."[2] The students' list of Harvard's corporate misdeeds was endless: the Harvard Management Company's highest-paid fund manager earning 180 times more than entry-level Harvard employees; outsourcing a significant portion of its staff jobs under the pretext of efficiency and adopting oppressive anti-union policies; purchasing African lands at low prices and subsequently removing indigenous peoples from their homes and devastating their environment; investing in rogue corporations that "profit off the backbreaking labor of a non-union immigrant workforce"; refusing to maintain financial transparency despite their impact on local communities. Their list went on and on.

Tents in Harvard Yard; students demanded fundamental changes in Harvard's management.

Students argued that Harvard needs to become a university for the 99 percent. For this goal, they demanded the university offer: "academic opportunities to assess responses to socioeconomic inequality outside the scope of mainstream economics"; implementation of "debt relief for students who suffer from excessive loan burdens"; commitment to "increasing the diversity" of Harvard's faculty and students; an end to admission privileges given to legacy students; and implementation of "a policy requiring faculty to declare conflicts of interest."

When news of Harvard students' campus occupation got out, Occupy Boston participants and interested neighbors gathered near Harvard Square in order to show their support to the students. Afraid of the movement's possible growth, Harvard University locked the gates to Harvard Yard and allowed only people with a Harvard identity card to enter. Although administrators claimed that this was a measure to protect Harvard students, it was clear that their claim was an excuse to curtail the movement's growth. Harvard University mobilized not only their own security guards but also the Cambridge police, who asked everyone attempting to enter to present a university ID card. Even reporters were denied entrance. Ordinarily something of a tourist attraction, visitors were now summarily dismissed, receiving nothing but the explanation that Harvard was "private property" as a reason for being denied entry.

As this campus lockdown continued, not only students but also professors began to rally in support of Occupy Harvard participants. More than a hundred professors signed a statement supporting them. As expected, there were members of Harvard who did not support this movement. In particular, the *Harvard Crimson* printed an editorial strongly critical of the Occupy Harvard movement, calling it a "disgrace" to the school's name. It stood flatly opposed to the students' stance that Harvard should become a "university for the 99 percent."

A Harvard degree opens an avenue to American society's 1 percent, and it is a ticket that allows us to achieve almost anything we set our minds to. As students of an elite institution, we have been given the tools to succeed in all walks of life—whether that success is defined in strictly financial terms or not.[3]

According to the *Crimson* editorial, Harvard students never entered an institution for the 99 percent in the first place; it would be a contradiction in terms if students demanded Harvard to become one. I wonder what these Harvard students learn if they consider a Harvard degree merely a ticket to climb the ladder of success. This editorial also claimed that the Occupy Wall Street movement is rooted in people's frustration in times of depression, that their anger towards the 1 percent simply reflects "the fears and concerns of a group looking for something better than what they have." It is frightening to think that this is how some of the future American elite and world leaders think.

In mid-December, Occupy Harvard chose to dismantle its Harvard Yard camp, citing frigid winter weather and their desire for the Yard's gates to reopen. They continued to maintain one information tent, a single weatherproof dome. The university administration welcomed this decision and declared that it would open the gates from 7 a.m. to 10 p.m.. In mid-January, though, as soon as students returned from winter vacation, Harvard surreptitiously took down the single remaining tent. Students protested with a sign, "You Cannot Evict an Idea."

This Occupy Harvard movement has a deeper significance than previous campus occupations by Harvard students. Its demands were more

A sign protesting Harvard's taking down the information tent.

about a fundamental change in the philosophy of the university's management than single issues like raising staff salaries or improving financial aid. This is most likely why the media and local communities alike paid attention to their movement. As has always been the case, Harvard's policies will have significant impact on other educational institutions. Unfortunately, Harvard has not always made the right decision when faced with protests—whether they come from within or from the outside. Among many events, the Martin Peretz incident of 2011 is a prime illustration.

Honoring a "Racist Fool"

On September 25, 2011, the 50th anniversary celebration of Harvard's Social Studies program was held at Harvard's Science Center in Cambridge. Along with the auspices of the occasion, this anniversary was particularly notable in that it was chosen to honor Martin Peretz for the launch of a $650,000 research fund in his name. In response, over a hundred members of the Harvard community along with local community activists gathered in front of the building holding placards and pickets to confront Peretz. They followed him for several minutes, chanting the slogan "Harvard, Harvard, shame on you for honoring a racist fool!"

So who is Martin Peretz? An American publisher who received his BA from Brandeis University and his MA and PhD from Harvard, Peretz purchased the *New Republic* in 1974 and served as its editor-in-chief for almost four decades. Under his leadership, the *New Republic* maintained neoliberal positions on economic and social issues, and assumed pro-Israel stances in foreign affairs, openly attacking those who advocated policies unfavorable to Israel or in favor of Palestine. When Professor Safran's CIA scandal broke out in the mid-1980s, he defended Safran, saying he was "a remarkably honest, dispassionate scholar." Consistently antagonistic towards non-whites, especially Muslims, Peretz posted a very provocative editorial online in early September 2011:

> But, frankly, Muslim life is cheap, most notably to Muslims. And among those Muslims led by Imam Rauf there is hardly one who has

"The stark fact is that the educated black middle and upper-middle classes do not go museums, and they do go to concerts either"

The New Republic, February 6th 1995

Martin Peretz (right) and protesters.

raised a fuss about the routine and random bloodshed that defines their brotherhood. So, yes, I wonder whether I need honor these people and pretend that they are worthy of the privileges of the First Amendment, which I have in my gut the sense that they will abuse.[4]

His article raised a huge controversy. Major media outlets and netizens strongly denounced his position. Peretz responded by issuing a statement on September 13. Regarding his statement about Muslims and the First Amendment he said, "I wrote that, but I do not believe that." Peretz also claimed that his comment that "Muslim life is cheap, most notably to Muslims" was "a statement of fact, not of value."

Nonetheless, Harvard decided to honor him on the 50th anniversary of its Social Studies program. Peretz and his cohorts collected $500,000 to commemorate his past career as an assistant professor in this program, and the university honored him by launching the fund in his name. When this plan was revealed, many argued that it should be immediately halted. They watched Harvard's response carefully.

As denouncements mounted among students, alumni, and local communities, Harvard decided to exclude Peretz from the event's speakers. But, claiming "free speech," Harvard decided to proceed with its original plan to create an undergraduate research fund in his name. The following is an excerpt from Harvard's statement: "It is central to the mission of a university to protect and affirm free speech, including the rights of Dr. Peretz, as well as those who disagree with him, to express their views. . . .

The fund [in honor of Peretz] will enable undergraduates to undertake significant research experiences as part of the social sciences curriculum and strengthen our commitment to rigorous intellectual inquiry."[5]

Harvard's statement began with "free speech," but ended with the importance of the fund. In short, Harvard was saying that it could not give up $500,000. Even more comically, as the public outcry persisted, Peretz's friends collected more donations, raising the total to $650,000. Despite continuing opposition, Harvard maintained its position, angering members of the Harvard community: "[Martin Peretz] has been very vocal about his hatred and his bigotry towards people of color. But Harvard doesn't have a right to honor him in her name. We think it is a scandal that, after so much controversy and so much anger expressed, Harvard's still going to continue with this."[6]

This was not, however, the first instance of Harvard accepting money somewhat shamelessly. On September 26, 2001, when everyone was still shaken by the events of 9/11, the BBC reported that Harvard received millions of dollars in donations from the family of Osama Bin Laden in the 1990s. The Cambridge City Council voted for a proposal that the university donate the entire $5 million it had received from the Bin Ladens to support the 9/11 victims' families. Harvard, however, replied that it had already set aside $1 million in a fund for scholarships for the victims' families, and that the Bin Laden family had only given $2 million total to the university.[7]

Like many people, I find the way Harvard handled the Martin Peretz scandal deplorable. Whether renowned individuals like Al Gore donated in Peretz's honor or not is inessential to the matter. Harvard should have condemned the values Peretz's racist and bigoted article implied. Peretz has the right to "free speech," but as an elite educational institution, Harvard should have been mindful of its responsibilities when making policy decisions. Due to Harvard's handling of this incident, it ended up betraying its own effort of the last several decades to become a truly all-embracing global university.

In 2011, Harvard University shocked the world again when a research study announced that Harvard was clandestinely buying vast areas of African farmland through hedge funds. One result of some of their purchases would be to force thousands of people off their land. The actions of one of the world's elite institutions make us wonder what is the true purpose of universities, and of higher education in general.

A Factory of "Red Guards" for the Empire

Since the financial crisis of 2008, we have witnessed a number of signs of the decline of the United States. At the end of World War II, Harvard University ascended together with the American empire, so it may not be so surprising that it has been subject to disgraceful scandals over and over. Yet this dynamic is not true only of Harvard. Harvard's crisis signifies the crisis of American higher education itself.

For the past three decades, the process of corporatizing universities has accelerated as neoliberal structures have firmly taken root in society. While universities have been busy making money, basic studies have been withering. We can now find expressions like "ivory tower" or "palace of knowledge" only in ancient encyclopedias. Under a neoliberal system, universities have become corporations marketing education for the sole purpose of producing profit. Scholars who should be engaging students in critical thinking are instead shuttling back and forth between universities and industries as industrial spies and consultants.

In ancient societies like Greece and China, education was offered only to a handful of aristocrats for the purpose of reproducing the ruling class. This was true of early America as well. But the third president of the United States, Thomas Jefferson, raised a question about this practice. In a letter to John Adams, Jefferson wrote that education should be given to the "natural aristocracy" based on "virtue and talents" rather than the "artificial aristocracy founded on wealth and birth."[8] In other words, Jefferson believed that people should be given equal access to education. His wish materialized through the system of public education.

James Conant, who became president of Harvard in 1933, is often considered to have actively put Jeffersonian ideas into practice. He believed that more students with talents should be given the opportunity to receive a high quality education. Thus, he actively used tests like the SAT in order to find better-qualified students. Of course, this "opportunity" was limited to students with talent, and an educational system based on elitism took root. To Conant, a typical power-hungry intellectual, power was as important for a university as scholarship.

University education became widely available to the general public during World War II. The Servicemen's Readjustment Act (the GI Bill) was legislated in 1944, and it included cash payments of tuition and living expenses for returning soldiers and veterans to attend college, high school, or vocational school. By the end of the program in 1956, roughly 2.2 million veterans had used the GI Bill's education benefits in order to attend college or university. University education was no longer an exceptional privilege given to a small minority. Behind the U.S. government's encouragement was its intention to build a stronger country through education. As a result, education became a tool to produce "red guards" of the American empire.

Professor Noam Chomsky observed, "If you're going to Oxford or Cambridge, part of the elite, you just have inculcated into you the understanding there are certain things it wouldn't do to say. For that matter, you don't even think, that is the primary, that's the indoctrinating function of universities."[9]

Since the 1970s, when neoliberalism was introduced and tuition began to soar, people could no longer go to college without worrying about the costs. These days, most American students graduate from college with enormous student loan debts. According to a November 2, 2011, *New York Times* article, "students who graduated from college in 2010 with student loans owed an average of $25,250."[10] Students were also facing "an unemployment rate for new college graduates of 9.1 percent, the highest in recent years." The myth of the so-called "American dream" repeatedly propagated through cultural media like Hollywood movies is now possible only in stories.

Professor Chomsky discusses political intentions hidden behind this brutal tuition burden. Noticing that countries with lower national per capita income often offer free higher education, he argues that today's high tuition is a sort of control mechanism rather than the result of economic necessity.

> It [raising tuition] is not economically necessary. I mean, for example, there's Mexico. It's a poor country. Now they have a quite good national university—several in fact. They are free. . . . In a poor country, it's free. If you go to a rich country, say, California, richest place in the world, maybe, the tuition is astronomical. [It is] to control. It's partly a form of segregation. You keep the wrong people out. But, partly it's just a system of control. A young person decides to go to law school to be a public interest lawyer and they come out of law school, with $100,000 in debt. They are going to work in a corporate law firm because they have no choice. And once you're in it, it's very hard to get out of. You internalize the culture.[11]

Complaints about heavy tuition costs erupted all over the world even before the Occupy Wall Street movement. In March 2010, for example, students in California led a statewide protest against education budget cuts and tuition hikes. Led by UC Berkeley students, Oakland area students occupied a nearby highway for four days. Around the same period, students in about a hundred universities in thirty-two U.S. states protested against tuition raises through strikes and rallies. In Britain, after the Conservative-Liberal Democrat coalition government had announced that it decided to raise the cap on tuition fees from £3,290 to £9,000, some fifty-two thousand university students marched on the streets of central London, protesting against planned spending cuts to higher education and a raised cap on tuition fees. Students declared in a statement that they were against "the marketization of education" and "the Tory system of attacking the poor and helping the rich." They also declared, "This is only the beginning."[12]

A Poison Called Elitism

In 1936, Harvard sent invitations to a host of scholars, politicians, and other VIPs to its 300th anniversary celebration. Not all invitees accepted. Albert Einstein declined the invitation to protest against Harvard's guest list, which included scholars who had collaborated with the Nazis. Dramatist George Bernard Shaw went further and sent a provocative letter of reply: "If Harvard would celebrate its 300th anniversary by burning itself to the ground and sowing its site with salt, the ceremony would give me the liveliest satisfaction as an example to all the other famous corrupters of youth, including Yale, Oxford, Cambridge, the Sorbonne, etc. etc. etc."[13]

This commentary contains a witty but solemn warning against elitism, in which renowned universities produce the ruling elite and diplomas determine one's social class. Despite warnings like these, though, elitism has intensified since then, and elite universities have grown tremendously. Among them, so-called Ivy League colleges including Harvard University have an exceptional influence on our society.

The Ivy League includes eight elite New England universities: Harvard, Yale, Brown, Columbia, Cornell, Dartmouth, Princeton, and Penn. Traditionally, these eight universities have almost exclusively produced important political and economic figures in America, and nowadays, they produce a large share of world leaders. A diploma from these colleges is considered a gold ticket guaranteeing one's bright future, and so the competition to enter these colleges is fierce. The policy adopted by these colleges of offering preferences to legacy students enables the inheritance of power and wealth, and reproduces the current state of inequality in the American university education system.

Given the privileges awaiting graduates of these Ivy League colleges, our society's obsession with them is not surprising at all. Professor emeritus of education Charles Willie, a Harvard sociologist, contended in my interview with him that the biggest problem facing contemporary education is that it offers only one definition of excellence. Willie argues that although grades are used to measure an individual's excellence, they are only one standard to judge an individual's potential.

Professor Willie, a close friend of Dr. Martin Luther King Jr., illustrated his point through an episode involving Reverend King. As is well known, King was a world-renowned leader and orator. His "I Have a Dream" speech is remembered as one of the finest in modern human history. King was not an all-A student during college, however. He even got a C on a public speech course. Professor Willie laughed, saying that something must have been wrong with the class or its standard for excellence. He emphasized that small colleges or state universities have advantages over Harvard in some areas, so it is unreasonable to compare all educational institutions equally.

Many different educational institutions can contribute to society with their different strengths.[14]

Unfortunately, universities are hierarchized, allegedly allowing entrance based on merit while a small minority of elite university graduates monopolizes power. Those who stand at the top after passing through their courses act as if they, the elite and professionals, are the only ones who know how to handle the truth. Their beliefs are distributed through media columns and textbooks, and solidified as absolute truths. Knowledge that does not conform to mainstream discourse is fated to abandonment and dereliction. Professor Chomsky considers an intellectual someone who analyzes and interprets social reality, a sort of an arbiter in that sense. Pointing out that intellectual interpretations are often systematically distorted, Chomsky provides a warning of the ideological controls behind such distortions.

> ...one must be careful not to give the impression, which in any event is false, that only intellectuals equipped with special training are capable of such analytic work. In fact that is just what the intelligentsia would often like us to think: they pretend to be engaged in an esoteric enterprise, inaccessible to simple people. But that's nonsense. The social sciences generally, and above all the analysis of contemporary affairs, are quite accessible to anyone who wants to take an interest in these matters. The alleged complexity, depth, and obscurity of these questions is part of the illusion propagated by the system of ideological control... in the analysis of social and political issues it is sufficient to face the facts and to be willing to follow a rational line of argument.[15]

As society becomes more specialized and fractured, intellectuals have a more important role to play. Their policies have far-reaching consequences. During my interview with John Trumpbour, he argued that we should look at educational institutions more critically than we are used to doing. He especially felt that, although we tend to automatically think of Harvard when considering the world's top universities, Harvard has not always chosen excellence over power. On the contrary, Harvard sometimes sacrificed excellence in order to serve power. Dr. Trumpbour rhetorically asks who else, other than those "excellent" Harvard men, could be responsible for the current crisis since numerous Harvard men control the destiny of the world's financial systems. We have to carefully watch the actions and policies of elite educational institutions in order to become better able to build a fairer society.

Harvard at a Crossroads

Can Harvard change and become a university for the 99 percent? Many wonder if, indeed, it can. On December 7, 2011, at Harvard's Science Center and in the midst of the Occupy movement, Harvard students and local

Teach-in discussing Harvard's future direction.

residents hosted a teach-in to investigate this possibility. Nine people
made brief presentations on different topics and discussions followed. The discussion topics were
as follows:

- Fear and Power
- Why Has Inequality Grown in
  America? And What Should We
  Do About it?
- The Occupy Movement and
  Student Debt Refusal
- Heterodox Economics: Alternatives to Mankiw's Ideology
- Wall Street's Role in the European Financial Crisis
- Booms and Busts: The Legal Dynamics of Modern Money
- Slavery and American Capitalism
- Economics for the 99 percent
- Vigilance, Inquiry, Alienation & Hope at Harvard and in the USA

Harvard students participating in the Occupy movement had organized the event, which reflected the students' serious intentions to explore
the movement's direction and realistic alternatives to the current system
at Harvard and in American society. One anonymous audience member
expressed his surprise and happiness regarding the general atmosphere of
the public forum, saying this was the first serious and sincere discussion he

had attended since the anti–Vietnam War era. There were many students who expressed their frustrations at the lack of progress after a month's participation in the Occupy movement. One student was on the verge of tears, saying that a security guard had written down his name and major on the first day of the occupation under the university administration's order. He was worried that he might be disadvantaged in the next semester's financial aid program.

Some might ask if a handful of students' camping-out could bring change to Harvard, or, even if that were to happen, if change at Harvard could bring change to the world. I have heard these questions many times at the screenings of my documentary film *Verita$: Everybody Loves Harvard*. Still, I believe that Harvard will change. Just imagine Harvard a hundred years ago. There were eugenicists. Women were not allowed entrance into Harvard. African American students were not allowed to live in dorms. And Harvard students went to bust workers' strikes. Harvard gentlemen of that time might pass out if they saw Harvard today. Harvard has been changing and is still changing. For example, although selection of Harvard's president has always been the exclusive business of Harvard fellows and overseers, after the dishonorable resignation of Lawrence Summers, Harvard changed this practice slightly to include a handful of students and professors in the selection process.

Substantial changes, of course, cannot happen overnight. They are products of constant demands and struggles, the combined efforts of the students, faculty, and staff members. This struggle is happening even at this very moment. Therefore, it is not entirely impossible for Harvard to become a university for the 99 percent in the next century.

The most important reasons why I believe in the possibility of Harvard changing is that it does not want to discard its traditional image as a progressive institution, and that it enjoys enormous human and material resources. Professor Maple Razsa (Global Studies, Colby College), one of the leaders of the 2001 Harvard living wage campaign, said that he felt shocked when he entered Harvard graduate school after attending a much smaller college. He found Harvard students arrogant and the magnitude of available material resources vastly different from his own experience. To him, it was like the difference between night and day. Due to the advantages he witnessed at Harvard, Professor Razsa argues Harvard is in a better position to carry out subversive activities and to generate a greater public interest in them. As university students' movements enabled Nike to become the symbol of overseas sweatshops, Harvard could lead public opinion on major social issues.

Another reason why I believe in the possibility of change at Harvard is that many intellectuals of the world gather there. Of course, many of them will taste and enjoy the power and privilege that only Harvard can

Bread and Puppet Theater performance in support of the Occupy Movement.

offer and become pro-American elites. But it is also possible that they could open their horizons and nurture their interests in global issues through their interactions with others. As Dr. Elaine Bernard observed:

> People with various viewpoints come from all over the world to Harvard. Harvard professors and administrators might think that they come to learn from us. But the best things they learn is what they, people from all over the world, learn from one another during their brief stay here. Some might be happy that they achieved their lifelong goal, and others could be disappointed in Harvard's reality, finding it different from what they expected. Others might also be shouting joyfully for having this opportunity to meet people from all kinds of backgrounds. Where else could we meet people with so many different viewpoints? Harvard might think that these outsiders learn from us, but it is more likely that they are not really interested in Harvard itself, because we're declining.[16]

On January 25, 2012, a performance by Bread and Puppet Theater was held in support of the Occupy Movements of the world in front of the John Harvard statue in Harvard Yard.[17] Audience members and participants had criticized the university's surprise take-down of the Occupy Movement tent and declared that this was only a beginning of their struggle. In their pamphlet they parodied Harvard's badge of *veritas*. They replaced "*veritas*" with "occupy" and encapsulated it with the Latin declaration *Corruptio Optimi Pessima*—"the corruption of the best is the worst of all."

At Harvard's 375th anniversary, a poster on campus features the Occupy Harvard logo with the proverb "The corruption of the best is the worst of all."

It was an original and strongly worded slogan, summarizing the significance of the Occupy movement well. It was ironic, though, that they still called themselves "the best," possibly revealing some shades of their own lingering sense of elitism.

On October 14, 2011, Harvard celebrated its 375th anniversary with a school festival. Unfortunately, it rained heavily that day, turning a festive occasion into a fairly messy affair. The Harvard lawn turned into mud, and various events had to be postponed under the pouring rain. A netizen left a comment on the events of the day, saying it served Harvard right.

Do you remember George Bernard Shaw's comment that he would have been happy if, to celebrate its anniversary, Harvard burned itself to the ground? If members of Harvard University don't want to be subject to the kind of sneers they received as their anniversary went awry, then perhaps they should explore a new direction as an educational institution rather than as a power group. If there are those who still take privileges of the top 1 percent for granted and set their entrance to that group as their priority, then they should remember the lessons of the French Revolution.

TIME TO STOP THE MAD DASH

"The more a ruling class is able to assimilate the foremost minds of a ruled class, the more stable and dangerous becomes its rule."
—Karl Marx

In the fall of 2005, I was studying English at Harvard Extension School. One day, the instructor brought a video of a politician's address together with a printout of his words. That was the first time I learned about Barack Obama. His speech was impressive—powerful and persuasive. It was as if John F. Kennedy had been reincarnated. Even more impressive, however, were my teacher's words at the end of the class: "Remember this politician. He will be an important figure within a few years."

My instructor may not have had anything specific in mind, but I immediately felt that Obama had a chance of becoming the next president. When I told my classmates, they all seemed skeptical. Hillary Clinton had been preparing for her candidacy for some time. Obama was merely a young rising star who could deliver a good speech. Within three years, Obama had accomplished what seemed impossible and won the Democratic Party nomination. When Obama was elected president in the winter of 2008, the world celebrated, talking of hope and change in America. I was not at all surprised. It just confirmed to me Harvard's firm influence on the world.

Higher Education Goes Astray

The world's most renowned university. The place where the best and the brightest gather. The highest brand of the higher education. These are some of the epithets used to describe Harvard University. When we examine Harvard's history, we cannot help feeling shocked by its true identity. These questions have to do with the question of higher education's larger purpose.

The twentieth century was a period during which higher education expanded more widely than any time in human history. We might call it the century of education. But, what is the result of higher education's expansion? Those with education form critical social networks and monopolize money and power. Although getting a secure job through the knowledge and technology acquired in university is one of many reasons why people get educations, many consider this the only reason.

Education is a process of growth, a process of developing and materializing an individual's potential, and a process through which an individual learns to understand others, society, history, culture, and nature more deeply and to embrace them. Shouldn't the ultimate goal of higher education be creating a civil society in which more people live equally and happily?

Some might argue that we should pay attention, above all, to the issue of "equal opportunity" in higher education. However, "equal opportunity" can serve as an excuse to make us gloss over the system in which elitism intensifies and deepens so many other inequalities. What's really important is to change the system in which education is used simply as a stepping-stone for success. Learning should not only be a means of moving up in social class, but a joy in and of itself. We feel happy because we can be liberated through learning about ourselves and the world around us.

Shameful Past Mostly Covered Up

It has been a while since education was subsumed by capitalism and the university became a training site for the elite ruling class. The university has become a reactionary institution that works to maintain and safeguard the status quo. If in the past it was one's family that decided one's class, these days it is one's education that decides it. Together with one's economic situation, education has become one of the absolute measures defining one's worth as a human being. This is true globally. In Ankara, where I screened my documentary, *Verita$: Everybody Loves Harvard*, the mostly university student audience noted that the problems of Harvard were often the same as theirs.

This is no surprise, as quite a few universities in the world are modeled after American universities—and Harvard University in particular. Perhaps because *veritas* is Harvard's motto, many universities across the world feature the word in their motto as well. The motto of Seoul National University, the top university in Korea, for example, is *"veritas lux mea."* It was probably modeled after Harvard's *"veritas"* and Yale's *"lux et veritas."* On the Harvard campus, we can find *"veritas"* inscribed everywhere—on the buildings and even on trash cans. Perhaps that is how deeply and proudly Harvard University feels about its commitment to truth.

Yet, as we have examined in this book, Harvard University seems to have been busy pursuing power and capital rather than truth. The public's belief that Harvard University is a progressive institution pursuing truth and freedom is only half true. Ascending along with the American empire, Harvard has played a key role as a strategic institute, producing ruling ideologies for the empire. This fact is mostly ignored or concealed, partly due to the enormous influence and reputation of Harvard.

The Veritas logo is found everywhere on the Harvard campus.

People still passionately yearn for the renowned educational institution that is Harvard. The gleaming left foot of the John Harvard statue, rubbed raw by so many aspiring visitors, is proof of these longings. How many of these tourists return to their homes with the knowledge of the true reality of Harvard? It is not easy to comprehend Harvard's true identity, so well hidden behind its prestigious name. Coming to an accurate understanding of Harvard, though, could be the first step to understanding today's U.S. and capital-centered world.

ABOUT THE AUTHOR

Shin Eun-jung was both a film director and an author. She was born in Gwangju, South Korea, in 1972. Her hometown's historic uprising against the South Korean military dictatorship in 1980 had a profound effect on her, propelling her into a lifetime of activism. While studying psychology at Chonnam National University, she participated in Korea's legendary student movement. After graduation, she worked as a television news writer for nine years at the Korean Broadcast System and Gwangju Broadcast Company. From 2000 to 2004, she directed the Gwangju Human Rights Film Festival, which screened documentaries from around the world. For five years, she taught college courses in TV scriptwriting in addition to other classes.

In 2004, she married American scholar-activist George Katsiaficas and moved to Boston. In the summer of 2005, she studied English—her first encounter with Harvard University. She attended many public events sponsored by Harvard's Kennedy School, the Korea Institute, and other Harvard and MIT sites. Back in Gwangju from 2008 to 2009, she taught documentary filmmaking at the Media Center in Gwangju. Her students there inspired her to make her own documentaries.

In 2009, she collaborated on two films. The first, produced with Choi Seong-uk, dealt with a serious dispute over demolition of the old Provincial Hall building, site of the last stand of the 1980 uprising. The building was slated to be torn down for construction of a mammoth Asian Cultural Center (designed by a Harvard graduate). A struggle led by family members of those who had been killed in the military's assault secured the preservation of part of it. Together with a women's media group, her second film portrayed the lives of female merchants who had worked for decades in Dae-in market, one of the oldest traditional markets in Gwangju. Returning to Boston in 2010, she finished a ten-minute English-language video about the Gwangju Uprising. That film was shown as the opening movie at an international conference commemorating the uprising's thirtieth anniversary and is available on YouTube (http://www.youtube.com/watch?v=iNPljovArCg).

After she returned to Boston in 2010, she initiated a new documentary project about Harvard University. As she came to realize Harvard's

Shin Eun-jung.

incredible influence, she wanted to uncover the origin of its enormous powers. For more than a year, she conducted extensive research and interviewed many American intellectuals. Through *Verita$: Everybody Loves Harvard*, her hope was to help people understand Harvard's real history, which is all too often unrecognized in public discussions. For *Verita$*, she was awarded Best Director of a Documentary at the 2011 New York International Film Festival. The film was also selected and screened in festivals in Turkey, Korea, and San Francisco.

Shin Eun-jung's work always sought to find truth and seek justice by challenging views that do not penetrate surface appearances. In less than two years before her tragic death in 2012, she produced Korean and English versions of *Verita$*, published a Korean book version that expanded upon the film, and began translating that book into English.

In her memory, the Director Shin Eun-jung Documentary Prize was established. More information can be found at the website for her films, VeritasTheFilm.com

ACKNOWLEDGEMENTS

This book was originally published in 2011 in Korean. Before she suddenly passed away in November 2012, Shin Eun-jung was hard at work translating the book with the help of Cassandra Katsiaficas. Seung Hee Jeon completed the translation. John Trumpbour and George Katsiaficas lightly edited the manuscript. Inez Hedges and Victor Wallace updated and revised the chapter on Harvard's Role in Russian Economic "Reform." Thomas Kleczka constructed a website, VeritasTheFilm.com, where Shin Eun-jung's films can be found.

Interviews with the following people were immensely helpful:

Ngo Vinh Long, Harvard College Class of 1968, currently professor of history, University of Maine: 9/18/10.

Noam Chomsky, Harvard University Society of Fellows 1951–1955, professor emeritus of linguistics and philosophy, MIT: 11/5/10; 9/10/11.

Wayne Langley, higher education director, Service Employees Union: 11/12/10.

John Trumpbour, Harvard University PhD in history, currently research director, Labor and Worklife Program, Harvard Law School: 7/22/10; 8/12/10; 9/9/10; 9/19/10.

Richard Levins, professor of population sciences at Harvard School of Public Health: 11/2/10

Margaret Gullette, Harvard University PhD, currently a resident scholar at the Women's Studies Research Center at Brandeis University: 11/19/10.

Michael Ansara, Harvard College class of 1968, co-chair and regional organizer for SDS: 9/16/10.

Maple Razsa, Harvard University PhD in anthropology, 2007; professor, Colby College, 9/17/10.

Victor Wallis, Harvard College class of 1958, currently professor of general education, Berklee College of Music: 9/8/10.

Edward J. Baker, former Associate Director of the Harvard-Yenching Institute: 8/21/10.

Janine R. Wedel, university professor in the School of Public Policy at George Mason University and a Senior Research Fellow of the New America Foundation: 10/23/10.

George Katsiaficas, associate in research, Harvard Korea Institute, 2006–2008; visiting scholar, Harvard Center for European Studies, 1993–94; currently Professor of Humanities at Wentworth Institute of Technology: 9/24/10.

David McCann, Harvard University professor of Korean literature: 10/5/10.

Jonathan Beckwith, professor in the Department of Microbiology and Molecular Genetics at Harvard Medical School: 11/1/10.

Charles Willie, Harvard University professor emeritus of education: 1/6/11.

Joshua Humphreys taught at Harvard, Princeton, and NYU; currently a fellow at Tellus Institute: 11/18/10.

PHOTO SOURCES

Prologue
p.2   Choi Seong-uk
p.2   Choi Seong-uk
p.2   Choi Seong-uk
p.3   Choi Seong-uk

Chapter 1 Profiling Harvard
p.8   Image of cartoon, NEA, Inc., 1966: found in Harvard University Archives, UAV 605 (NAH 4) Box 100
p.10   Shin Eun-jung
p.11   John Quincy Adams George Peter Alexander Healy (Public Domain) http://en.wikipedia.org/wiki/File:US_Navy_031029-N-6236G-001_A_painting_of_President_John_Adams_(1735-1826),_2nd_president_of_the_United_States,_by_Asher_B._Durand_(1767-1845)-crop.jpg
p.11   Mathew Brady (Public Domain) http://en.wikipedia.org/wiki/File:President_Rutherford_Hayes_1870_-_1880.jpg
p.11   Pach Brothers (Public Domain) http://en.wikipedia.org/wiki/File:President_Theodore_Roosevelt,_1904.jpg
p.11   Elias Goldensky (Public Domain) http://en.wikipedia.org/wiki/File:FDR_in_1933.jpg
p.11   U.S. federal government (Public Domain) http://en.wikipedia.org/wiki/File:John_F._Kennedy,_White_House_color_photo_portrait.jpg
p.11   U.S. federal government (Public Domain) http://en.wikipedia.org/wiki/File:George-W-Bush.jpeg
p.11   U.S. federal government (Public Domain) http://en.wikipedia.org/wiki/File:Barack_Obama_at_Cairo_University_cropped.jpg
p.13   http://saintpetersbasilica.org/Statues/StPeter/StPeter.htm
p.13   Choi Seung-uk
p.14   Shin Eun-jung
p.15   William A. Crafts (1876), Pioneers in the settlement of America: from Florida in 1510 to California in 1849 (Pioneers in the settlement of America: from Florida in 1510 to California in 1849. ed.), Boston: Published by Samuel Walker and Company (Public Domain) http://en.wikipedia.org/wiki/File:Witchcraft_at_Salem_Village.jpg
p.15   Peter Pelham (Public Domain) http://en.wikipedia.org/wiki/File:Cotton_Mather.jpg
p.17   Original uploader was Ktsquare at en.wikipedia (Public Domain) http://en.wikipedia.org/wiki/File:Charles_William_Eliot.jpg

Chapter 2 Governing Harvard

p.24 U.S. federal government (Public Domain) http://en.wikipedia.org/wiki/ File:Harvard_President_Drew_Faust_US_Navy_110304-N-5549O-204.jpg

p.24 Harvard Factbook (2007-08); http://www.bibliotecapleyades.net/sociopolitica/ elite/uni_org5.gif

p.25 http://www.hcs.harvard.edu/~pslm/livingwage/portal.html

p.27 *Moody's* magazine (Public Domain) http://en.wikipedia.org/wiki/ File:J.P._Morgan_and_J.P._Morgan_Jr.png

p.32 Portrait of Derek Bok, 1969 (W615121_1): Harvard University Archives, UAV 605 (frame 6A) Box 32

Chapter 3 The Harvard Tradition: Rich, White, and Male

p.40 Lewis Wickes Hine, *Little Spinner in a Carolina Cotton Mill, 1908*

p.40 http://womhist.binghamton.edu/teacher/DBQlaw2.htm(National Child Labor Committee. Public domain) http://ko.wikipedia.org/wiki/ percent ED percent 8C percent 8C percent EC percent 9D percent BC:1912_Lawrence_Textile_Strike_1.jpg

p.41 http://en.wikipedia.org/wiki/File:Abott_Lawrence_Lowell_by_John_Singer_ Sargent_1923.jpeg

p.41 Portrait of James Bryant Conant ca. 1958 (W614758_1): Harvard University Archives, UAV 605 (Conant, James) Box 1

p.43 *The Harvard Crimson*

p.46 Harry H. Laughlin, The Second International Exhibition of Eugenics held September 22 to October 22, 1921, in connection with the Second International Congress of Eugenics in the American Museum of Natural History, New York (Baltimore: William & Wilkins Co., 1923). (Public Domain) http://en.wikipedia. org/wiki/File:Eugenics_congress_logo.png

p.46 "The Second International Congress of Eugenics," *Scientific Monthly* 13:5 (Nov 1921), 476, on 479. Cropped from larger photograph (Public Domain) http:// en.wikipedia.org/wiki/File:Charles_Davenport_1921.jpg

p.47 Fastfission (Public Domain) http://en.wikipedia.org/wiki/File:European_immi- gration_to_the_United_States_1881-1940.png

p.47 U.S. federal government (Public Domain) http://en.wikipedia.org/wiki/ File:CalvinCoolidgeimmigration3.jpg

p.50 Harvard University Archives W376389_1 available at http://ids.lib.harvard.edu/ ids/view/7477527?buttons=y

p.51 Bundesarchiv Bild 102-14080, 21 June 1932, Berlin, Hitler, Göring und Hanfstaengl. jpg From Wikipedia, the free encyclopedia http://en.wikipedia.org/wiki/ File:Bundesarchiv_Bild_102-14080,_Berlin,_Hitler,_Göring_und_Hanfstaengl.jpg

p.53 U.S. federal government (Public Domain) http://en.wikipedia.org/wiki/ File:Project_Paperclip_Team_at_Fort_Bliss.jpg

p.55 http://www.picturehistory.com/product/id/3703 (Public Domain) http:// en.wikipedia.org/wiki/File:Louis_Agassiz_H6.jpg

p.55 http://en.wikipedia.org/wiki/File:Helen_KellerA.jpg (Public Domain)

p.56 Shin Eun-jung

p.57 U.S. federal government (Public Domain) http://en.wikipedia.org/wiki/File:Alice_ Hamilton.jpg

Chapter 4 Pentagon University

p.61 Navy Supply School students marching through Harvard Yard, 1943 (W615117_1): Harvard University Archives, UAV 605.442 (N-155) Box 2

p.64 Returning veteran students, 1946, (W616235_1): Harvard University Archives, HUPSF World War II (248) p.65　Harvard University Archives, HUPSF Student Life (40)

p.66　Noam Chomsky, Laura Nader, Immanuel Wallerstein, Richard Lewontin and Richard Ohmann, eds., *The Cold War & the University: Toward an Intellectual History of the Postwar Years*, New Press, 1998.

p.67　Photograph of ceremony honoring Winston Churchill, 1943: Harvard University Archives, UAV 605 (Churchill) Box 31

p.67　George Marshall at Harvard Commencement, 1947 (W614728_1): Harvard University Archives, UAV 605 (U1717) Box 31

p.70　Library of Congress (Public Domain) http://en.wikipedia.org/wiki/File:Joseph_McCarthy.jpg

p.70　Marion S. Trikosko (Public Domain) http://en.wikipedia.org/wiki/File:Hoover-JEdgar-LOC.jpg

p.71　Library of Congress. New York World-Telegram & Sun Collection. http://hdl.loc.gov/loc.pnp/cph.3c30365 (Public Domain) http://en.wikipedia.org/wiki/File:Hiss01.jpg

p.72　U.S. federal government (Public Domain) http://en.wikipedia.org/wiki/File:McGeorge_Bundy.jpg

p.73　Roger Higgins, photographer from "New York World-Telegram and the Sun" (Public Domain) http://en.wikipedia.org/wiki/File:Julius_and_Ethel_Rosenberg_NYWTS.jpg

p.75　Portrait of Harvard president Nathan Marsh Pusey, ca. 1960 (W616235_1): Harvard University Archives, HUP Pusey, Nathan (39)

p.81　Courtesy of the Boston Public Library, Print Department

p.84　Harvard University Archives, UAV 605 (NAH 23) Box 100

p.87　U.S. federal government (Public Domain) http://en.wikipedia.org/wiki/File:Defoliation_agent_spraying.jpg

Chapter 5 Harvard and Foreign Policy

p.93　Portrait of Archibald Cary Coolidge ca. 1925 (W614759_1): Harvard University Archives, UAV 605 (F2225) Box 3

p.94　Harris & Ewing (Public Domain) http://en.wikipedia.org/wiki/File:George_F._Kennan_1947.jpg

p.99　U.S. federal government (Public Domain) http://en.wikipedia.org/wiki/File:Brzezinski_1977.jpg

p.99　U.S. federal government (Public Domain) http://en.wikipedia.org/wiki/File:JimmyCarterPortrait2.jpg

p.102　U.S. federal government (Public Domain) http://en.wikipedia.org/wiki/File:Paul_Nitze.jpeg

Chapter 6 Harvard in Crisis: The Anti-war Movement

p.107　U.S. federal government (Public Domain) http://en.wikipedia.org/wiki/File:Rosaparks.jpg

p.109　Shin Eun-jung

p.110　Choi Seong-uk

p.115　http://www.weforum.org http://en.wikipedia.org/wiki/File:Samuel_P._Huntington_(2004_World_Economic_Forum).jpg

p.115　Marion S. Trikosko (Public Domain) http://en.wikipedia.org/wiki/File:Henry_Kissinger.jpg

p.118　Library of the Harvard Center for International Affairs, 1970 (W615122_1): Harvard University Archives, UAV 605.295.7p Box 5

p.119　*How Harvard Rules*

p.120　Choi Seong-uk

p.121 Ted Dully, *Boston Globe*
p.122 John Filo
p.123 Diogo
p.126 Shin Eun-jung
p.128 Portrait of three Harvard presidents, 1971 (W615120_1): Harvard University Archives, UAV 605 (frame 34) Box 32
p.130 *How Harvard Rules*
p.133 Choi Seong-uk

Chapter 7 Harvard's Role in Russian Economic "Reform"

p.140 Palácio do Planalto do Brasil (Public Domain) http://en.wikipedia.org/wiki/File:Jeffrey_sachs_in_Brazil.jpg
p.141 http://en.wikipedia.org/wiki/File:Voucher.jpg (Public Domain)
p.141 Jürg Vollmer/Maiakinfo
p.143 Wikipedia Commons
p.144 Wikipedia "Demographics of Russia"
p.145 USAID, U.S. federal government (Public Domain) http://en.wikipedia.org/wiki/File:USAID-Identity.svg
p.148 *The Nation*
p.149 http://www.kremlin.ru/sdocs/news.shtml?day=31&month=12&year=1999&Submit.x=0&Submit.y=0&value_from=&value_to=&date=&stype=&dayRequired=no&day_enable=true# http://en.wikipedia.org/wiki/File:Boris_Yeltsin-2.jpg
p.149 RIA Novosti archive, image #100306, http://visualrian.ru/ru/site/gallery/#100306 http://en.wikipedia.org/wiki/File:RIAN_archive_100306_Vladimir_Putin,_Federal_Security_Service_Director.jpg
p.151 U.S. federal government (Public Domain) http://en.wikipedia.org/wiki/File:Lawrence_Summers_Treasury_portrait.jpg

Chapter 8 Harvard's Labor Policy and the 2001 Occupation

p.155 Campaign to revoke South African investment, ca. 1985 (W615125_1): Harvard University Archives, UAV 605.295.6p, Box 2
p.160 http://www.hcs.harvard.edu/~pslm/livingwage/portal.html
p.161 Choi Seong-uk
p.162 Shin Eun-jung
p.164 http://www.hcs.harvard.edu http://www.hcs.harvard.edu/~pslm/livingwage/portal.html
p.165 Shin Eun-jung

Chapter 9 A Hedge Fund with Libraries: The Financial Crisis of 2008

p.169 The Friedman Foundation for Educational Choice http://en.wikipedia.org/wiki/File:Portrait_of_Milton_Friedman.jpg
p.174 "Educational Endowments and the Financial Crisis: Social Costs and Systemic Risks in the Shadow Banking System"
p.176 Tellus Institute Report
p.178 Shin Eun-jung
p.179 Tellus Institute Report
p.180 Marilyn Humphries
p.182 Choi Seong-uk
p.182 Shin Eun-jung

Chapter 10 Harvard at a Crossroads

p.192 Victor Wallis

p.194 Shin Eun-jung
p.195 Choi Seong-uk
p.201 Shin Eun-jung
p.203 Shin Eun-jung
p.204 Shin Eun-jung

Epilogue
p.207 Shin Eun-jung

NOTES

Introduction

1   Yang Keun-man, "Former Jeongyojo Teachers to Be Reinstated," April 28, 2002, at http://english.chosun.com/site/data/html_dir/2002/04/28/2002042861020.html.

2   Ramsay Liem, "I will forever be enriched by the example of her life and her incredible spirit," in *Bada, Across the Border* (2013), a privately published collection of eulogies and tributes to Shin Eun-jung (pages 320–22). For the teachers' strike, see in the same collection Park Sumi, "Like a nomad who never stays in the same place for long," (245–46).

3   Gi-Wook Shin and Kyung Moon Hwang, *Contentious Kwangju: The May 18th Uprising in Korea's Past and Present* (Lanham, MD: Rowman & Littlefield, 2003), xvii. For a discussion of the debate on the death toll, see the extended note in George Katsiaficas, *Asia's Unknown Uprisings, Vol. 1: South Korean Social Movements in the 20th Century* (Oakland: PM Press, 2012), 214–15n.1. See also Asia Watch Committee, *Human Rights in Korea* (New York: Asia Watch, 1986), 42.

4   Bruce Cumings, "Introduction" to Lee Jae-eui, *Kwangju Diary: Beyond Death, Beyond the Darkness of the Age* (Los Angeles: UCLA Asia Pacific Monograph Series, 1999), 27.

5   Ibid., 25. See also Tim Shorrock, "Debacle in Kwangju: Were Washington Cables Read as a Green Light for the 1980 Korean Massacre?," *The Nation*, December 9, 1996, 19–22.

6   Cumings, "Introduction," 25; and Gregory Henderson, "Harvard's Korean Grant: Dreams of Reason and Spectres," *Harvard Crimson*, January 5, 1977.

7   Alex Beam, "Gillette, Who Are They?," *Boston Globe*, July 13, 1988, 67. Beam notes that Colman Mockler, then CEO of Gillette, helped run Harvard as a member of the Harvard Corporation. As for Gillette, "It is perhaps no accident that six of the company's 10 American directors hold degrees from the World's Greatest University."

8   Jon Plender, "Endowments Can Learn a Lesson from Yale," *Financial Times*, September 29, 2014, 13. In fiscal 2014, the Yale endowment grew 20.2 percent, compared with Harvard's 15.4 percent performance. Yale's ten-year annual return as of June 2014 was 11.0 percent and Harvard trailed with an 8.9 percent ten-year return. See Dan Fitzpatrick, "Global Finance: A Harvard Insider to Run Endowment," *Wall Street Journal*, September 25, 2014, C3, and Dan Fitzpatrick, "Harvard Endowment Earns 15.4% Return in Fiscal 2014," *Wall Street Journal Online*, September 23, 2014, at http://online.wsj.com/articles/harvard-endowment-earns-15-4-return-for-fiscal-2014-1411506002.

9   Madeline W. Lissner, "Going Global: Harvard's Stamp Abroad," *Harvard Crimson*, June 6, 2007.

10 For the global listing of alumni clubs and official alumni contacts, see the websites of the Harvard and Yale alumni associations. Commenting on upper-class networking, C. Wright Mills long ago made the point that people coming from prestigious private secondary schools and then belonging to the most exclusive social clubs end up

having a very different Harvard experience from the vast majority of student strivers. See *The Power Elite* (New York: Oxford University Press, 1978 [1956]), 67.

11 The genre includes Andrew Hacker and Claudia Dreifus in *Higher Education? How Colleges Are Wasting Our Money and Failing Our Kids—and What We Can Do about It* (2010) and the many essays of William Deresiewicz, culminating in his *Excellent Sheep: The Miseducation of the American Elite and the Way to a Meaningful Life* (2014), the latter a condemnation of what he calls the HYPSter schools (Harvard, Yale, Princeton, and Stanford). Despite the Harvard-centric lens of her documentary film and companion book originally for a Korean audience, Eun-jung was also curious about other elite universities, especially their student movements. In addition to exploring the 1969 pamphlet *How Harvard Rules* and the 1989 volume *How Harvard Rules: Reason in the Service of Empire*, as a former student activist, she took delight in unearthing the radical guides *Go to School, Learn to Rule: The Yale Method* (ca. 1970) and *Who Rules Columbia?* (1968).

12 Hacker and Dreifus, *Higher Education?*, 59.

13 Noam Chomsky and Michel Foucault, *The Chomsky-Foucault Debate: On Human Nature* (New York: The New Press, 2006), 40.

14 See Kingman Brewster Jr., *The Report of the President* (Yale University, 1967-68), 38. Brewster was also quoted by *Go to School, Learn to Rule: The Yale Method* (pamphlet, ca. 1970), 22.

15 Nathan Pusey, *Cambridge and Harvard* (pamphlet, 1959), 12.

16 Bundy quoted in *How Harvard Rules* (pamphlet, 1969), 35.

17 Navy Secretary Ray E. Mabus quoted on Faust's "total commitment" to NROTC by Nikita Kansra and Samuel Y. Weinstock, "U.S. Navy Awards Faust for Welcoming ROTC," *Harvard Crimson*, March 15, 2013.

18 See "Third Annual Harvard National Security Fellow—ROTC Student Breakfast" at http://www.advocatesforrotc.org/harvard/04nsf.html.

19 British Prime Minister David Cameron likes to contrast what he calls "muscular liberalism" with flabby state multiculturalism. Faust's mélange of feminism and enthusiasm for the military and corporations might be regarded as a variant of Cameron's thematic innovations.

20 Gary J. Bass, *The Blood Telegram: Nixon, Kissinger, and a Forgotten Genocide* (New York: Vintage Books, 2013), xii.

21 Lt. Gen. J.F.R. Jacob, *Surrender at Dacca: Birth of a Nation* (New Delhi: Manmohan Publishers, 1997), 100.

22 Bass, *Blood Telegram*, xvi.

23 Niall Ferguson et al., "Eric Hobsbawm—A Historian's Historian," *The Guardian*, October 1, 2012, http://www.theguardian.com/commentisfree/2012/oct/01/eric-hobsbawm-historian.

24 According to Media Matters, Limbaugh called Gates an "angry racist" on July 27, 2009, http://mediamatters.org/research/2009/10/13/limbaughs-colorblind-history-of-racially-charge/155659.

25 Condoleezza Rice's Harvard lecture series from 2010 can be viewed at http://hutchinscenter.fas.harvard.edu/node/1141.

26 An example of this estimate of invasions is on display in Euny Hong, *The Birth of Korean Cool: How One Nation Is Conquering the World through Pop Culture* (New York: Picador, 2014), 51.

27 Micah Zenko, *Reforming U.S. Drone Strike Policies* (Council on Foreign Relations Special Report No. 65), January 2013, 8.

28 Michael Hastings, "Killer Drones: How America Goes to War in Secret," *Rolling Stone*, April 26, 2012, 40-47 and 82.

29   Ashton B. Carter and William J. Perry, "If Necessary, Strike and Destroy: North Korea Cannot Be Allowed to Test This Missile," *Washington Post*, June 22, 2006, A29. See also Michael Crowley, "Can a Wonk Run a War? Ash Carter Is a Scholar, a Bureaucrat—and the Opposite of Chuck Hagel," *Politico*, December 3, 2014, http://www.politico.com/story/2014/12/ashton-carter-secretary-of-defense-113283.html.

30   Jonathan Alter, *The Promise: President Obama, Year One* (New York: Simon & Schuster, 2010), 64.

31   Chris Floyd, "The Moral Blindness of Our Leading Liberals," *CounterPunch*, October 29, 2014, http://www.counterpunch.org/2014/10/29/the-moral-blindness-of-our-leading-liberals/.

32   Stefan Stern, "A 100-Year Health Check for Harvard: Unrattled by the Financial Turmoil, the Pre-eminent Business School Used Its Centennial Celebration to Debate Its Role in the Solution," *Financial Times* (London edition), October 21, 2008, 18.

33   Ferguson quoted by Prateek Kumar, "Harvard Business School Marks 100th Anniversary: Business School Alumni Look for Answers to Recent Market Crisis," *Harvard Crimson*, October 13, 2008.

34   Stern, "100-Year Health Check," 18.

35   John Summers, "All the Privileged Must Have Prizes," *Times Higher Education Supplement*, July 10, 2008, 42 and 44. This essay was republished in a wider format in "History as a Vocation" in Summers, *Every Fury on Earth* (Aurora, CO: PenMark Press, 2009), 3–21.

Chapter 1 Profiling Harvard

1   John Trumpbour, ed., *How Harvard Rules: Reason in the Service of Empire* (Boston: South End Press, 1989), 4.

2   Richard Norton Smith, *The Harvard Century: The Making of a University to a Nation* (New York: Simon and Schuster, 1986), 11.

3   Sam Dillon, "Elite Korean Schools, Forging Ivy League Skills," *New York Times*, April 27, 2008.

4   Marie Thibault, "Billionaire University," *Forbes*, August 14, 2009.

5   Randy Cohen, "Should You Give to Harvard?," *New York Times*, September 28, 2009.

6   *How Harvard Rules: Being a Total Critique of Harvard University*, booklet published by Harvard students, 1969, 5.

7   Donn M. Kurtz II, "Harvard and Oxford," *Global Study Magazine*, http://www.globalstudymagazine.com/site/articles/525/.

8   Ibid.

9   "A Harvard Chronology," *Harvard Magazine*, September–October 1986.

10   Andrew Schlesinger, *Veritas: Harvard College and the American Experience* (Chicago: Ivan R. Dee, 2005), 18.

11   Henry Adams, *The Education of Henry Adams: An Autobiography* (New York: Houghton Mifflin Company, 1918), 54.

12   Stephan Thernstrom, "Poor but Hopeful Scholars," *Harvard Magazine*, September–October 1986.

13   Ibid.

14   John T. Bethell, *Harvard Observed* (Cambridge, MA: Harvard University Press, 1998), 14.

15   See the commencement video in the film *Verita$: Everybody Loves Harvard*.

16   Interview with John Trumpbour.

17   Ellen Schrecker, *No Ivory Tower* (New York: Oxford University Press, 1986), 340.

18   Richard Cravatts, "Kennedy School: Conservative Hotbed," *New York Times*, July 15, 1988, A31.

19   Noam Chomsky, *Necessary Illusions* (Boston: South End Press, 1989), 22.

20 Interview with Noam Chomsky.
21 Interview with Richard Levins.
22 It is sometimes pointed out that Harvard professor Stephen Marglin is a radical economist, but it is commonly noted that he achieved tenure largely by masking his politics in his early academic production.

Chapter 2 Governing Harvard

1 Robert Weissman, "How Harvard Is Ruled," in Trumpbour, *How Harvard Rules*, 33.
2 Interview with Trumpbour.
3 Trumpbour, *How Harvard Rules*, 44.
4 Chester Hartman and Robert Paul Wolff, "Democracy Harvard Style: The (S)Election of Overseers" in ibid., 411.
5 Schlesinger, *Veritas*, 249.
6 Interview with Trumpbour.
7 Interview with Trumpbour; Henry Rosovsky, *The University: An Owner's Manual* (New York: W.W. Norton and Co., 1991).
8 Clyde W. Barrow, *Universities and the Capitalist State: Corporate Liberalism and the Reconstruction of American Higher Education, 1894-1928* (Madison: University of Wisconsin Press, 1990), 42.
9 Trumpbour, *How Harvard Rules*, 142-43.
10 Donald Macedo, introduction to Noam Chomsky, *Chomsky on MisEducation* (Lanham, MD: Rowman & Littlefield, 2000), 4-5. Macedo is quoting Chomsky and Paulo Freire, respectively.
11 Paul Krugman, "The Great Divide," *New York Times*, January 29, 2002.
12 Interview with Edward J. Baker.
13 Robert Weissman, "How Harvard Is Ruled," as quoted in *How Harvard Rules*, 44.
14 Schlesinger, *Veritas*, 106-7.
15 Elias J. Groll, Zoe A.Y. Weinberg, and William N. White, "Harvard Corporation Announces Historic Overhaul to Governance Structure," *Harvard Crimson*, December 6, 2010.
16 Paul Fain, "Harvard U. Overhauls Governing Board in Recession's Wake, a First after 360 Years," *Chronicle of Higher Education*, December 6, 2010.

Chapter 3 The Harvard Tradition: Rich, White, and Male

1 *How Harvard Rules: Being a Total Critique of Harvard University*, 4.
2 Schlesinger, *Veritas*, 166.
3 Ibid., 129-30.
4 Primus V, "Blockheads" from "The College Pump" column, *Harvard Magazine* (January-February 2006): 80.
5 Trumpbour, *How Harvard Rules*, 3-4.
6 Herbert H. Denton Jr., "Behind the Velvet Curtain," *Harvard Crimson*, May 25, 1965. Denton cites one of FDR's biographers who regarded this as "one of the most devastating set-backs of his life."
7 James MacGregor Burns, *Roosevelt: The Lion and the Fox, 1882-1940* (New York: Harcourt, 1984 [1956]), 18.
8 Interview with Victor Wallis.
9 Justin C. Worland, "Legacy Admit Rate at 30 Percent," *Harvard Crimson*, May 11, 2011.
10 *How Harvard Rules: Being a Total Critique of Harvard University*, 5.
11 Interview with Wayne Langley.
12 Schlesinger, *Veritas*, 170.
13 Ibid.
14 Smith, *Harvard Century*, 117.

15 The Immigration Restriction League was founded in 1894 by people who opposed the influx of "undesirable immigrants" coming from Southern and Eastern Europe.

16 Morton Keller and Phyllis Keller, *Making Harvard Modern: The Rise of America's University* (New York: Oxford University Press, 2001), 49.

17 Schlesinger, *Veritas*, 161.

18 Corydon Ireland, "Harvard and Slavery," *Harvard Gazette*, November 18, 2011.

19 Interview with Jonathan Beckwith.

20 Interview with Charles V. Willie.

21 Jonathan Beckwith, "The Science of Racism," in Trumpbour, *How Harvard Rules*, 243.

22 Interview with Levins.

23 Beckwith, "Science of Racism," 244-45.

24 Interview with Jonathan Beckwith.

25 Edwin Black, *War against the Weak: Eugenics and America's Campaign to Create a Master Race* (New York: Thunder's Mouth Press, 2004), 73.

26 Ibid., 74.

27 Ibid.

28 Ibid., 58.

29 Ibid., 59.

30 Daniel Kevles, *In the Name of Eugenics: Genetics and the Uses of Human Heredity* (New York: Knopf, 1985), 111.

31 Black, *War Against the Weak*, 259.

32 Interview with Levins.

33 Jonathan Beckwith, *Making Genes, Making Waves: A Social Activist in Science* (Cambridge, MA: Harvard University Press, 2002), 109.

34 Black, *War Against the Weak*, 277.

35 Interview with Beckwith.

36 Stephen H. Norwood, *The Third Reich in the Ivory Tower: Complicity and Conflict on American Campuses* (Cambridge: Cambridge University Press, 2004), 48.

37 Ibid., 50.

38 Ibid.

39 Ibid., 53.

40 Ibid., 57-58.

41 Song Hongbing, *Currency Wars*, from Korean Translation (Seoul: Random House Korea, 2008), 207.

42 Sigmund Diamond, *Compromised Campus* (New York: Oxford University Press), 92-93.

43 Schlesinger, *Veritas*, 129-30.

44 Barbara Sicherman, *Alice Hamilton: A Life in Letters* (Chicago: University of Illinois Press, 2003 [1984]), 5.

45 Interview with Margaret Gullette (Radcliffe Class of 1962, cultural critic).

46 Ibid.

47 Harvard University Office of the Senior Vice Provost Faculty Development & Diversity, 2011 Annual Report.

Chapter 4 Pentagon University

1 Smith, *Harvard Century*, 151.

2 *How Harvard Rules: Being a Total Critique of Harvard University*, 35.

3 Interview with Chomsky.

4 Noam Chomsky, Laura Nader, Immanuel Wallerstein, Richard Lewontin, and Richard Ohmann, eds., *The Cold War & the University: Toward an Intellectual History of the Postwar Years* (New York: The New Press, 1998), 172.

5 Schlesinger, *Veritas*, 187.

6   Ibid.

7   Quotes from Schlesinger, 187–91.

8   Selected Documents on Truman's Decision to Use the Atomic Bomb, 1945, Harry S. Truman Presidential Library, http://www.trumanlibrary.org.

9   Howard Zinn, *Passionate Declarations: Essays on War and Justice* (New York, Harper Perennial, 2003). "The U.S. Strategic Bombing Survey, which interviewed 700 Japanese military and political officials after the war, came to this conclusion: 'Based on a detailed investigation of all the facts and supported by the testimony of the surviving Japanese leaders involved, it is the Survey's opinion that certainly prior to 31 December 1945, and in all probability prior to 1 November 1945, Japan would have surrendered even if the atomic bombs had not been dropped, even if Russia had not entered the war, and even if no invasion had been planned or contemplated.'" (24).

10 Trumpbour, *How Harvard Rules*, 62.

11 Ibid., 63.

12 Chomsky et al., *The Cold War and the University*, 13.

13 Trumpbour, *How Harvard Rules*, 52.

14 Interview with Noam Chomsky.

15 Trumpbour, *How Harvard Rules*, 53.

16 Ibid., 63.

17 *How Harvard Rules: Being a Total Critique of Harvard University*, 35–36.

18 Interview with Ngo Vinh Long.

19 Ellen Schrecker, "Political Tests for Professors: Academic Freedom during the McCarthy Years," October 7, 1999, http://sunsite.berkeley.edu/uchistory/archives_ exhibits/loyaltyoath/symposium/schrecker.html.

20 Schlesinger, *Veritas*, 203.

21 Elizabeth Mehren, "Harvard's Loyalty Oath Still Stings Opponent," *Los Angeles Times*, April 5, 2001.

22 Diamond, *Compromised Campus*, 18.

23 "The rights and responsibilities of universities and their faculties," Statement by the AAU, March 24, 1953.

24 Schrecker, "Political Tests for Professors."

25 Chomsky et al., *The Cold War and the University*, 43.

26 Diamond, *Compromised Campus*, 112.

27 Bethell, *Harvard Observed*, 190.

28 Smith, *Harvard Century*, 186.

29 Schlesinger, *Veritas*, 204.

30 Ibid.

31 Interview with Levins.

32 *How Harvard Rules: Being a Total Critique of Harvard University*, 15.

33 Chomsky et al., *The Cold War and the University*, 179.

34 Interview with Chomsky.

35 Chomsky uses this term on many occasions, but he credits Gramsci for developing it. See "Equality: Language Development, Human Intelligence, and Social Organization" in *The Chomsky Reader* (New York, Pantheon, 1987), 201. For examples of many experts in legitimation, see also discussion by Trumpbour, *How Harvard Rules*, 55–56.

36 Interview with George Katsiaficas.

37 Interview with Levins.

38 Trumpbour, *How Harvard Rules*, 54.

39 Ibid., 52.

40 Ibid., 54.

41 Interview with Chomsky.

42 Chomsky et al., *The Cold War and the University*, 198.

43 Ibid., 201–2.

44 Trumpbour, *How Harvard Rules*, 81.

45 Chomsky et al., *The Cold War and the University*, 197.

46 CMES annual report quoted by Trumpbour, *How Harvard Rules*, 88.

47 Chomsky et al., *The Cold War and the University*, 207.

48 Ibid., 220.

49 This is the famous phrase that Kennedy delivered during his inaugural speech, but it is not his original work. There were various similar versions. In 1916, Warren G. Harding (twenty-ninth president, 1921–1923) said at the Republican convention, "We must have a citizenship less concerned about what the government can do for it and more anxious about what it can do for the nation."

50 Interview with Michael Ansara.

51 Interview with Chomsky.

52 The Bay of Pigs Invasion was the failed attempt to invade Cuba by CIA-trained Cuban exiles attempting to overthrow Fidel Castro's government in April 1961. It severely embarrassed the Kennedy Administration and made Castro keenly aware of continuing U.S. intervention in Cuba.

53 Trumpbour, *How Harvard Rules*, 77.

54 Ibid., 77–78.

55 Interview with Chomsky.

Chapter 5 Harvard and Foreign Policy

1 Colin Campbell, "The Harvard Factor," *New York Times*, July 20, 1986.

2 *How Harvard Rules: Being a Total Critique of Harvard University*, 13.

3 Trumpbour, *How Harvard Rules*, 57.

4 Interview with Trumpbour.

5 Trumpbour, *How Harvard Rules*, 57.

6 Ibid., 58.

7 Ibid.

8 Interview with Trumpbour.

9 Michael Parenti, *The Assassination of Julius Caesar* (New York: The New Press, 2004), 19.

10 Interview with Chomsky; "The United States Has Essentially a One-Party System," *Spiegel Online*, October 10, 2008.

11 Trumpbour, *How Harvard Rules*, 65–66.

12 Bowman quotation and the Rockefeller funding is discussed at the CFR's official website: http://www.cfr.org/about/history/cfr/war_peace.html.

13 Noam Chomsky, "Dominance and Its Dilemmas," *Boston Review*, 2003.

14 Interview with Noam Chomsky by David Barsamian, "Telling the Truth about Imperialism," *International Socialist Review* 32 (November–December 2003), available at http://www.isreview.org/issues/32/chomsky.shtml.

15 Trumpbour, *How Harvard Rules*, 59.

16 The Trilateral Commission: http://www.trilateral.org.

17 Noam Chomsky, "The Carter Administration, Myth and Reality," *Radical Priorities*, 3rd ed. (Oakland: AK Press, 2003), 137.

18 Trumpbour, *How Harvard Rules*, 60.

19 George Katsiaficas, "Neoliberalism and the Gwangju Uprising," *Korea Policy Review*, John F. Kennedy School of Government, Harvard University, Volume II, 2006, 32, http://eroseffect.com/articles/neoliberalismgwangju.htm.

20 Ibid., 33.

21 Ibid.

22   Interview with Trumpbour.

23   Trumpbour, *How Harvard Rules*, 60–61.

24   Ibid.

25   Interview with Trumpbour.

26   CPD: www.committeeonthepresentdanger.org.

27   Charles Feldman & Stan Wilson, "Ex-CIA director: U.S. faces 'World War IV,'" http://
     www.cnn.com/2003/US/04/03/sprj.irq.woolsey.world.war/index.html.

28   Trumpbour, *How Harvard Rules*, 64.

29   Ibid., 65.

30   Ibid.

Chapter 6 Harvard in Crisis: The Anti-war Movement

1   Clark Kerr, *The Uses of the University* (Cambridge, MA: Harvard University Press,
     1963), 124.

2   Howard Zinn, *Passionate Declarations: Essays on War and Justice* (New York, Harper
     Perennial, 2003), 131.

3   Interview with Ansara.

4   Schlesinger, *Veritas*, 222.

5   Interview with Ngo Vinh Long.

6   Samuel P. Huntington, "The Bases of Accommodation," *Foreign Affairs* 46, no. 4 (July
     1968): 652.

7   Interview with Katsiaficas.

8   Interview with Ngo Vinh Long.

9   Interview with Ansara.

10   Christopher Hitchens, *The Trial of Henry Kissinger* (London, Verso, 2001), 13.

11   Ibid., 41.

12   Ibid., 35.

13   Interview with Chomsky.

14   Hitchens, *The Trial of Henry Kissinger*, 34–35.

15   Interview with Katsiaficas.

16   Interview with Chomsky.

17   Schlesinger, *Veritas*, 228.

18   Interview with Ansara.

19   Schlesinger, *Veritas*, 230.

20   Ibid., 209.

21   Interview with Ansara.

22   Michael Ansara, in Trumpbour, *How Harvard Rules*, 232–33.

23   George Katsiaficas, *The Imagination of the New Left: A Global Analysis of 1968* (Boston:
     South End Press, 1987), 120.

24   Interview with Katsiaficas.

25   Schlesinger, *Veritas*, 209.

26   Donald Macedo, introduction to Noam Chomsky, *Chomsky on MisEducation* (Lanham,
     MD: Rowman & Littlefield, 2000), 2.

27   Interview with Chomsky.

28   "Nixon Cutbacks Could Threaten Harvard Plan," *Harvard Crimson*, February 23, 1973.

29   Interview with Gullette.

30   Interview with Joshua Humphreys.

31   Carl A. Vigeland, "The Making of Harvard's Fortune," *Harvard Magazine*, September–
     October 1986.

32   Interview with Katsiaficas.

33   Ernest Volkman, "Spies on Campus," http://www.cia-on-campus.org/volkman.html.
     This article originally appeared in *Penthouse*, October 1979.

34 Trumpbour, *How Harvard Rules*, 28–33.

35 Volkman, "Spies on Campus."

36 The 700 percent growth in funds was from $2 billion in 1977 to $13.2 billion in 1988.

37 Fox Butterfield, "Scaling Back Growth at Harvard's Kennedy School," *New York Times*, December 18, 1991.

38 http://article.joinsmsn.com/news/article/article.asp?total_id=5386170&ctg=1000.

39 Interview with Trumpbour.

40 Interview with David R. McCann.

41 Ibid.

Chapter 7 Harvard's Role in Russian Economic "Reform"

1   David McClintock, "How Harvard Lost Russia," *Institutional Investor Magazine*, January 24, 2006, http://janinewedel.info/harvardinvestigative_InstInvestorMag. pdf.

2   Janine R. Wedel, *Collision and Collusion: The Strange Case of Western Aid to Eastern Europe* (New York: Palgrave, 2001), p.276 n.80. The report is based on a letter summarizing the meeting by Harvard Professor Graham Allison.

3   Interview with Janine R. Wedel.

4   Wedel, *Collision and Collusion*, 131, 238.

5   Ibid., 241.

6   Ibid.

7   Boris Kagarlitsky, who served on the Moscow City Council from 1992 to 1993, noted that on November 24, 1992, after the "liberation of prices" of meat, the cost of a worker's lunch tripled in one day. The factory then attempted to place the workers on a vegetarian diet. See Boris Kagarlitsky, *Square Wheels: How Russian Democracy Got Derailed* (New York: Monthly Review Press, 1994), 179.

8   Marshall I. Goldman, *The Piratization of Russia: Russian Reform Goes Awry* (London: Routledge, 2003), 88.

9   Peter Rutland, "Neoliberalism and the Russian Transition," *Review of International Political Economy* 20, no. 2 (2013): 343.

10 Maxim Boycko, Andrei Shleifer, and Robert W. Vishny, "Privatization," *Journal of Financial Economics* 35 (1994): 249.

11 Ibid., 261.

12 McClintock, "How Harvard Lost Russia."

13 Janine R. Wedel, "The Harvard Boys Do Russia," *The Nation*, June 1, 1998, 15.

14 Ibid., 14.

15 Rutland, "Neoliberalism and the Russian Transition," 343.

16 Ho Kwang-jun, "Russia Kaehyog-gigwanch'a t'alson," *Sisa-journal*, December 11, 1997.

17 Richard Sakwa, *Russian Politics and Society* (London: Routledge, 2002), 89.

18 Song Hongbing, *Currency Wars*, trans. Cha Hye-jong (Seoul: Random House Korea, 2008), 245.

19 On the general decline of living conditions associated with privatization, see Hans Aage, "The Triumph of Capitalism in Russia and Eastern Europe and Its Western Apologetics," *Socialism and Democracy* 19, no. 2 (July 2005): 3–36.

20 Anne Williamson, "Testimony before the Committee on Banking and Financial Services of the House of Representatives, September 21, 1999," 13.

21 Wedel, *Collision and Collusion*, 147.

22 Ibid.

23 "Russia Says IMF Loans Were Not Misused," BBC September 2, 1999.

24 Interview with Wedel.

25 Wedel, "The Harvard Boys Do Russia," 14.

26   Wedel, *Collision and Collusion*, 132.

27   McClintock, "How Harvard Lost Russia."

28   Cho Chun-sang, "IMF-ui ch'ibuga turonanda," *Hangyoreh 21* (September 3, 1998).

29   McClintock, "How Harvard Lost Russia."

30   Ibid.

31   James Risen, "Gore Rejected C.I.A. Evidence of Russian Corruption," *New York Times*, November 23, 1998.

32   Stephen F. Cohen, *Failed Crusade: America and the Tragedy of Post-Communist Russia* (New York: W.W. Norton, 2000), 28.

33   Sara Ivry, "Did an Exposé Help to Sink Harvard's President?," *New York Times*, February 27, 2006.

34   Interview with Wedel.

Chapter 8 Harvard's Labor Policy and the 2001 Occupation

1   Interview with Wallis.

2   Vladimir Escalante, "A History of University Labor Struggle," in Trumpbour, *How Harvard Rules*, 211–12.

3   Ibid., 200.

4   Ibid., 202.

5   Ibid., 205–6.

6   Ibid., 211–12.

7   Ibid., 210–11.

8   John Hoerr, "Solidaritas at Harvard," *American Prospect* 4, no. 14 (June 23, 1993), available at http://prospect.org/article/solidaritas-harvard.

9   Harvard Information for Employees, "Labor and Employee Relations," http://hr.harvard.edu/labor-and-employee-relations-department/.

10   D. Joseph Menn, "Saving Money or Jeopardizing Jobs?," *Harvard Crimson*, April 2, 1984.

11   Interview with Maple Razsa.

12   Ibid.

13   Ibid.

Chapter 9 A Hedge Fund with Libraries: The Financial Crisis of 2008

1   Interview with Trumpbour.

2   Interview with Langley.

3   See "An Open Letter to Greg Mankiw," *Harvard Political Review*, November 2, 2011, available at http://harvardpolitics.com/harvard/an-open-letter-to-greg-mankiw/.

4   James Petras, "Turkey and Latin America: Reaction and Revolution," *Dissident Voice*, September 1, 2007.

5   George Katsiaficas, "Neoliberalism and the Gwangju Uprising," *Korea Policy Review*, John F. Kennedy School of Government, Harvard University, Volume II, 2006, 32, available at http://eroseffect.com/articles/neoliberalismgwangju.htm.

6   Ibid.

7   United Nations Human Development Report 1999 (New York: Oxford University Press, 1999), 37, available at http://hdr.undp.org/en/content/human-development-report-1999.

8   Interview with Humphreys.

9   Ibid.

10   Ibid.

11   Stephen Strom, "Harvard Money Manager's Pay Criticized," *New York Times*, June 4, 2004.

12 Cho Nam-gyu, "Wolga 3nyonmane 'tamyogui janchi' . . . siwie 'girum' ["Greedy Party" at Wall Street three years later . . . pouring gasoline onto demonstration]," *Segye Ilbo*, October 9, 2011.

13 Interview with Humphreys.

14 Lee Chyen Yee & Samuel Shen, "China's CIC in Talks with Harvard on Property Funds," *Wall Street Journal*, August 4, 2010.

15 Tracy Jan, "Harvard to Lay Off 275," *Boston Globe*, June 23, 2009.

16 Interview with Langley.

17 Summers made a similar remark at a 2003 Harvard School of Public Health panel discussion. His entire speech including this remark can be found at http://www. harvard.edu/president/speeches/summers_2003/africa.php.

18 Charles Ferguson, "Larry Summers and the Subversion of Economics," *Chronicle of Higher Education*, October 3, 2010.

19 Beth Healy, "Ex-employee Says She Warned Harvard of Risky Moves," *Boston Globe*, April 3, 2009.

20 Ferguson, "Larry Summers and the Subversion of Economics."

21 Travis Waldron, "Wall Street Traders Have Profited More under Obama than in Eight Years under Bush," *THINKPROGRESS*, November 7, 2011.

22 "Harvard, Vanderbilt, Spelman Exposed for Taking Part in 'Africa Land Grab,'" *Democracy Now!*, June 20, 2011.

23 Ibid.

24 Interview with Humphreys.

25 Ferguson, "Larry Summers and the Subversion of Economics."

26 Duff Wilson, "Harvard Medical School in Ethic Quandary," *New York Times*, March 3, 2009.

Chapter 10 Harvard at a Crossroads

1 *The Occupy Harvard Crimson*, 2011.

2 "Harvard Joins the Occupy Movement," *The Nation*, November 10, 2011.

3 Evan Ribot, "The Disgrace of Occupy Harvard," *Harvard Crimson*, November 16, 2011.

4 Martin Peretz, "*The New York Times* Laments 'A Sadly Wary Misunderstanding of Muslim-Americans,' but Really Is It 'Sadly Wary' or a 'Misunderstanding' at All?," *New Republic*, September 4, 2010.

5 Benjamin Sarlin, "Harvard's Marty Peretz Problem," *Daily Beast*, September 15, 2010.

6 Interview with Maryam Monalisa Garabi.

7 "Bin Laden Family's Harvard Donations," *BBC NEWS*, September 26, 2001.

8 Thomas Jefferson's letter to John Adams, "Natural and Artificial Aristocracy," October 28, 1813.

9 Interview with Chomsky.

10 Tamar Lewin, "College Graduates' Debt Burden Grew, Yet Again, in 2010," *New York Times*, November 2, 2011.

11 Interview with Chomsky.

12 "Demo 2010 Student Protests," *The Guardian*, November 10, 2010, http://www. guardian.co.uk/uk/blog/2010/nov/10/demo-2010-student-protests-live.

13 Smith, *Harvard Century*, 124.

14 Interview with Willie.

15 Noam Chomsky and Michel Foucault, *The Chomsky–Foucault Debate on Human Nature* (New York: The New Press, 2006), 70.

16 Interview with Elaine Bernard.

17 The Bread and Puppet Theater is a politically radical puppet theater, active since the 1960s, currently based in Vermont.

INDEX

"Passim" (literally "scattered") indicates intermittent discussion of a topic over a cluster of pages.

VERITA$ THE FILM

Links for all of Shin Eun-jung's films, including the award-winning documentary upon which this book is based, can be found at veritasthefilm.com.

ABOUT PM PRESS

PM Press was founded at the end of 2007 by a small collection of folks with decades of publishing, media, and organizing experience. PM Press co-conspirators have published and distributed hundreds of books, pamphlets, CDs, and DVDs. Members of PM have founded enduring book fairs, spearheaded victorious tenant organizing campaigns, and worked closely with bookstores, academic conferences, and even rock bands to deliver political and challenging ideas to all walks of life. We're old enough to know what we're doing and young enough to know what's at stake.

We seek to create radical and stimulating fiction and non-fiction books, pamphlets, T-shirts, visual and audio materials to entertain, educate, and inspire you. We aim to distribute these through every available channel with every available technology—whether that means you are seeing anarchist classics at our bookfair stalls; reading our latest vegan cookbook at the café; downloading geeky fiction e-books; or digging new music and timely videos from our website.

PM Press is always on the lookout for talented and skilled volunteers, artists, activists, and writers to work with. If you have a great idea for a project or can contribute in some way, please get in touch.

PM Press
PO Box 23912
Oakland, CA 94623
www.pmpress.org

FRIENDS OF PM PRESS

These are indisputably momentous times—the financial system is melting down globally and the Empire is stumbling. Now more than ever there is a vital need for radical ideas.

In the seven years since its founding—and on a mere shoestring—PM Press has risen to the formidable challenge of publishing and distributing knowledge and entertainment for the struggles ahead. With over 300 releases to date, we have published an impressive and stimulating array of literature, art, music, politics, and culture. Using every available medium, we've succeeded in connecting those hungry for ideas and information to those putting them into practice.

Friends of PM allows you to directly help impact, amplify, and revitalize the discourse and actions of radical writers, filmmakers, and artists. It provides us with a stable foundation from which we can build upon our early successes and provides a much-needed subsidy for the materials that can't necessarily pay their own way. You can help make that happen—and receive every new title automatically delivered to your door once a month—by joining as a Friend of PM Press. And, we'll throw in a free T-shirt when you sign up.

Here are your options:

- **$30 a month** Get all books and pamphlets plus 50% discount on all webstore purchases

- **$40 a month** Get all PM Press releases (including CDs and DVDs) plus 50% discount on all webstore purchases

- **$100 a month** Superstar—Everything plus PM merchandise, free downloads, and 50% discount on all webstore purchases

For those who can't afford $30 or more a month, we're introducing **Sustainer Rates** at $15, $10 and $5. Sustainers get a free PM Press T-shirt and a 50% discount on all purchases from our website.

Your Visa or Mastercard will be billed once a month, until you tell us to stop. Or until our efforts succeed in bringing the revolution around. Or the financial meltdown of Capital makes plastic redundant. Whichever comes first.

Asia's Unknown Uprisings
Volume 1: South Korean Social Movements in the 20th Century

George Katsiaficas

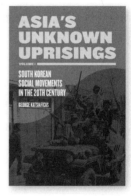

ISBN: 978-1-60486-457-1
$26.95   480 pages

Using social movements as a prism to illuminate the oft-hidden history of 20th century Korea, this book provides detailed analysis of major uprisings that have patterned that country's politics and society. From the 1894 Tonghak Uprising through the March 1, 1919, independence movement and anti-Japanese resistance, a direct line is traced to the popular opposition to U.S. division of Korea after World War Two. The overthrow of Syngman Rhee in 1960, resistance to Park Chung-hee, the 1980 Gwangju Uprising, as well as student, labor, and feminist movements are all recounted with attention to their economic and political contexts. South Korean opposition to neoliberalism is portrayed in detail, as is an analysis of neoliberalism's rise and effects. With a central focus on the Gwangju Uprising (that ultimately proved decisive in South Korea's democratization), the author uses Korean experiences as a baseboard to extrapolate into the possibilities of global social movements in the 21st century.

Previous English language sources have emphasized leaders—whether Korean, Japanese, or American. This book emphasizes grassroots crystallization of counter-elite dynamics and notes how the intelligence of ordinary people surpasses that of political and economic leaders holding the reins of power. It is the first volume in a two-part study that concludes by analyzing in rich detail uprisings in nine other places: the Philippines, Burma, Tibet, China, Taiwan, Bangladesh, Nepal, Thailand, and Indonesia. Richly illustrated, with tables, charts, graphs, index, and footnotes.

"George Katsiaficas has written a majestic account of political uprisings and social movements in Asia—an important contribution to the literature on both Asian studies and social change that is highly-recommended reading for anyone concerned with these fields of interest. The work is well-researched, clearly-argued, and beautifully written, accessible to both academic and general readers."
—Prof. Carl Boggs, author of *The Crimes of Empire* and *Imperial Delusions*

"This book makes a unique contribution to Korean Studies because of its social movements' prism. It will resonate well in Korea and will also serve as a good introduction to Korea for outsiders. By providing details on 20th century uprisings, Katsiaficas provides insights into the trajectory of social movements in the future."
—Na Kahn-chae, Director, May 18 Institute, Gwangju, South Korea

Asia's Unknown Uprisings
Volume 2
People Power in the Philippines, Burma, Tibet, China, Taiwan, Bangladesh, Nepal, Thailand, and Indonesia, 1947–2009

George Katsiaficas

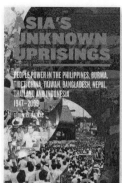

ISBN: 978-1-60486-488-5
$26.95   520 pages

Ten years in the making, this book provides a unique perspective on uprisings in nine places in East Asia in the 1980s and 1990s. While the 2011 Arab Spring is well known, the wave of uprisings that swept East Asia in the 1980s became hardly visible. This book begins with an overview of late 20th-century history—the context within which Asian uprisings arose. Through a critique of Samuel Huntington's notion of a "Third Wave" of democratization, the author relates Asian uprisings to predecessors in 1968 and shows their subsequent influence on the wave of uprisings that swept Eastern Europe at the end of the 1980s. By empirically reconstructing the specific history of each Asian uprising, significant insight into major constituencies of change and the trajectories of these societies becomes visible.

It is difficult to find comprehensive histories of any one of these uprisings, yet this book provides detailed histories of uprisings in nine places (the Philippines, Burma, Tibet, China, Taiwan, Bangladesh, Nepal, Thailand, and Indonesia) as well as introductory and concluding chapters that place them in a global context and analyze them in light of major sociological theories. Richly illustrated, with tables, charts, chronologies, graphs, index, and footnotes.

"George Katsiaficas has written a majestic account of political uprisings and social movements in Asia—an important contribution to the literature on both Asian studies and social change that is highly-recommended reading for anyone concerned with these fields of interest. The work is well-researched, clearly-argued, and beautifully written, accessible to both academic and general readers."
—Carl Boggs, author of *The Crimes of Empire and Imperial Delusions*

"George Katsiaficas is America's leading practitioner of the method of 'participant-observation,' acting with and observing the movements that he is studying. This study of People Power is a brilliant narrative of the present as history from below. It is a detailed account of the struggle for freedom and social justice, encompassing the different currents, both reformist and revolutionary, in a balanced study that combines objectivity and commitment. Above all, he presents the beauty of popular movements in the process of self-emancipation."
—James Petras, professor of sociology at Binghamton University

Anarchism and Education:
A Philosophical Perspective

Judith Suissa

ISBN: 978-1-60486-114-3
$19.95   184 pages

While there have been historical accounts of the
anarchist school movement, there has been no
systematic work on the philosophical underpinnings of
anarchist educational ideas—until now.

Anarchism and Education offers a philosophical account of the neglected tradition
of anarchist thought on education. Although few anarchist thinkers wrote
systematically on education, this analysis is based largely on a reconstruction
of the educational thought of anarchist thinkers gleaned from their various
ethical, philosophical, and popular writings. Primarily drawing on the work of the
nineteenth-century anarchist theorists such as Bakunin, Kropotkin, and Proudhon,
the book also covers twentieth-century anarchist thinkers such as Noam Chomsky,
Paul Goodman, Daniel Guerin, and Colin Ward.

This original work will interest philosophers of education and educationalist
thinkers as well as those with a general interest in anarchism.

*"This is an excellent book that deals with important issues through the lens of anarchist
theories and practices of education... The book tackles a number of issues that are
relevant to anybody who is trying to come to terms with the philosophy of education."*
—*Higher Education Review*